MILITARY LIFE

MILITARY LIFE

The Psychology of Serving in Peace and Combat

Volume 4: Military Culture

Edited by Thomas W. Britt, Amy B. Adler, and Carl Andrew Castro

PRAEGER SECURITY INTERNATIONAL
Westport, Connecticut · London

Library of Congress Cataloging-in-Publication Data

Military life: the psychology of serving in peace and combat / edited
  by Thomas W. Britt, Amy B. Adler, and Carl Andrew Castro.
    p. cm.
  Includes bibliographical references and index.
  ISBN 0-275-98300-5 ((set) : alk. paper)—ISBN 0-275-98301-3 ((v. 1) :
    alk. paper)—ISBN 0-275-98302-1 ((v. 2) : alk. paper)—ISBN
    0-275-98303-X ((v. 3) : alk. paper)—ISBN 0-275-98304-8 ((v. 4) :
    alk. paper)
  1. Psychology, Military. 2. War—Psychological aspects. 3. Combat—
    Psychological aspects. 4. Peace—Psychological aspects. 5. United
    States—Army—Military life. 6. Combat disorders. 7. Post-traumatic
    stress disorder. I. Britt, Thomas W., 1966– II. Adler, Amy B., 1963–
    III. Castro, Carl Andrew.
  U22.3.M485 2006
  355.1'0973—dc22   2005017484

British Library Cataloguing in Publication Data is available.

Library of Congress Catalog Card Number: 2005017484
ISBN: 0–275–98300–5 (set)
    0–275–98301–3 (vol. 1)
    0–275–98302–1 (vol. 2)
    0–275–98303–X (vol. 3)
    0–275–98304–8 (vol. 4)

First published in 2006

Praeger Security International, 88 Post Road West, Westport, CT 06881
An imprint of Greenwood Publishing Group, Inc.
www.praeger.com

Printed in the United States of America

The paper used in this book complies with the
Permanent Paper Standard issued by the National
Information Standards Organization (Z39.48–1984).

10 9 8 7 6 5 4 3 2 1

To my dad, Col. (ret.) Thomas W. Britt —TWB

To Matthias —ABA

To Jerry W. Rudy —CAC

CONTENTS

PREFACE

The psychological health and well-being of military personnel is important to the effectiveness of a nation's military, the adjustment of military families, and the integration of military personnel into the larger civilian community. A careful examination of the psychological issues confronting military personnel must necessarily be broad in scope and include a range of disciplines within psychology and the social sciences to provide a comprehensive assessment of the factors that affect the performance, health, and well-being of military personnel and their families. Such a multidisciplinary approach ensures researchers, military leaders, policy makers, and health care providers with a framework for understanding key factors relevant to modern military operations.

This four-volume set, *Military Life: The Psychology of Serving in Peace and Combat*, is organized around four defining fields of applied military psychology: military performance, operational stress, the military family, and military culture. Each volume begins with a riveting account of an individual's experience. These first-person accounts leave no doubt that the topics covered in this set are real, relevant, and deeply felt. The accounts are from the front line: the war and home front, as told by a veteran of Vietnam, the Gulf War, and Iraq; the precarious mental health of military personnel in a combat zone, as told by a military psychiatrist who served alongside Marines in combat; the anxiety and hope of military families on the front line of family separation, as told by an Army wife and mother of two service members turned military sociologist; and a psychologist with a front-row seat to observing the U.S. military's cultural shifts from Vietnam to the global war on terror. The stories told in these first-person accounts are stories of the authors' personal struggles with the challenges wrought by military conflict, incorporating the perspective that comes from their expertise, compassion, and humor. Three parts follow each of these first-person accounts. The chapters in each section are written by authorities selected for their knowledge in the field of military psychology, sociology, and other social sciences and shed light on the reality of life in the armed forces.

This set integrates the diverse influences on the well-being and performance of military personnel by developing separate volumes that address different facets of military psychology. By focusing on *Military Performance*, the first volume addresses the need to understand the determinants of how military personnel think, react, and behave on military operations. Several of the chapters in Volume 1 also have implications for the well-being of military personnel—such as the consequences of killing, how stress affects decision making, and how sleep loss affects operational effectiveness. Newly emerging issues in the armed forces are also discussed, including the role of terrorism, psychological operations, and advances in optimizing cognition on the battlefield. The impact of morale, the small military unit, and individual personality also provide insight into what influences the well-being and performance of military personnel.

The second volume in the set, *Operational Stress*, examines issues related to preparing military personnel to meet operational demands, details the psychological consequences of potentially traumatic events experienced on deployment, and reviews possible interventions that can support military personnel as they face such events. This volume includes descriptions of the experience of combat stress control teams on deployment, prisoners of war and the challenge of repatriation, the secular and spiritual role of military chaplains, the impact of military leaders, and the enduring role of small unit climate.

The third volume in the set takes an in-depth look at *The Military Family*. This comprehensive volume tackles the major stressors facing military families head on: family separation, family relocation, and dealing with the death of a service member. The particular issues confronting single parents, military children, and dual-military couples are also addressed. Another chapter addresses the balance between military work and family life. The problem of military family violence is the topic of the next chapter. A final chapter focuses on strategies for reducing military family conflict.

The fourth volume in the set, *Military Culture*, addresses the wider context of values, group diversity, and perceptions of the military, each of which has potential implications for the well-being and performance of military personnel. The role of values is explored in three chapters that address crosscultural values, the link between military values and performance, and the concept of courage. The next section explores specific groups within the military and the larger cultural trends that affect these groups: military reservists, women in the military, and the issue of gays serving in the armed forces. The final section of the volume examines how the military is perceived: the attitudes of service members about quality of life in the military, the role of the media in covering military operations, and the development of public attitudes toward the military and how these attitudes influence recruiting.

Producing this set required the effort and support of numerous people. In addition to thanking the authors for their outstanding chapters, we would like to thank Judy Pham, Hayley Brooks, Whitney Bryan, and Sarah Brink for their technical assistance in formatting the chapters. We would also like to thank Debbie Carvalko and the team at Praeger for providing valuable support and encouragement throughout the project. Finally, we appreciate the support provided by the Military Operational Medicine Directorate of the U.S. Army Medical Research and Materiel Command, Fort Detrick, Maryland. Note that the views expressed in this set are those of the authors and do not reflect the official policy or position of the Department of the Army, Department of Defense, or the U.S. Government.

We express our gratitude to the military personnel who have served their country in times of war and the families who have supported them. We hope this set in some small way can improve the lives of the next generation of service members and their families.

PART I

FIRST PERSON

CHAPTER 1

MILITARY CULTURE AND VALUES: A PERSONAL VIEW

Guy L. Siebold

Many years ago, as a young airman, I was waiting in the Los Angeles bus terminal to go up the coast to my new assignment at Vandenberg Air Force Base. I sat there in my dress blue uniform. The bus terminal at that time was a somewhat seedy place, periodically frequented by derelicts and many with shabby attire and limited etiquette. While I was waiting, a young mother with two small children approached me and asked if she and her children could sit next to me. She explained that she was concerned about being alone in the terminal and that she would feel safe being near a military man in uniform. Of course, I agreed. Up to that time, I had not thought much about what people in real life thought about men and women in uniform. It felt good to be respected, appreciated, and in uniform. The incident reflected a different message from what I received from the major media and some in academia.

Military Life in Garrison

During my stay at Vandenberg, I was introduced to garrison culture and values. There were two worlds—the accounting and finance office where I worked and the administrative unit in which I was housed. In the former, the top noncommissioned officer (NCO) in the office ruled. If he thought you worked hard, tried hard, and were trustworthy, things went well, and he would "cut you some slack," as we used

The views and opinions expressed herein are those of the author and not necessarily those of the U.S. Army Research Institute for the Behavioral and Social Sciences, the Department of the Army, or the Department of Defense.

to say back then. In my case, that meant more independent work, being allowed to smoke a cigar (with window open), and getting time off, for example, to compete in a national karate tournament. On the other hand, if you didn't work hard or were untrustworthy, you were typically put under the close oversight of a mid-level NCO and were more likely to get assigned to less desirable tasks such as auditing pay records or reconciling discrepancies. In a perverse twist, a less productive airman might get special benefits such as being sent offsite for computer training because he was the type of person the office could more easily afford to lose.

In all, the people in my finance office worked hard and would bend over backwards to make sure that their fellow airmen got paid on time and correctly. On rare occasions when there was a widely despised or destructive person, it would not be surprising to discover his pay records had been misplaced or lost in transit when he traveled to a new station. To our discredit, it was also not unheard of for those working the customer service counter during payday to eat a substantial amount of raw onions with their hamburgers at lunch. The theory was that people with pay problems would then try to minimize their time with those onion-breath airmen helping them at the counter. (These were still the days of conscript service; the draft ended in 1974.) The onion goal was to minimize the work of the airmen rather than to serve as many customers as possible in a limited time frame.

Onion-breath service was an exception. The general work group values were to learn your job and do it well (i.e., job competence), try to be helpful (i.e., be responsive and show initiative but not by volunteering), and don't do dumb things (e.g., be consistently late, make a lot of mistakes, talk disrespectfully, or be any kind of problem). Leaders were expected to be knowledgeable, treat people fairly, and be consistent and firm without throwing their weight around. In one instance, I achieved the maximum score on a knowledge test in accounting and finance. As a result, along with other high scorers in their specialties, I participated in a base-wide ceremony in which the top NCO in my office took the opportunity to present me with a certificate and have our picture taken with higher leaders. The downside to this was that the lower-ranking NCO who did all the job training in the office received no public recognition at all and was noticeably upset for weeks about his boss taking the credit for the training success. To him, it wasn't fair.

To most airmen, leaders were "lifers," career people in the service for their prime working life. The term was a means of ego-compensation for the conscript airmen who had less pay, benefits, status, and power, as well as, in particular, less freedom. In context, the term also helped draw lines in an us-versus-them distinction. It was the lifer's duty to look out for the organization, rules, and regulations. The airmen were conscripts, or more precisely, mostly people who were draft-motivated volunteers that joined the Air Force to avoid being drafted into the Army or Marines. These airmen did not think that it was their duty necessarily to look out for the organization, and the rules and regulations were to be complied with to avoid sanctions, not to be particularly punctilious. Although there were many differently nuanced relationships among the people in the office, it was divided socially primarily into two major groups: lifers and first-term airmen. There were no officers and only a couple civilians, who for the most part worked and lived in different circles. The airmen categorized the NCO lifers as "good and knowledgeable," "good with less knowledge," and "others," with one or more generally recognized character flaws. Interaction with the latter was avoided when possible. Presumably the NCOs similarly divided the airmen into categories.

Life in the headquarters administrative unit that controlled our nonworking hours was a different matter. Leaders in that unit could do little to help or reward someone but a lot to punish and restrict him. What mattered about leaders at headquarters was that they were fair. The unit was controlled by the top NCO. The few officers were not relevant unless you got into serious trouble. Most airmen, including me, tried to maintain friendly relations with the top unit NCO but to avoid him or being noticed by him as much as possible. My only negative encounter with him was when, on a weekend pass, I went to San Francisco, which was beyond the geographical limit of the pass. Of course, in the middle of that city, whom would I run into but an airman clerk who worked directly for the top NCO in the headquarters unit. Fortunately the only punishment I got for exceeding the pass limit was being put on laundry detail for a few weeks. While not upset with this punishment, I was greatly displeased that a fellow airman voluntarily squealed on me to the higher ups instead of siding with his own kind. On the other hand, I avoided guilt by association when the top NCO walked into my barrack room one day to find my roommate taking apart and cleaning his motorcycle in the middle of the floor. But that's another story.

Life in the barracks was not much different from that of a dormitory in an educational institution, except that the occupants were responsible for keeping it very clean and orderly. Unit leaders made sure of that. Rooms could be personalized but only so far. Social relationships were based on with whom one worked, the physical proximity of rooms, personalities, preferred off-duty activities, and exchanges of different sorts of skills and capabilities, such as transportation if one owned a vehicle. Overall, the social relations were friendly among the airmen, but there was little sense of being a group. Rather, we just had in common that we were all in the same situation together. Neither trust nor mutual dependency was unusually high. Nonetheless, we banded together at times to hit the beaches or go camping in the Sierra Nevada Mountains. A couple of times a portion of the unit was selected to help fight wildfires in nearby mountain areas. It is amazing how you can be fifteen feet from a line of fire and not feel a thing; but be ten feet away from the advancing fire line and feel the blazing heat. Fighting the fires built common experiences but not a sense of unity. While most airmen were glad to be helpful, the net effect of fighting the fires was that you then had to spend extra time cleaning ash from your boots and polishing them to wear in public.

Military Life in a Combat Zone

After two years of Vandenberg, having "done" California, and being curious by nature, I volunteered for and received combat zone duty in Nha trang, Vietnam. There I received my introduction to combat zone culture and values. There are many excellent descriptions of the culture, norms, and values of small combat units. My experiences were with a finance support unit rather than direct combat, although my finance office and base were shelled by the enemy often enough to be annoying. It was my hypothesis, based on observations, that the local enemy units had a quota by which they were required to shoot rockets or other weapons at my base once a month but no more. We never knew what day the enemy was going to attack, but it was never more than once a month. Fortunately the enemy usually attacked the planes on the flight line rather than the clubs, chow hall, BX, or latrines where they could have done some real damage. Our only extended combat period was during the Tet Offensive in 1968. To illustrate, one of my office NCOs lived in a rented house in town. During Tet, some soldiers set up a heavy machine gun position on his front porch. The NCO felt it imprudent to ask which side they were on and merely waited inside a couple days until the soldiers left.

My first impression of Vietnam was that we had a large logistic build-up there. With the exception of the periodic shelling and the presence of Vietnamese working on the base in many capacities, the base probably looked like any number of places throughout the world with the same general climate. Most of the Vietnamese were fine people, although it was not uncommon for local teenagers to try to ride by on a moped and steal a watch off an unwary arm. Nonetheless, there was not complete trust between the American military men and their South Vietnamese counterparts. For example, during Tet, I was told, South Vietnamese gate guards managed to let a small truck full of enemy soldiers into the area headquarters of the Military Assistance Command, Vietnam. The enemy overran the building. An Army captain, who was a friend of mine from karate class (taught by neighboring Korean troops), had his hands tied behind his back, was forced to kneel, and was shot in the head. On the other hand, I heard stories of South Vietnamese and soldiers of other nations risking their lives for Americans.

While the accounting and finance airmen were not battle-hardened combat troops, we did try to take care of those more directly exposed to combat. When a pilot would come in from an extended stay in the field and be due a large amount of back pay, I would, as was done in the Roman legions, often give him a partial payment on the spot and ask him to come back the next day when I would have the much larger, exact balance computed and available for him. That way, he could, if desired, blow the initial payment as he chose that night and come back the next day for a more rational disposition of the bulk of his pay. Actually, to describe us as "not battle-hardened" is an overstatement. The leaders locked up all our weapons and ammunition, which would only be available in a serious emergency. I think they were afraid that we were more likely to shoot ourselves than the enemy or that we would lose our weapons if they were handed out. (At least Deputy Sheriff Barney Fife from TV's *The Andy Griffith Show* got to carry a bullet in his shirt pocket!)

A combat zone is a dangerous place. However, for most of us the air base was relatively safe; the danger from enemy indirect fire was random. As a consequence, for example, people typically went about their business on the air base individually. But when people went downtown, off the air base where they could run into trouble, they often went in small groups. One time when I wrangled a free trip on a courier plane to Hong Kong, a stray shell hit the finance office. A fellow airman filling in for me in the officer's pay area received shrapnel in his face. One piece of the shrapnel had to stay in place because it was too close to a nerve to remove. During another attack, another of my Tae Kwon Do classmates was shredded. Given the random nature of the danger, there was no particular benefit to banding together with tight cohesion as in a small combat infantry unit. There was only a background or latent level of cohesion as a result of being together in a combat zone but not much more, although there were groups with special interests or activities that supported each other and small groups of friends that hung out together. When under attack by rockets or other indirect fire, we all stampeded to our respective sand bag bunkers en masse. When possible we hastily picked up goodies to take in the bunker because we were not sure how long it would be before the situation was all clear. There, it was not uncommon to exchange swigs of Jack Daniels bourbon and chocolate chip cookies from home. The offerings, in other words, were eclectic.

During my tour, I saw two instances of exemplary leadership. One occurred after the assassination of Martin Luther King. Upon learning of the event, the base commander and other senior officers immediately went down among the troops, particularly with the African-American airmen, and discussed what people were feeling and thinking. While showing empathy, the leaders helped the airmen transcend the tragedy and focus on the importance and value of their military service to the country as a whole. Another example occurred when we were allowed to volunteer to help take some Vietnamese orphans on a boat ride, picnic, and beach party on a nearby island. The purpose on one level was just to allow the kids to have some fun. On a more abstract plane, the purpose was to take the orphans out of the harsh and danger-filled world that they knew in the hope that they would experience, for a while, a better world that they could support and work towards as they grew up. It was at least one attempt by the leaders to build positive motivation and relationships with the people we were in the country to defend. We wanted the kids to cast their future with their government rather than with the enemy. This incident follows my view that the essence of leadership is to articulate and promote (to adopt the style of General MacArthur) the mission, the mission, and the mission. Ideology was not a major discussion topic in my circles, but I believe there was at least a background or latent level of support for the stated purposes of our being in South Vietnam. Most informal talk was about more basic matters or about getting back to the "world" (the United States).

Assessing Military Culture and Values

Perhaps surprisingly, the culture and values in my office in the combat zone were not that different from the office back in the States. Overall, there appeared to be five primary values: (1) *job competence*, (2) *honesty*, (3) *helpfulness*, (4) *fairness*, and (5) *respect*. Job competence was important. You had to know what you were doing and where to go for help if you needed it. You had to do a reasonable amount of work. If you couldn't carry your weight and do it consistently, someone else had to pick up the slack or risk. Honesty was fundamental. There wasn't time to worry about whether someone was exaggerating, holding back information, or outright lying. If you couldn't be trusted, you were written off and isolated. Helpfulness meant that you made time to help someone who needed it and weren't always bitching when someone asked you to do something. You were expected to show initiative but not go overboard or make a habit of volunteering. As John Wayne over-heroics were not appreciated on the battlefield, over-zealous behavior was seen as "brown-nosing" and an indication that you were better than others or, worse, that you were a "suck-up" who did not identify with your fellow airmen. Such behavior was rare. Fairness was key, especially if you were a leader. Nothing destroyed motivation and morale faster than blatant favoritism or the appearance that someone was getting special treatment or that you (as a leader) were delegating all the tough work to subordinates while you took it easy.

In the final analysis, people wanted to be treated with respect and appreciated for their contributions. This did not mean exhibiting touchy-feely nurturing but a clear showing that you (leaders especially) felt someone was hard-working and competent, honest, helpful, and fair. All who were contributing should receive their share of the credit. Such values were fundamental to the way in which military personnel judged their environment and leaders. If these basic values were upheld, then most people were satisfied and motivated. If not, both direct and second order problems could be generated. Although we junior enlisted did not use terms such as values, we knew that competence, honesty, helpfulness, fairness, and respect mattered.

Two decades later, I learned that top leaders considered values quite important to military culture and needed to be reflected in military policy. Specifically, I found myself as lead scientist on a project on Army values requested by the Secretary of the Army and Chief of Staff of the Army. The project asked, What were the values held by soldiers of all ranks and their Army civilian counterparts? The top level backing of the project was important because we got all the support we needed. The downside was that they wanted an answer in 30 days.

One fundamental finding of the project was that first-term soldiers came into the volunteer Army with high expectations and good support for core military values but became on average somewhat disillusioned in their first year or so as they adjusted to the reality of everyday military life. Another finding was that on the whole, the strongest support was for the value of *freedom*. Almost all soldiers (96 percent) felt freedom was very important or extremely important to them. In comparing the lower ranks with the higher grades and with the civilians (whether they served in the continental United States or overseas), we found the perceived importance of freedom was uniformly strong throughout. Three other values that 90 percent or more of soldiers said were very or extremely important to them were *self-respect* (92 percent), *family security* (91 percent), and *standing up for what is right* (91 percent). Interestingly, other research showed that after they completed their service obligation and had some time back in civilian life, almost all first-term soldiers (87 percent) looked back on their service experience in a positive light and were proud to have served (95 percent).

As part of the project on Army values, we conducted research with American soldiers and civilians stationed in Europe. During interviews, we found that the same work group values were important to them—competence, honesty, helpfulness, fairness, and respect. In asking how to improve things, a number of soldiers mentioned that you needed to get rid of any poor performers ("slugs") who disproportionately damaged the group. Also mentioned was a need to appreciate the contributions of military wives. For example, a wife might be required to stay up until midnight sewing on patches or ironing a uniform for her husband's inspection the next day.

In the middle of the research, American planes carried out a retaliatory air raid on Libya. Immediately the American forces in Europe went on alert; officers and NCOs pulled additional duty such as patrolling the military housing areas. An analysis of the data showed clearly that, after the bombing, the lower enlisted soldiers expressed a much higher opinion of their leaders' abilities and contributions as well as greater support for core military values. With the potential for combat substantially heightened, there was no room for a distinction between the lifers and those in their first term of enlistment.

The Broad View

A consistent interest and theme of my research since I began serving in the military has been the question of how individuals coordinate and integrate their actions with others in the context of their social environments. Indeed the question is central to social psychology. Most interaction in the military and in other organizations occurs in pairs of individuals or small work groups such as fire teams, crews, squads, and staffs. Coordination involves the recognition of others and their actions; integration involves the mutual interaction with others to achieve common goals. In these social processes, values, norms, rules, regulations, and the wider culture within which they operate are crucial to success. The services have their stated values, and they are on target and important. These values derive from the culture, history, and functions of the military services. Nonetheless, part of the foundation for these military values is the common experience of service members (in combat, training for combat, and support) and the required coordination and integration of action. Thus I believe the basic small work group values noted above to be key and a mandatory focus for continuing investigation. From my experience, I feel these values approach being universal imperatives because small work groups cannot function effectively without them, and a social environment which encourages and supports these values frees up human energy for productive activity. I see the values as relatively timeless and not much changed since the era of the hoplite soldiers of ancient Greece. They are just as applicable today to the small work groups engaged in Afghanistan, Iraq, and other places across the globe. In a given context, these small work group values may not be all the values that need emphasis and support, but they are likely to be necessary ones.

On the other hand, compared to my active duty time, what is new in this so-called post-modern age is the apparently recognized need to make a special effort to formally teach military values to service members. Further, unlike in prior times, service members discuss these values widely, either by implication or directly, on the Internet or by other electronic means. In Army basic training for example, instruction on the Soldier's Creed now includes attention to each of the Army values: *loyalty, duty, respect, selfless service, honor, integrity,* and *personal courage.* In the field, including deployments in such locations as Afghanistan, Iraq, and Kosovo, many soldiers have Internet access via Army Knowledge Online to electronic forums, groups, and chat rooms to bring up problems, discuss issues, share lessons, and learn from each other. In the Vietnam War era, such conversations were personal and limited and would usually occur only within a service member's primary work group or over beers at the club. One thing though still irks service members and can be heard in their comments on the Internet; that is their perception that the mainstream media presents a negative picture of what is going on and concentrates on the sensational rather than the many good and positive things that are being accomplished. Such perceived distortions undercut morale because they detract from the meaning of the missions and importance of service member contributions.

In looking at military culture and values, one has to consider the service member as the focal centerpiece. It is the character of the service member that matters, as shaped, developed, and reinforced in small work group culture and values. Whether risking their lives to protect their country or that of others, providing medical assistance to local country civilians, or passing out chocolate bars to their children, the American service members are contributing their all in productive and meaningful ways. One cannot help but be impressed by their demeanor or their deeds, from their answering the unit telephone with "Alpha Company, PFC Smith speaking, may I help you sir or ma'am," to their working together as a squad to clear out a high-rise building with potential hostile combatants that usually would be cleared by a full platoon. Their demeanor and exemplary deeds are not new but reflect the history of those who came before such as my father-in-law, uncle-in-law, two neighbors, a supervisor, and related others who rest now in Arlington National Cemetery. To paraphrase de Tocqueville, the American military is great because it is good. I believe it is good because of the character and values of its service members. American military service members are not just great people; they are good people. They are the kind that a young mother with two children would feel safe sitting next to at a bus station. I am proud to be associated with them.

PART II

MILITARY VALUES

CHAPTER 2

CULTURE'S CONSEQUENCES IN THE MILITARY

Joseph L. Soeters, Cristina-Rodica Poponete, and Joseph T. Page Jr.

In the world of international business it has become clear that management in an international context has its own peculiarities. International management needs to take into account that consumers and workforces in different countries are alike in many aspects but are unlike in many other aspects (Boyacigiller & Adler, 1991; Hill, 2001). If multinational companies fail to translate these differences into their production and marketing policies, they will undoubtedly face serious difficulties in their global operations. It has been demonstrated empirically that people differ with respect to values and attitudes along national borders. Systematic national differences, for instance, have been demonstrated with regard to the way people deal with hierarchies and rules in organizations (Hofstede, 1991, 2001). Despite globalization and McDonaldization, those national cultural differences seem to be fairly persistent, as many recent studies have confirmed (House, Hanges, Javidan, Dorfman, & Gupta, 2004; van Oudhoven, 2001; Vinken, Soeters, & Ester, 2004; see also Harrison & Huntington, 2000).

The military is experiencing basically the same developments as multinational companies. Internationalization is taking place in at least two ways: the military is increasingly engaged in places all over the world, whereas national armed forces are no longer capable of executing operations on their own. Even the U.S. armed forces, the largest and most advanced in the world, need allies from around the globe (e.g., NATO, Japan) to perform their duties in large-scale operations, such as in Afghanistan and Iraq. In Europe, the tendency for national armed forces to work together has already merited structural binational or multinational arrangements. The German Bundeswehr, for example, has been divided into various parts, each of which have merged with other national forces. As a consequence, the first German/Dutch Corps, the Eurocorps (with military from Germany, France, Spain, and Belgium), the Multinational Corps North East (containing military from Germany, Denmark, and Poland) and others have been formed.

The structural internationalization of the workforce (for instance in multinational headquarters), the multinational character of military contingents during deployments, and the variety of local populations the military have to deal with, have become predominant features of current military activities. Similar to multinational companies, the current military may face serious difficulties in terms of interoperability, efficiency, effectiveness, and legitimacy if they are not capable of dealing adequately with the cultural factor. This is a real change as compared to previous times when armed forces were above all based on national sovereignty. Given this fairly recent development, it comes as no surprise that the cultural factor in the military has recently started to attract the attention of both practitioners in the field and scholars of military sciences (Duffey, 2000).

In this chapter we aim to describe the results of those first studies dealing with the cultural factors in the military. We will use these results to interpret a number of observations stemming from recent international military operations. First, we will present the results of three studies that have tried to measure cultural dimensions in the military. Then we intend to delve deeper into the implications of these findings. Cultural differences seem to be fairly soft and intangible at first glance (basically these differences are only words), but in reality differences may be hard in their consequences. For instance, it has been demonstrated that aircraft accidents may result as a consequence of specific national cultural characteristics (Hofstede, 1991, 2001; Soeters & Boer, 2000). Relevance of the cultural factor may be seen particularly in national styles in fighting, warring, and the controlling of a foreign occupied area. The way nations deal with conflicts reflects basic national cultural characteristics. Data evidencing these differences not only stem from the present, but also—and perhaps predominantly—from the past, i.e., the colonial era.

Subsequently, we will focus on issues that come to the fore in current multinational actions and missions. These consequences relate to a variety of issues such as safety policies, force protection styles, and the importance of bureaucratic procedures as to the command and control and the setup of military missions. All these issues, if not dealt with properly, may be detrimental to the successful collaboration of military units of different countries (Elron, Halevy, Ben Ari, & Shamir, 2003; Elron, Shamir, & Ben-Ari, 1999). We will close this chapter with some points of discussion, recommendations for commanders, and avenues for future research. In Table 2.1 we have depicted the line of the argument in this chapter.

Before we begin, however, one preliminary remark needs to be made. Although the impact of the cultural factor in military as well as civilian aviation has been demonstrated unequivocally (Helmreich & Merritt, 1998; Soeters & Boer, 2000), we will focus on army operations only. In the air forces uniformity in technologies (for instance F-15 or F-16 technology) reduces the impact of the cultural factor. Besides, air forces more often cooperate internationally. In armies, however, technology is far less dominating, and hence the people or cultural factor creates more difficulties and

Table 2.1
Chapter Overview

National military cultures	⇒	Styles of dealing with conflicts	⇒	Safety policies/force protection International military cooperation The need for intercultural training

challenges at the same time. Besides, armies are far less experienced in multinational military cooperation than air forces.

Values in Military Academies and the Military at Large

The first large-scale attempt to measure culture in organizations dates back to the 1970s. In this period the Dutch social psychologist Geert Hofstede (1980; 1991; 2001) collected data from over 100,000 respondents, all of whom were workers in more than 50 national subsidiaries of the American corporation IBM. Later he added data from an additional ten countries. Hofstede found that cultural differences between countries may be distinguished on the basis of five dimensions or cultural yardsticks. These five dimensions include:

1. *Power distance*, which refers to differences in the way people deal with social (in)equality, hierarchy in organizations, and the relation to authority;

2. *Individualism*, which describes cultures where the ties between individuals are loose and where everyone is supposed to look after himself or herself, as contrasted to *collectivism*, in which people are integrated in strong, cohesive groups;

3. *Masculinity*, which basically refers to achievement motivation ("going for gold," "winner takes it all") versus caring for others and striving for quality of life (which is called *femininity*);

4. *Uncertainty avoidance*, which pertains to primary dilemmas and conflicts and ways of dealing with them, e.g., through rules and regulations; and

5. *Long-term orientation*, which refers to the level of perseverance and acceptance of gradual change in a society or community.

The fifth dimension has not been constructed on the basis of the IBM data. Hofstede derived the fifth dimension from an additional study together with Asian academics who wanted to identify typical Asian cultural aspects, which exist, in varying degrees throughout the whole world.

In 1997 Soeters published a study applying these cultural yardsticks to the military. He used samples of cadet-officers of military academies in 18 countries as respondents (see also Soeters & Recht, 1998). The academies in the original North American Treaty Organization (NATO) countries (except Greece and Turkey) participated in the study, as did some additional countries like Belarus, Brazil, and

Argentina. Later Poponete (work in progress) did the same study in one more country, Romania, which is a new NATO member-state as of 2004. To demonstrate the relevance of Hofstede's work more clearly, Soeters connected the four original dimensions (long-term orientation was not included in this study) to the well-known Institutional-Occupational Model (Moskos & Wood, 1988).

This model refers to the attitude of soldiers toward their work in the military. This attitude may be institutional, which relates to a vocational orientation reflecting patriotism and a total dedication to the military organization. On the other hand, soldiers' attitudes may be occupational, which refers to seeing working in the military as "just another job" (Moskos & Wood, 1988). This latter attitude, for instance, implies that military personnel are not solely focused on the internal labor market of the military. Soeters assumed that high degrees of individualism, indicating that people feel fairly independent of the organization, and masculinity, reflecting the wish to earn high salaries, are indicators of occupationalism.

The other two cultural dimensions, power distance and uncertainty avoidance, were assumed to be indicators of organizational regimes: high degrees of power distance and uncertainty avoidance were seen as manifestations of classic machine bureaucracies with tall pyramids and a large degree of rule orientation and formal paperwork. Low degrees of these cultural dimensions were assumed to be representing more modern working organizations stressing flexibility and results orientation.

The study among the military academies showed that, compared to their compatriots in the civilian sector, the cadet-officers in general yielded higher scores on power distance and lower scores on individualism and masculinity (see Table 2.2). These results confirm common notions about differences between civilian and military workers and organizations. In the military, hierarchies and power distances are known to be more elaborate and fundamental to the structure of the organization than they are in the business sector. In the military, collectivism (i.e.,, group orientation, interdependency, and cohesion) is clearly a more important concept than it is among average civilian organizations. In the military, finally, earning high salaries and striving for individual merit is not valued as much as in business corporations. The dimension of uncertainty avoidance (rule orientation, formalization, the wish to continue to work for the military) showed mixed results: some academies such as the ones in Germany, Italy, Denmark, the United Kingdom and especially the United States (i.e.,, West Point) exhibited higher degrees of this dimension, which had been expected, but there were also a number of academies (in the Netherlands, Canada, and Norway) that scored lower on this particular dimension. We were not able to fully interpret these latter specific results.

By and large, the results proved to be in accordance with basic ideas and common knowledge about cultural differences between the civilian and the military sector. *These results clearly demonstrate that in the military—in contrast to civilian organizations—indeed something like a supranational culture exists. This supranational military culture is more collectivistic, more hierarchy-oriented, and less salary-driven than the average civilian working culture.* The consequence of this is that military personnel

Table 2.2
Cultural Differences between Military and Civilian Organizations

Cultural dimension	*Military organizations as compared to civilian organizations*
Power Distance (hierarchy orientation)	Higher
Individualism (independence of the organization)	Lower
Masculinity (achievement orientation, in particular, striving for high wages)	Lower
Uncertainty Avoidance (rule orientation)	Mixed Results

Source: Soeters, 1997.

of different origins can often function and get along with each other without too many problems (Elron et al., 1999). Moskos (1976, personal communication, April 15, 2002) even claims that military personnel from different countries seem to be better suited to work together than with civilian personnel from nongovernmental organizations (NGOs) or local agencies.

However, there are substantial cultural differences among the military of different countries as well. In the academy study, interesting results in this respect came to the fore (see Table 2.3). First, a so-called *Latin* cluster consisting of academies in France, Italy, Belgium, Spain, and Brazil could be discerned (Soeters, 1997; Soeters & Recht, 1998). This cluster was characterized by a high level of power distance and a large degree of uncertainty avoidance. This grouping of countries with a Latin background can also be found in Hofstede's work (1980, 2001) in the business sector as well as in various replications (e.g., House, Hanges, Javidan, Dorfman, & Gupta, 2004) of that study. As heirs of the Roman Empire, all these countries are still homogeneous with respect to religion; they are all predominantly Roman Catholic. A large pyramidal structure and corresponding administrative style belong to the hallmarks of that church. The statement *Roma locuta, causa finita* (when Rome has spoken, the matter has been closed) aptly expresses that administrative style. The later measurement in the academies in Romania (Poponete, work in progress) proved to fit in perfectly well into this cluster. This comes as no surprise since Romania used to be the favorite colony among Roman settlers during the heydays of the Roman Empire. The Norwegian and Canadian academies, on the other hand, yielded comparatively low scores on these dimensions, suggesting a fairly modern working culture.

Hybrid forms could be found in the British academy, where the power distance scores between the various ranks proved to be remarkably high (the highest among all academies in the study!), as well as in the American academy and the German defense university, where the degree of uncertainty avoidance was especially high. In the latter result one may recognize the outspoken tendency of both the American

Table 2.3
Examples of Cultural Configurations within the Military

Cultural configuration	High on both dimensions	Hybrid	Low on both dimensions
Power Distance and Uncertainty Avoidance	French, Italian, Belgian, Spanish, Brazilian, Romanian	British (high on power distance), American and German (high on uncertainty avoidance)	Norwegian and Canadian
Individualism (independence) and Masculinity (achievement orientation, in particular, striving for high wages)	Norwegian, Canadian, American, Danish	Romanian (high on striving for high wages)	Italian and Belgian

Sources: Page, 2003; Poponete, work in progress; Soeters, 1997; Soeters & Recht, 1998.
* According to Page (2003), Germany is also high on power distance and masculinity.

and German armed forces to work by the book, to obey orders, and to comply most and for all with military law.

Again in the academies in Norway and Canada, but this time accompanied by the American and the Danish academies, the two other dimensions conveyed a relatively modern military culture in which independence of the organization, i.e., individualism, as well as the goal to earn high salaries, i.e., masculinity, are dominant features. In the academies of these countries, occupationalism clearly prevails. Actually, the recruiting and promotion policies in these countries are directly geared toward establishing such an occupational military culture. On the other hand, in some continental European countries such as Italy and Belgium, both dimensions scored comparatively low. This suggests that the loyalty to the military (i.e., collectivism) looms large, whereas the need to earn high salaries does not seem to be very substantial. The Romanian study indicated that the local academy culture is somewhat hybrid as far as the individualism-collectivism dimension is concerned, whereas the ambition to earn higher salaries is fairly large. Probably, this latter result should be connected to the generally low wage level in that country. Apparently, the ambition to gain more money is particularly strong in the post-Communist era.

Recently, Page (2003) did a similar study applying Hofstede's cultural yardsticks to samples of military personnel. These were career officers (or officer-equivalent personnel) who, at the time of the study, were mostly attending international courses or conferences in Europe. Included were a number of NATO countries (Belgium, the Netherlands, Canada, Germany, Norway, the United Kingdom, and the United States) as well as a number of Partnership for Peace (PfP) countries (Georgia, Romania, Slovakia, and Slovenia). As another earlier study had also demonstrated (Soeters & Recht, 2001), the new results with regard to the NATO countries largely confirmed the earlier academy findings (Page, 2003, p. 102). There was one clear exception, though. In the Page study the German career officers displayed far higher levels of power distance and masculinity as compared to the results of the German student-officers in the academy study. Once again, the U.S. military proved to be high on masculinity and uncertainty avoidance. As to long-term orientation, which was not measured in the academy study, no significant differences were found among the NATO career officers nor was there a clear pattern with respect to the differences between military and civilian organizations.

Among the four PfP countries, the cultural differences on all dimensions were larger than the differences between the NATO countries. Comparing the NATO and PfP countries, the results indicated that the career military personnel of the NATO countries are significantly more culturally homogeneous (i.e., more similar) as a group than are career military personnel in PfP countries (Page, 2003, p. 96). The differences between the PfP group of countries and others were largely due to the exceptional scores (in virtually all dimensions) of Georgia, being a part of the former Soviet Union and situated in Asia at a large distance from the other countries in the study. That the NATO countries, despite their cultural differences, also display a certain cultural homogeneity may be seen as the outcome of the alliance's lengthy history of more than 50 years. Perhaps the PfP organization was divergent because of its briefer history; the PfP program was initiated in 1994.

In summary, the studies demonstrated that especially among NATO military there is something like a supranational military culture, enabling military of different origins within NATO to work together fairly smoothly (see also Elron et al., 1999). Notwithstanding, there are substantial national cultural differences, even within NATO, as well. What consequences do these cultural differences have?

National Styles in Dealing with Conflicts

Countries display differing levels of violence within their national borders. These differences occur with respect to state-related political violence as well as spontaneous violence such as murders. These differences have been shown to be culturally influenced. For instance, in countries with a masculine culture there is more political violence; this effect is unrelated to other factors such as population size and economic development (van de Vliert et al., 1999). Countries deal with political, social, and economic problems in varying ways, applying more or less forceful pressure. A comparative analysis (Faure & Rubin, 1993) of the resolution of water disputes demonstrates this. Different problem-solving styles were clearly related to the cultural profiles of the countries in the respective water basins.

Some countries, like Belgium, have pursued a complete political turnaround, in this case the introduction of a federal-state structure, without one single drop of blood being spilled (Soeters, 1996). Other countries having similar population-related tensions, like Belgium has had between the Flemish- and the French-speaking parts, seem to be able to deal with such strains only in a violent, conflict-driven manner. The obvious example is the former Yugoslavia. From Hofstede's work (1994) it has become clear that all population groups within this Balkan country have a cultural profile that combines three elements: (a) high power distance providing the leaders with ample influence and discretionary power to do whatever they prefer to do; (b) high collectivism, which is conducive to the development of strong, cohesive groups; and, (c) a high degree of uncertainty avoidance impacting the development of, among others, xenophobia. This combination may lead to the development of fierce us-versus-them thinking, especially if social and economic conditions are unfavorable. In the words of a Yugoslav sociologist written almost 60 years ago,

> Rivalries and hostilities are paralleled by attachment and subservience to those in power —a situation that breeds both treachery and loyalty, feud and solidarity, factionalism and ethnocentrism, a general feeling of insecurity of life and property, and endless strife. 'He who has no enemy is not a man,' they say. These are the conditions which made Balkan herdsmen excel in violence, villainy, and rebelliousness, as well in deeds of self-denial and patriotism. (Tomasic, 1946, pp. 132–133)

It does not require much imaginative power to recognize in these words the *explosive* combination of cultural elements that, according to Hofstede (1994), characterize the population groups in the former Yugoslavia (see also Duffey, 2000, pp. 152–153). The contrast between the former Yugoslavia and Belgium is reflected particularly in the far higher level of individualism among Belgium's two rival population groups, i.e.,, the Flemish and the Walloons. Interestingly enough, the explosive cultural profile also applies to Greece, Turkey, and other countries in the Middle East as well as many African countries. All these areas are relatively prone to conflict-driven solutions for social, economic, and political problems. The example of Greece and Turkey (with pertinacious conflicts over Cyprus and the border in the Aegean Sea) shows the conflict-prone style of solving problems in these two nations. However, this example also demonstrates that increasing wealth-related individualism and belonging to a larger alliance (NATO, for Greece also European Union) tend to de-fuse inclinations toward violence and conflict. The disputes between the two countries—although still existing—are nowadays unlikely to be dealt with through military conflict. As a consequence, both countries are considering reducing the duration of the periods military conscripts need to serve.

Going back in time, culture-related styles for dealing with issues of force and dominance can be observed as well. Lammers (2003a; 2003b) studied the way in which former colonial powers such as France, the United Kingdom, and the Netherlands developed different styles of governance in their respective colonies. The French tended toward forms of direct rule, while the British and the Dutch preferred a system of indirect rule. The French ruled through centralized, top-down governance with the aid of French and loyal local elites, whereas the British and the Dutch favored some sort of decentralized system of rule allowing native elites, either of a traditional or a modern bent, a fair deal of autonomy (Lammers, 2003b, p. 1395).

In correspondence with the French cultural profile as discerned by Hofstede (2001) and d'Iribarne (1989) and confirmed in the academy study, the French colonial governance style was characterized by authoritarian leadership and bureaucratic discipline, transforming the preexisting system of governance. Differences between the British and the Dutch colonial styles—as said, both inclined to indirect rule maintaining traditional systems of governance—related to the British being more detached and pragmatic and the Dutch being more closely involved in the way they ran their colonies. In addition, over centuries both the French and the British colonial powers had developed a governance style that was clearly based on the use of military force. One only needs to recall in this connection the persistent military actions of both countries in Africa and the British actions, in particular, in the Middle East (Turkey, Iraq, Syria, etc.).

This military approach was not standard among colonial powers, though. Except for the so-called policing actions in Indonesia in 1947 and 1948, the Dutch predominantly relied on trade and economic development as a means of gaining influence and governance (Voorhoeve, 1979). The Netherlands, although once a major colonial power, never has had a reputation of using indiscriminate military force. This may be a reflection of this country's high femininity score and further underscores the Dutch tendency toward quality of life and solidarity with the needy (Soeters, 2001; also Lammers, 2003b). It may come as no surprise that one of the earliest publications criticizing colonial practices from within, is a Dutch novel called *Max Havelaar*, published in 1860 (Hofstede, 1994). The current reluctance among the Dutch, both politicians and military, to have their military involved in high-intensity conflicts still reflects this aversion to strife and violence. Nowadays, the Dutch are known for their use of "soft, less robust tactics" during peacekeeping operations such as in Iraq in 2003–2004 (Onishi, 2004; Robberson, 2003). However, and this should be stressed as well, this Dutch style does not always produce adequate results as the Srebrenica massacre and other observations from Bosnia have demonstrated. In these hostile, warlike circumstances the Dutch military were unable to prove themselves equal to the dramatic crisis situation (e.g., Fitz-Gerald, 2003, p. 73; Sion, 2004; Soeters, 2001).

These observations support an important finding by Hofstede. Hofstede (1991, pp. 100–101; see also van de Vliert et al., 1999) has empirically demonstrated that the cultural dimension of masculinity statistically correlates with defense spending as a percentage of GNP. Masculine countries especially like the United Kingdom and the United States (and in previous times Japan, Germany and Italy) tend to try to resolve international conflicts by fighting, particularly through the use of military force. The way the United Kingdom "resolved" the Falkland conflict in the early 1980s provides a prime example in this respect. A dispute about a small, sparsely populated archipelago close to the Argentinean coast led to a real war with Argentina. The British chased off the Argentine occupiers, at the cost of (officially) 725 Argentine and 225 British lives, plus enormous financial expenses. Since then, the economy on the islands took a long time to recover and the archipelago is still in need of British military presence. This is the clear result of a clash between two masculine cultures, both unable to solve their disputes other than by the use of military violence. In much the same manner, the British still have not been able to solve the problems between Catholics and Protestants in Northern Ireland which still requires them to deploy large numbers of troops in that very small region of their nation.

A more or less similar conflict about a small group of islands between Finland and Sweden in the 1920s created an intense dispute between the two countries. Here, however, the end of the conflict was different. Despite the grim emotions, the conflict was resolved by negotiations only (Hofstede, 1991, pp. 100–101). According to Hofstede (1991, 2001) both countries (Finland and Sweden) are low on masculinity, which demonstrates the validity of this important finding.

This leads to the perhaps controversial conclusion that the current operations in Iraq and, in particular, the British and American decision to go to war in that country does not seem to be sheer coincidence. This war-prone policy seems to relate closely to the military tradition and cultural profile of both countries. Apparently, even current political and military decision making is likely to be a consequence of national cultural characteristics that seem to last for centuries. This is not the same as stating that culture is destiny. Social mechanisms like the implications of national cultural profiles have the character of probability, and are hence less deterministic than laws of natural sciences (Elster, 1993). On the other hand, these social mechanisms seem to be too important to be ignored.

Implications for the Military

Force Protection, Operational Goals and Military Styles

Previously, we have concluded that certainly within NATO a kind of supranational military culture exists which enables military personnel from different origins to work together fairly smoothly. At the same time, we have also noted that persistent cultural differences between national armed forces continue to exist. These differences even seem to impact present day decision making with regard to operations and policy maxims concerning the way these operations should be performed. This brings us to the operational level.

Since the end of the Cold War, many multinational military actions have taken place in such far-flung areas as Somalia, the former Yugoslavia, Afghanistan, and Iraq. These many large-scale operations provide us with a wealth of observations concerning the ways national armed forces act in their everyday operations. Soeters and Bos-Bakx (2003) have described a number of observations concerning Dutch-British and Danish-American interactions in the former Yugoslavia. Other interactions, between the Dutch, Germans, and Turks in the former Yugoslavia and Afghanistan, have been reported as well (Soeters & Moelker, 2003; Soeters, Tanerçan, Varoğlu, & Sigri, 2004).

It has been shown, for example, that British and Turkish officers want to be addressed by their subordinates in a manner that is different from the way Dutch or Danish officers are used to being approached by their soldiers. Turkish and British (but also German) officers do not expect to be contradicted, which is in line with the relatively high power distance in the armed forces of those countries. In the Dutch and Danish armed forces, on the contrary, open communication with and consultation of the lower ranks are even advocated as elements of an alleged "superior" commanding philosophy, the so-called Mission Oriented Command (Duine, 1998). Sometimes this particular cultural feature creates serious friction in the cooperation between the Dutch and the Germans during deployments such as in Kabul as well as in the headquarters of the German-Netherlands Corps (Soeters & Moelker, 2003). On the other hand, the Germans seem to experience problems with the even larger power distances in the French armed forces (Winslow, Kammhuber, & Soeters, 2004, p. 402).

All these observations illustrate that there are substantial differences in working styles between the military of various countries. This affects highly operational issues. In encounters between military from different nations, fierce debates are going on with respect to questions as how to patrol, how to carry one's weapon, how to approach the local population, and how to communicate with the local authorities. Further, there may be discussions about which safety measures to be taken and how to use spare time, including the ways of dealing with alcohol use (Winslow et al., 2004, pp. 401–402).

Specific peculiarities have been observed in the way the U.S. troops operate during peacekeeping as well as warfighting missions. In their everyday operating styles, their relative high scores on masculinity and uncertainty avoidance seem to be mirrored. The U.S. military generally seems to make a fairly tough impression with regard to their contact vis-à-vis the local population. This may be seen as an expression of masculinity. This operational style of the U.S. military has been observed in such differing actions as in Somalia, Haiti, and Iraq (Duffey, 2000, p. 154; Fitz-Gerald, 2003; Onishi, 2004; van Kesteren, 2004). Similar observations have been made about the robust style adopted by the Australians who had the lead in the operations in East Timor. They displayed an operational style that is relatively akin to the American way of operating (Duffey, 2000, p. 147). Not surprisingly, Australia is also fairly high on masculinity (Hofstede, 1991, 2001). Acting tough may be intentional, but this may also be the result of high levels of stress among the soldiers due to the ambitious goals their political leaders (and commanders) expect them to achieve. This may be seen as an indicator of masculinity in as far as it expresses a determinate will among U.S. politicians to strive for no less than the highest results ("no substitute for victory" as the famous quote goes). As a consequence, U.S. politicians seem to demand efforts and sacrifices from their military personnel that probably no other leaders in the Western hemisphere would be able to ask...nor would dare to exact.[1]

Toughness, however, may also be the consequence of another cultural characteristic. Observations from the Dutch area of responsibility in Iraq indicate that U.S. troops went straight through a small village where a religious ceremony was going on, despite recommendations by the Dutch to take a detour (Onishi, 2004; van Kesteren, 2004). Interesting is the American argument voiced to motivate this action: "We only need to stick to what we were ordered to do." Here one can clearly recognize the influence of the relatively high level of uncertainty avoidance among U.S. troops.

This cultural characteristic is fairly predominant: U.S. soldiers are trained to work by the book, to obey orders, and to tolerate no mistakes or defects. This attitude has also been observed in Bosnia and Kosovo (Caniglia, 2001; Fitz-Gerald, 2003, p. 71; Moskos, personal communication, April 15, 2002). Even U.S. general officers are not seen as having the authority to change policies and measures according to their own views. Strict and severe force protection policies clearly reflect this tendency toward uncertainty avoidance (see also Fitz-Gerald, 2003, p. 68 on the U.S. operations in Haiti). But at the same time there may be a relation to masculinity in the sense of achievement orientation and ambition (controlling a large nation that hosts many potential hostile elements). Such an ambition is fully in line with the American belief that people can really affect circumstances and influence future events (Boyacigiller & Adler, 1991, p. 272). But such ambitious goals may effect situations that are really life-threatening, and hence may strengthen among soldiers the tendencies of risk and uncertainty avoidance that are already in place.

In sum, America's military actions in Iraq seem to reflect the United States's culture. In this vein it may be interesting to note that America's culture is sometimes characterized with three C's: the C's of competition, conflict, and cracking. This description stems from a totally different realm, i.e., the field of municipalities and local democracy (Hendriks & Musso, 2004). But the connection is striking. This is not to say that these three C's (as contrasted with the famous Dutch three C's of consensus, consultation, and compromise) are bad or not valuable. On the contrary, the United States's ambitious culture leads to relatively high economic growth levels, many innovations in technologies (including military technologies) and the highest number of Nobel Prize winners throughout decades. Hence, the United States's ambitious culture produces impressive results. At the same time, in the field, it may lead to military performance that is not always conducive in reaching smooth solutions in difficult multicultural circumstances.

But cultural characteristics go further than operations at the soldier level. Importantly, they affect the cooperation in staff units as well as the relationships between commanders.

Command and Control and the Design of Operations

With respect to the lines of command in multinational military operations, the influence of the cultural factor can especially be experienced. It has been observed that armed forces from nations that are high on power distance, such as France and Italy, resent and ultimately refuse being placed under the operational command of other countries (Duffey, 2000, p. 154). Such national armed forces will continue to adhere to their national lines of command. This phenomenon is not exceptional.

In a Dutch-Turkish arrangement in Kosovo, a Turkish company was placed under the operational command of a Dutch battalion. (Turkey is also fairly high on power distance.) The Turks accepted being placed under Dutch command, but in everyday reality the Turkish company commander hardly ever contacted his Dutch superior. On the other hand, he often requested advice from a neighboring Turkish battalion commander and he frequently needed to "call Ankara" before deciding what to do (Soeters et al., 2004).

In the multinational headquarters of international operations, military from all kinds of origins work and live together. In such conditions, one can clearly experience the impact of the cultural factor. Military from countries that are relatively low on power distance and uncertainty avoidance, such as the Netherlands and Denmark, experience a real culture shock due to the micromanagement they encounter in their work. They are amazed by the wish of top level officials to control everything that is going on in their area of responsibility. Being accustomed to a fair degree of autonomy, Dutch officers tend to be surprised (and sometimes horrified) when confronted with detailed and precise instructions coming directly from the level of one- and two-star generals. During their deployment the Dutch officers get used to these strange (to them) working styles, but the initial shock never really seems to disappear (Duine, 1998).

Such culture shocks happen to servicemen in multinational headquarters, but also in international camps such as Camp Warehouse in Kabul (Afghanistan) during the International Security Assistance Force (ISAF) operation. In camps of this type, military of various origins are expected to work and live together in a small space. It comes as no surprise that this sometimes is simply asking too much. Friction and irritation about minor issues will abound; in such cases one is likely to dispute each other's behavior with respect to noise, the use of alcohol, food issues, leadership styles, safety matters, and the like. Even in such small camps people tend to retreat and isolate themselves in their own corners while simultaneously conducting non-stop complaining and gossiping about the others (Soeters & Moelker, 2003). How can these sometimes problematic interactions be resolved?

Encounters between groups of different origins and cultures may be solved in a number of ways. This depends on (a) whether or not one wants to maintain one's own culture and identity, and (b) the relationship sought among other groups (Berry, 2004). If one does not think one's own cultural identity is worth maintaining and if one does not seek to develop any relations with other groups (because these are not considered to be valuable), the result will be negative only. In similar encounters of profit companies (in the form of mergers, acquisitions and joint ventures), bankruptcies are likely to occur. In encounters of not-for-profit organizations such as the military, *chaos, obstruction, marginalization,* and *fragmentation* in the form of endless debates, negative stereotyping and quarrelling will likely develop. Clearly, such a situation should be avoided at all costs during multinational military missions.

If, however, one considers one's own cultural identity not so very important, whereas the other groups are deemed highly outstanding, then it would make sense to *assimilate* (Berry, 2004). Assimilation implies the development of cultural practices that arc akin to the other groups' cultural characteristics. Assimilation implies one group becoming similar to one or more other groups. The Dutch officers, who were complaining about the difference between the Dutch command practices at home and everyday reality in multinational headquarters, actually recommended the Dutch military adapt their command styles to what is common practice in the international military world. This recommendation was aimed to prevent cultural shocks among Dutch military who in the future will be going to be deployed in multinational headquarters. In general, the assimilation strategy tends to develop if one party clearly dominates the other. More often than not, the larger party implicitly or explicitly expects this to happen. If the other, smaller party agrees, this strategy generally works quite well. For instance, one can clearly observe this phenomenon among air forces that use the same (mostly United States-dominated) technology. Clearly, at internationally run airports in Afghanistan and elsewhere (Kabul, Kandahar, and Manas) the impact of cultural differences between the various national contingents is hardly noticeable, whereas such differences really do show themselves in the various camps of the land forces in the Kabul area (Camp Warehouse, Camp Julien). This presumably is related to the fact that among land forces the minority party does not feel comfortable when confronted with the expectation that it should adapt to another dominating party. In that case, another strategy will prove to be more successful.

If one is not inclined to give up on its own cultural practices and if one rejects the other groups' characteristics, then to actually *separate* may be the best thing to do. In military operations this is more or less common practice as we have seen in the many operations in the former Yugoslavia. In the Balkans, all national contingents of a certain size were assigned their own geographic area of responsibility. This means that every national group of military could work and live on its own and without continuously being confronted with other groups' practices and expectations. Actually, after the fairly problematic ISAF deployment of Dutch military in Camp Warehouse in Kabul, where the collaboration with the Germans deteriorated seriously, the Dutch decision to deploy to Iraq was felt as a certain relief. The Iraq deployment implied more autonomy since the Dutch were granted their own camps and area of responsibility (i.e., the southwestern part of Iraq). This separation strategy can be strengthened by giving each national contingent its own role in a system of international division of labor (Elron et al., 1999, p. 88). For instance, in Iraq the Dutch were working together with a Japanese contingent, but there was a strict division of roles: the Japanese were mainly performing civic activities (building power facilities and the like), whereas the Dutch were responsible for the core military tasks such as patrolling, security, and guarding.

How pragmatic the separation strategy in itself may seem, it never can be seen as the ultimate goal to achieve in regard to intercultural encounters. *Mutual accommodation* (Berry, 2004, p. 177) would be the best strategy, because this leads to true integration in which the best of many worlds are used and merged into something that is better than all previous contributing cultures. This strategy involves the acceptance by dominant and nondominant groups of a new way of working based on the input of all. But to achieve such an ideal situation, power relations should be balanced to prevent domination of some over others. At the same time, people involved should be adept at working within intercultural environments. Hence, there is a need for intercultural training (Fitz-Gerald, 2003).

Intercultural Training: About Bonding and Bridging

As mentioned earlier, soldiers experience difficulties when dealing with military from other countries. This has repeatedly been observed despite the fact that, at least within NATO, a certain supranational military culture seems to exist. True enough, this supranational military culture enables military from different origins to work together fairly smoothly most of the time (Moskos, 1976, personal communication, April 15, 2002). But, depending on the circumstances, cooperation between military from different nations is sometimes perceived as very problematic. Encounters with other military are pervasive depending on the living accommodations. In Camp Warehouse for instance, the military of a large variety of nations worked and lived together in relatively small camps from which one could not leave during free time as a consequence of strict force protection regulations. Evading other nationals in such circumstances is therefore almost impossible. Hence, experiencing problems with those other nationals seems hardly avoidable, as we saw above (Soeters & Moelker, 2003).

This may particularly apply to military that belong to elite units such as paratroopers, special forces and air mobile units. Elite units are known for their high levels of cohesion (Manning & Fullerton, 1988). Cohesion implies the development of strong emotional ties among members of the in-group. However advantageous cohesion in military units may be, it has serious problematic sides as well. If cohesion in a group is strongly developed, the members of the group are less inclined to interact with members of outside groups and they do not tend to value ideas that come from outside. In fact, they are quite critical toward outsiders and their practices. In general, people from a highly cohesive group tend to display less mental flexibility (Granovetter, 1983). On average, if people are strong in bonding, they are relatively weak in bridging to outsiders. These insights stem from general social science (Granovetter, 1973, 1983), but they apply remarkably well to the military in multinational operations. Hence, it comes as no surprise that problems are experienced, especially by elite units when they are forced to interact with others from outside their own units. In Kabul it has been demonstrated that military personnel from staff units and less elitist units faced relatively fewer problems when interacting with military from other national units. Among elite units of various nations, however, there has been considerably more friction and irritation, and less acceptance of other people's views (Soeters & Moelker, 2003).

This situation poses a specific responsibility on the shoulders of commanders, including junior commanders. Being used to the ideal of bonding with their own personnel, commanders tend to take the side of their soldiers in matters of dispute with others. In international military cooperation, however, this attitude may not always be very productive. In such situations, commanders, including junior commanders, may need to remain objective and deliberately aloof from their subordinates, and they would need to be mindful of interests that go beyond those of their own unit.

Elron et al. (2003) have attempted to summarize the recommendations that could be of use to commanders in international military cooperation. First, commanders should map differences between the various national contingents by addressing task-specific differences and engage in socially based cultural stories and comparisons (talking for instance about how life is in Turkey and how it is in the Netherlands). Second, they would need to emphasize commonness (the superordinate goals of the mission) and shared commonalities, such as the same military professional background, common lessons learned, shared mission-specific experiences, and the basic commonalities such as eating, drinking, and sleeping. In general, commanders would need to strive for a common in-group identity among the various national units engaged in the mission (Gaertner & Dovidio, 2000). In addition, in dealing with problems they would need to search for integrative solutions and compromises in which different angles, arguments, and perspectives may be considered. Finally, commanders should work on developing an attitude among their soldiers to tolerate and accept differences; in other words to give cultural space, suspend quick judgements, and to avoid treading on others' cultural comfort zone (such as not ridiculing people's religious customs and practices).

These are no easy recommendations, and surely these methods are at odds with common military practices stressing unit uniqueness, cohesion, and sometimes even unit superiority. Therefore, commanders—but actually military from all ranks— should receive some intercultural training before being deployed. This has also been emphasized by retired Major-General Robert Scales, Jr., before the U.S. House Armed Services Committee; in his address he has stressed that cultural awareness can serve all military personnel in better understanding and dealing with friends and foes alike (Scales, 2003). Such training should preferably entail learning from authentic and relevant problem situations. This implies that the problems presented should be real and not invented. Preferably, the problems should be available in a tool kit containing evocative small films on CD-ROM or DVD. The training should, in addition, integrate multiple perspectives and not emphasize one single "truth." Finally, it should provide space for reflection and articulation of assumptions. The German Bundeswehr has ample experience with this type of intercultural training that was used before deployments to, among others, Somalia and Indonesia (East Timor). Despite this extensive experience, however, even here the impact in everyday reality was deemed not fully satisfactory (Winslow et al., 2004, pp. 403–409). One of the recommendations was that such intercultural training should be anchored in the overall training and preparation program that all military personnel have to go through before being deployed. Besides, it remains important to study the effectiveness of this type of training throughout the whole organization.

One more issue needs mentioning in this connection. Cultural differences not only pertain to operational and command styles, but they most definitely also impact issues of a more ethical nature (Winslow et al., 2004, p. 400). How should military men treat women in the local population and interact with female soldiers, and how should military decide whether or not to participate in the local black market and react to attempts of bribery by locals (invitations to drinks or offering of money and prostitution)? These are all problems that military from different nations are not likely to approach in a similar fashion. Therefore, it would be wise to develop some supranational understanding of what is appropriate and what is not appropriate behavior in such circumstances. This could hardly be done by issuing a code of conduct, because such a document would prove to be too general and abstract. Perhaps one could learn from experiences in multinational business in this respect.

In multinational business, for instance international banking (van Nimwegen, Soeters, & Luijk, 2004), preventing unethical behavior is of predominant importance since unethical behavior may affect business results in a dramatic way.[2]

To prevent this from happening, multinational companies have developed methods not unlike the aforementioned procedure developed by the German Bundeswehr. Through these methods they create a common awareness of ethical values on the basis of experience in dealing with actual problems. In presenting those problems in a lively manner to all employees worldwide, the international workforce is put in a position where they can discuss the issues and draw conclusions on the basis of these discussions. These conclusions are then put on the web where everyone can access and learn from them. On the basis of all this bottom-up input, more general conclusions can be inferred and disseminated among the international work force of the organization. In such a way, the multinational company creates a kind of participatory learning and mutual adjustment of ideas of what is good (acceptable) and bad behavior (Holden, 2002).

Although this may seem somewhat idealistic, it would be worthwhile to implement such approaches when setting up military missions to areas which are culturally distant and that involve national contingents which have not been working together before. Ideally, the training tool kit to be used should be the same in all countries, whenever and wherever military units are preparing for deployment. For now, this idea may seem to be unthinkable, but perhaps in ten years from now this idea will have proven not to be so outrageous after all.

Future Directions

In the foregoing we have attempted to describe and analyze the impact of the cultural factor in multinational military operations. We have demonstrated that national armed forces are alike in many aspects, especially if a dominating technology reduces behavioral variance, which is the case in many air forces. As compared to the civilian sector, the military displays common cultural characteristics (collectivism, importance of hierarchy) that cross national borders. Hence, some kind of supranational military culture truly does exist, especially within NATO. On the other hand, there are (even within NATO) conspicuous differences between national armed forces. These divergences come to the fore in multinational operations as they impact a large number of command and operational issues.

It is important to be aware of this double-edged character of the cultural factor in the military. Therefore, one should not sweep the cultural factor under the carpet and be blind to cultural differences. But neither should one exaggerate its importance. If the cultural factor is not addressed properly, new stereotypes will arise "evoked by managers to explain others and themselves" (Moss Kanter & Corn, 1994, p. 5). Downplaying cultural differences may prevent the development of stereotypes within the organization (Holden, 2002). If anything, the cultural factor requires a sober and wise attitude of commanders, irrespective of their level in the chain of command. Also, and perhaps especially, junior commanders should be able to deal with this factor in a competent way. For junior commanders and NCOs in particular it is important to realize that they no longer can afford to exclusively take the side of their own personnel. They will need to balance between fostering the cohesion in their unit and creating an open mindset among their personnel, thus enabling them to collaborate and cohabitate with military and civilian personnel of other nations.

In order to achieve this ideal, intercultural training is important, not only for multinational peacekeeping missions but also as part of the "train as you fight" doctrine. The latter may be particularly important since a recent study has demonstrated that experiencing life-threatening events (for instance attacks) impacts the willingness to cooperate with military from other nations negatively. These findings from Afghanistan are fully in line with basic social-psychological theories stressing the inverse relation between death awareness and openness to others (Dechesne, Berg, & Soeters, 2004). As the probabilities that Western militaries will be facing such events increase, intercultural training will be needed that much more.

Many examples can be of use to show the way in this respect. But still, this seems a long way to go since many armed forces have not even begun to become aware of the importance of this factor. This is a serious problem. Approaching the cultural factor in a truly valuable manner can only be achieved if all participating countries in organizations such as NATO and other military coalitions actively take part in this type of intercultural training and dialogue. As long as all nations think that intercultural training is their own national business, a process of mutual accommodation is not likely to develop. If so, national contingents could better be deployed separately. But if separated deployment is not possible (because of geographical and operational reasons like in Kabul), then the various parties are sentenced to work and live together. This need not be a problem when, as earlier noted, commanders display a sober and wise attitude, not choosing between bonding within units or bridging to other units, but actively encouraging both bridging and bonding. Problems in these processes will doubtless occur. Commanders, aware of the interests at stake, should deal with these issues in a reflective and, most of all, rational and balanced way. If problems occur, commanders should not break off the communication altogether, nor should they start acting strategically against the interests of the partners in the mission, for instance, by striving for dominance. Acting strategically should be set aside to fight terrorists and other possible enemies.

If the military will engage in committed and responsible cooperation and cohabitation based on mutual recognition, then natural and pragmatic communication patterns are likely to evolve (Habermas, 2003). Only through permanent interaction and active dialogue about cultural issues and projects, will people from different nations be able to develop some form of shared meaning and mutual respect. In such processes one can not only learn about the truth and truthfulness of other people but also about the normative value of their deeds and thoughts, the latter being especially important in dealing with issues of an ethical nature.

War is serious business and the same can be said for global peace-enforcing and peacekeeping missions. All military organizations have multiple responsibilities to themselves and to others, friends and foes alike. Current global events provide a unique opportunity for those associated with the profession of arms to recognize, train for, and set a high standard in dealing with the special responsibilities associated with culture.

Notes

1. In the Netherlands, the general public and the families of the military are likely to demand immediate withdrawal of troops when the situation in a crisis area seems to become dangerous. This happened for instance in August 2004, when an ambush in Iraq caused one casualty and five wounded servicemen among the Dutch troops. In addition, deployments lasting longer than six months in most continental European armed forces are inconceivable. Clearly, these are huge differences compared with the policies in the U.S. Armed Forces.
2. See the dramatic fall of the British Barings Bank due to the lack of integrity of one of the bank's key employees.

References

Berry, J. W. (2004). Fundamental psychological processes in intercultural relations. In D. Landis, J.M. Bennett, and M.J. Bennett (Eds.), *Handbook of intercultural training*. (3rd ed., pp. 166–184). Thousand Oaks, CA: Sage.

Boyacigiller, N. A., & Adler, N. J. (1991). The parochial dinosaur: Organizational science in a global context. *Academy of Management Review, 16*, 262–290.

Caniglia, R. R. (2001). U.S. and British approaches to force protection. *Military Review, 79*, 73–81.

Dechesne, M., Berg, C. van den, & Soeters, J. (2004). *International collaboration under threat: A field study in Kabul.* (Manuscript submitted for publication.)

d'Iribarne, P. (1989). *La logique de l'honneur: Gestion des entrepresies et traditions nationals (Honor's logic: Business and national traditions)*. Paris: Editions Du Seuil.

Duffey, T. (2000). Cultural issues in contemporary peacekeeping. *International Peacekeeping, 7*, 142–168.

Duine, J. (1998). Werken en leven in HQ SFOR (Working and living in HQ SFOR). *Militaire Spectator, 167*, 451–455.

Elron, E., Shamir, B., & Ben-Ari, E. (1999). Why don't they fight each other? Cultural diversity and operational unity in multinational forces. *Armed Forces and Society, 26*, 73–97.

Elron, E., Halevy, N., Ben Ari, E., & Shamir, B. (2003). Cooperation and coordination across cultures in the peacekeeping forces: individual and organizational integrating mechanisms. In T. Britt & A. B. Adler (Eds.), *The psychology of the peacekeeper: Lessons from the field* (pp. 261–282). Westport, CT: Praeger.

Elster, J. (1993). *Nuts and bolts for the social sciences.* Cambridge: Cambridge University Press.

Faure, G. O., & Rubin, J. Z. (1993). *Culture and negotiation: The resolution of water disputes.* Newbury Park, CA: Sage.

Fitz-Gerald, A. (2003). Multinational landforce interoperability: Meeting the challenge of different backgrounds in chapter VI peace support operations. *Journal of Conflict Studies, 23*, 60–85.

Gaertner, S. L., & Dovidio, J. F. (2000). *Reducing intergroup bias: The common ingroup identity model.* Sussex: Taylor & Francis.

Granovetter, M. (1973). The strength of weak ties. *American Journal of Sociology, 78*, 1360–1380.

Granovetter, M. (1983). The strength of weak ties: A network theory revisited, *Sociological Theory, 1*, 201–233.

Habermas, J. (2003). *On the pragmatics of communication.* Cambridge: Polity Press.

Harrison, L. E., & Huntington, S. P. (Eds.). (2000). *Culture matters: How values shape human progress.* New York: Basic Books.

Helmreich, R. L., & Merritt, A. C. (1998). *Culture at work in aviation and medicine.* Aldershot: Ashgate.

Hendriks, F., & Musso, J. (2004). Making local democracy work, neighborhood-oriented reform in Los Angeles and the Dutch Randstad. In R. Bogason, S. Kensen, & H. Miller (Eds.), *Tampering with tradition: The unrealized authority of democratic agency* (pp. 39–63). New York: Lexington.

Hill, C. (2001). *International business: Competing in the global marketplace: Postscript 2001* (3rd ed.). Boston: McGraw-Hill.

Hofstede, G. H. (1980). *Culture's consequences: International differences in work-related values.* Thousand Oaks, CA: Sage.

Hofstede, G. H. (1991). *Cultures and organizations: Software of the mind.* London: McGraw-Hill.

Hofstede, G .H. (1994). Images of Europe. *Netherlands' Journal of Social Sciences, 30*, 63–82.

Hofstede, G. H. (1994). The merchant and the preacher, as pictured by Max Havelaar (1860). In B. Czarniawska-Joerges & P. Guillet de Monthoux (Eds.), *Good novels, better management: Reading organizational realities* (pp. 138–153). London/New York: Harwood Publishers.

Hofstede, G. H. (2001). *Culture's consequences: Comparing values, behaviors, institutions, and organizations across nations.* Thousand Oaks, CA: Sage.

Holden, N. (2002). *Cross-cultural management. A knowledge management perspective.* Essex, UK: Prentice Hall.

House, R. J., Hanges, P. J., Javidan, M., Dorfman, P. W., & Gupta V. (Eds.). (2004). *Culture, leadership, and organizations. The globe study of 62 societies.* Thousand Oaks, CA: Sage.

Kesteren, G. van (2004, March). Forget about the hearts and minds. *NRC Handelsblad.*

Lammers, C. J. (2003a). Mutiny in comparative perspective. *International Review of Social History, 48*, 473–482.

Lammers, C. J. (2003b). Occupation regimes alike and unlike: British, Dutch and French patterns of interorganizational control of foreign territories. *Organization Studies, 24*, 1379–1403.

Manning, F. J., & Fullerton, T. D. (1988). Health and well-being in highly cohesive units of the U.S. Army. *Journal of Applied Social Psychology, 18*, 503–519.

Moskos, C. (1976). *Peace soldiers: The sociology of a United Nations military force*. Chicago: Chicago University Press.

Moskos, C., & Wood, F. R. (1988). *The military: More than just a job?*. Washington, DC: Pergamon-Brassey's.

Moss Kanter, R., & Corn, R. (1994). Do cultural differences make a business difference? Contextual factors affecting cross-cultural relationship success. *Journal of Management Development, 13*, 5–23.

Nimwegen, T. van, Soeters, J., & Luijk, H. van (2004). Managing values and ethics in an international bank. *International Journal of Cross-Cultural Management, 4*, 101–122.

Onishi, N. (2004, October 30). Dutch soldiers find smiles protect as well as armor. *The New York Times*.

Operation Iraqi Freedom: Outside Perspectives. (October 21, 2003). *Hearings before the House Armed Services Committee United States House of Representatives* (testimony of R. H. Scales Jr., First Session of the 108th Congress).

Page, J. T. (2003). *Culture and the profession of arms in the 21st century: An application of Hofstede's theory within the North Atlantic Treaty Organization (NATO) and the Partnership for Peace (PfP) military cultures*. Unpublished doctoral dissertation, Nova Southeastern University, Baden Wuerttemburg, Germany.

Poponete, C. (2007). *Culture in the Romanian armed forces*. Doctoral dissertation in progress, Henri Coanda Romanian Air Force Academy, Brasov, Romania.

Robberson, T. (2003, December 24). The Dutch model: Troops show how to lower tensions in Iraq. *The Dallas Morning News*.

Sion, L. (2004). *"Changing from green to blue beret": Dutch peacekeepers in Bosnia and Kosovo*. Unpublished doctoral dissertation, Free University of Amsterdam.

Soeters, J. (1996). Culture and conflict: An application of Hofstede's theory to the conflict in the former Yugoslavia. *Peace and Conflict: Journal of Peace Psychology, 2*, 233–244.

Soeters, J. (1997). Values in military academies: A thirteen country study. *Armed Forces and Society, 24*, 7–32.

Soeters, J. (2001). The Dutch military and the use of violence. *Netherlands' Journal of Social Sciences, 37*, 24–37.

Soeters, J., & Boer, P. (2000). Culture and flight safety in military aviation. *The International Journal of Aviation Psychology, 10*, 111–133.

Soeters, J., & Bos-Bakx, M. (2003). Cross-cultural issues in peacekeeping operations. In T. W. Britt & A. B. Adler (Eds.), *The psychology of the peacekeeper: Lessons from the field* (pp. 283–298). Westport, CT: Praeger.

Soeters, J. & Moelker, R. (2003). German-Dutch cooperation in the heat of Kabul. In G. Kümmel and S. Colmer (Eds.), *Soldat – Militär – Politik – Gesellschaft* (pp. 63–75). Baden-Baden: Nomos.

Soeters, J. & Recht, R. (1998). Culture and discipline in military academies: An international comparison. *Journal of Political and Military Sociology, 26*, 169–189.

Soeters, J. & Recht, R. (2001). Convergence or divergence in the multinational classroom? Experiences from the military. *International Journal of Intercultural Relations, 25*, 423–440.

Soeters, J., Tanerçan, E., Varoğlu, A., & Sigri, Ű. (2004). Turkish-Dutch encounters during peacekeeping. *International Peacekeeping, 11*, 354–368.

Tomasic, D. (1946). The structure of Balkan society. *American Journal of Sociology, 52*, 132–140.

Van Oudenhoven, J. P. (2001). Do organizations reflect national cultures? A 10-nation study. *International Journal of Intercultural Relations, 25*, 89–107.

Vinken, H., Soeters, J., & Ester, P. (Eds.). (2004). *Comparing cultures. Dimensions of culture in a comparative perspective*. Leiden, Netherlands: Brill.

Vliert, E. van de, et al. (1999). Temperature, cultural masculinity, and domestic political violence. *Journal of Cross-Cultural Psychology, 30*, 291–341.

Voorhoeve, J. C. (1979). *Peace, profits and principles: A study of Dutch foreign policy*. The Hague, Netherlands: Martinus Nijhoff.

Winslow, D., Kammhuber, S., & Soeters, J. (2004). Diversity management and training in non-American forces. In D. Landis, J. M. Bennett, & M. J. Bennett, *Handbook of intercultural training* (3rd ed., pp. 395–415). Thousand Oaks, CA: Sage.

CHAPTER 3

FROM VALUES TO PERFORMANCE: IT'S THE JOURNEY THAT CHANGES THE TRAVELER

Michael W. Grojean and Jeffrey L. Thomas

A journey of a thousand miles begins with a single step.

–Lao-tzu

Rocked by ethical scandals over the past two decades, three of the four U.S. Armed Services have made well-publicized rededications to core organizational values. The underlying assumption is that these scandals call attention to a critical systemic failure to properly develop, monitor, and moderate values, which in turn leads to behavioral indiscretions and performance decrements. As a result, each of the U.S. Armed Services clearly articulated its own core organizational values in the hopes of preventing further scandal, behavioral indiscretions, and performance decrements and reinforcing what the particular organization holds important in its service members. For example, the U.S. Army espoused seven core values of loyalty, duty, respect, selfless service, honesty, integrity, and personal courage, which cleverly make up the acronym, LDRSHIP.

Although identifying core organizational values is an important strategic gesture—one that informs service members and potential service members what a particular organization stands for—there is very little data to support the assumption that service members who endorse these values are better behaving or better performing than service members who do not. For example, a collaborative study conducted by the U.S. Army Center for Army Leadership and Walter Reed Army Institute of Research (Thomas, Bliese, & Bullis, 2001) found

The views expressed in this chapter are those of the authors and do not necessarily represent the official policy or position of the U.S. Army Medical Command or the U.S. Department of Defense.

that the Army values of selfless service, integrity, and respect were unrelated to a number of performance criteria using Campbell's (1990, 1999) multidimensional model of performance (e.g., task-specific, disciplined, demonstrating effort, contextual). As a further illustration of the difficulty of linking values to behavior or performance directly, Thomas, Dickson, and Bliese (2001) conducted a study using broader value orientations that were not defined by the organization, but were selected rather because they were hypothesized to be linked to the *Leader Motive Profile* of successful leader performance (McClelland & Burnham, 1976). Results showed that Leader Motive Profile value orientations of power and affiliation were only weakly related to the rated leadership performance of Army cadets and that other variables mediated the link between values and performance.

Establishing a direct link between values (organizationally espoused or not) and behavior or performance is a difficult task, as these studies indicate. In terms of the core values for military organizations, we posit that such a relationship is significantly more complex than a simple values/behavior/performance link. Our belief is that this relationship is rooted in socialization and the identity development of service members. When an initial entry employee (e.g., military recruit) identifies with core organizational values, is socialized within the culture, and develops a role identity at the individual and group level, the stage is set for pro-organizational behavior and performance.

To describe this process, we will draw from the industrial and organizational psychology literature. Specifically, we will review relevant research on self-concept and role identity, organizational socialization, behavioral indicators of successful socialization, and performance. Drawing from these literatures, we argue that basic tendencies such as values are cognitive adaptations that are shaped by one's self-concept and socialization experiences. In turn, one's socialization and identity influence behavior and performance and in this manner serve as a primary mediator in linking values to behavior and performance. Thus, we suggest that organizationally espoused and inculcated values are relevant to specific performance criteria to the extent that they are linked to a self-concept activated by specific contextual and environmental cues (i.e., the process of organizational socialization). We propose that the relationship between values and performance in organizations chiefly occurs as illustrated in Figure 3.1.

This model will serve to facilitate the rest of the chapter. Specifically, we will discuss each element of the model, presenting brief reviews of each component and making the case for how each is an important part of the process in linking values to performance. Simultaneous to this process, we will use a vignette comparing two socialization scenarios—one unsuccessful and one successful—to illustrate the elements of the model and highlight its practical importance.

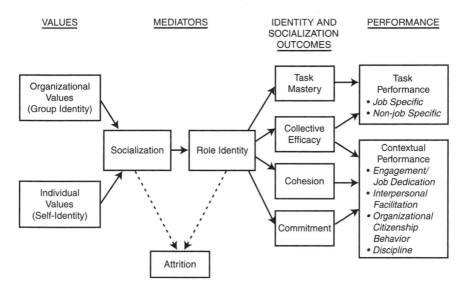

Figure 3.1
Values to Performance Process Model

Values to Performance Illustrated: The Story of Mr. Lewis and Mr. Clark

Perhaps the best way to understand the relationships we posit in our model is to illustrate them with a vignette of two young service members as they join the military. We assume that the process of identity formation as the means of linking values to performance works similarly across the different types of armed forces. Of note, some of these services may accomplish this feat better and with more ease due to multiple influences; type of service, manner of people attracted to that service, recruitment strategies, and geographic area of recruitment, to just name a few.

We start our story with two young people interested in serving in their nation's armed forces: Mr. Lewis and Mr. Clark.

Mr. Lewis was a success story in high school, physically fit and a superb athlete in sports that required individual effort and little teamwork. Determined to make a name for himself, perhaps the single most important value in his life was that of self-advancement, a combination of personal power and achievement striving. Mr. Lewis enlisted in the armed forces as he saw this as an opportunity to go to college and eventually advance his position in life.

Mr. Clark was a similar success story, except in his situation he was a consummate team player—he readily led the sports teams to which he belonged. He believed the greater good was to serve rather than to be served, which typified the driving value in his life; that of self-transcendence, the concept of service to others and ideals greater than one's self. Mr. Clark enlisted in the armed forces because he felt that it was his duty to participate in the service that defended his nation's freedom.

At first blush, it would appear that while both these young men make ideal candidates for entry into the military, Mr. Lewis, possesses a more self-centered focus that is not as conducive to the concepts of self-sacrifice and duty that are hallmark values in each branch of the military.

On the other hand, Mr. Clark seemed to have a head start on just such ideals with his valuing of service to others and a higher ideal. The intent of this illustration is to trace the potential paths of these two new military members and how they may lead to success or attrition depending on the path they walk through socialization and identity formation.

Although both receive their initial entry training at the same time, they are in separate training units with differing officers and noncommissioned officers in charge. In Mr. Lewis' case, his cadre is formed of veterans from previous conflicts—service members who understand and are committed to their branch's values and ideals. Mr. Lewis has a rough time of it at first, with his natural tendency to focus on himself drawing early attention. Certainly Lewis is moving from the anticipatory to the encounter stage of socialization. Based on discussion with his recruiter, television ads, and his Internet exploration, he assumed that he would just have to tolerate four years of service and he would be on his way with a great college fund established. What he was starting to find was that if he were to continue by focusing solely on himself, those would be a very long four years indeed. Lewis's cadre instructs him in the basic requirements of his service, but they do more. They model the values of his organization—demonstrating their own personal sacrifices through concern for his and the other recruits' development.

Tough and demanding, his cadre earns his trust, respect, and ultimately his admiration. Ultimately, the leadership team of this training unit provides a model for what is and what is not appropriate behavior expected from members in this service. They also describe not only what values are critical to the organization; they demonstrate how those values are enacted in role-appropriate behavior. Lewis now understands what it means to be a member of this organization, even if perhaps it is slightly at discord with his own personal values and preferences.

Clark's path is slightly different from Lewis's. His cadre consists of seasoned veterans as well, but in this case a sense of bitterness and cynicism permeates the leadership of his training unit. His desire to serve and well-intentioned enthusiasm is met with derision and ridicule from his training cadre. The message to Clark is as simple as the one to Lewis, although in the opposite direction: "you are merely a resource to be used and discarded by this organization as its leaders see fit."

Naturally, Clark is slightly disillusioned by this mismatch with his expectations. However he resolves to wait it out and see how things progress in his first unit. In his case, the anticipatory stage of socialization giving way to the encounter provides him with disconfirming information regarding the value and worth of his service.

Both entrants have moved from the anticipatory to the encounter stages of socialization, receiving somewhat conflicting information between their original expectations and what they perceive to be the ideals of the organization. Provided that the dissonance is not too severe, this encounter will likely continue into their first duty assignment, where they will ultimately enter the change and acquisition stage of socialization.

It is in this third stage that long-term changes will occur, where the role identity of the service member will form and either be adopted or rejected. Lewis is beginning to form the image that the ideal service member is a selfless individual who focuses on the needs of others. Clark, on the other hand, is developing the impression that service members are out for themselves, cynical about their service, and embittered about being overused. While neither of these emerging identities with their attendant values match the initial values possessed by the entrants, it is far more likely that Lewis will ultimately adopt the role identity due to the role modeling and positive intervention of his socialization agents (training cadre). Clark, on the other hand, will likely become disillusioned with his service if he continues to find confirming information regarding his perception of the service member role identity. Continued disillusionment will likely lead to his eventual attrition from the military.

Meanwhile, the question becomes one of performance. In this illustration, it is easy to assume that Lewis, adopting the role identity formed in his interaction with his training cadre (and subsequent unit assignment) would then be more likely to behave in organizationally endorsed behaviors. It is also easy to see Lewis more likely to contribute to the collective efficacy and cohesion and to possess higher levels of commitment to the organization as he continues to successfully participate in the unit's mission.

Clark on the other hand is likely a different story. As he rejects the role identity that he has formed based on his interactions with the socialization agents of his experience, he is likely to demonstrate far less commitment and dedication in his performance. There is little to make us believe that he will not perform to the best of his capability, indeed, his original value set will likely cause him to do his best regardless. However if nothing counters his beliefs of what is expected of service members, it is highly unlikely that he will contribute to the collective efficacy and cohesion we see with Lewis. It is unlikely, as well, that higher levels of commitment may be expected—and in fact, this lack of commitment will add to the likelihood that Clark will depart the organization.

This story of two entrants is intended to illustrate how individual values and organizational values mesh during the socialization process. In the first case, the individual possessed some values that were not conducive to proper military service, but through successful socialization developed a role identity that ultimately led to organizationally successful behavior.

In the second case, the entrant possessed values that the organization endorsed and desired in its members. However, through the failed socialization effort (misdirected socialization agents), this member formed a faulty role identity for the organization and refused to adopt it. Ultimately, this member would have exhibited lower levels of motivation, satisfaction, and commitment—all of which would have detracted from his overall performance and, in the end, caused attrition.

Values: Definition and Conceptualization

Value is the most invincible and impalpable of ghosts, and comes and goes unthought of while the visible and dense matter remains as it was.
                                        –W. Stanley Jevons, British Economist, Logician

The study of values and their impact has attracted many scholars over the past half century (e.g., Feather, 1995; Hofstede, 1980; House et al., 1999; Kluckhohn & Strodtbeck, 1961; Parsons & Shils, 1951; Rokeach, 1973; Schwartz, 1994; Schwartz & Bilsky, 1990). Hofstede defines values as "a broad tendency to prefer certain states of affairs over others" (1980, p. 18). He further posits that such preferences exist simultaneously in two elements; intensity and direction. For example, a person may believe in the value *avoidance of debt*. The first element is the intensity of the value, that is, how weakly, moderately, or strongly a person feels about it. The other element is the direction, which is in essence whether the person feels positively or negatively about the value. In the avoidance-of-debt example, a person may either feel strongly or weakly about being indebted, as well as in a positive or negative direction.

Rokeach (1973) provides a definition of values as well. A value is "an enduring belief that a specific mode of conduct or end-state of existence is personally or socially preferable to an opposite or converse mode of conduct or end-state of existence" (p. 5). Erez and Earley (1993) derive several characteristics of values from this definition. First they state that while an individual's values are stable and enduring, they are also malleable. Values are beliefs, which provide a basis to judge how desirable a mode of conduct or an end state is. Erez and Early also state that values can refer to either modes of conduct (instrumental) or end states (terminal) and that personal preference will be patterned in alignment with these values. Finally, they state that an individual conceives a value as something that is socially or personally preferable.

Given the amount of attention values have received, it is not surprising that definitions vary. For the purposes of this chapter, however, we will be relying on the definition of values presented by Schwartz (1994). Values are desirable goals that cross situations, vary in importance, and serve as a guiding influence in a person's life. He further identifies four implicit concepts embedded in this definition. In short, values (1) serve the interests of a social entity, (2) motivate action—providing direction and intensity, (3) function as standards for judging and justifying action, and (4) are acquired both through socialization to dominant group values and through the unique learning experiences of individuals.

As suggested by the definitions of values, researchers believe that a person's values are motivational (i.e., they provide valence) and can vary in intensity. They also serve as standards for judgment and justification of action. For example, Feather (1995, p. 1145) found strong support that "attractiveness of alternate courses of action were related to value types and that choice between alternatives was related to value types and valences." Further, Sagiv and Schwartz (1995) found that readiness for out-group social contact among Israeli Jews was most positive with the value of universalism and the most negative with the value of tradition.

One confounding issue that frequently arises in discussions of values relates to which level of analysis is appropriate for studying values. For example, Parsons and Shils (1951) and Hofstede (1980) were interested in values as they manifested themselves at a societal cultural level. Kluckhohn and Strodtbeck (1961) were interested in values that not only describe the individual as a part of a collective, but also form a belief set about the characteristics of mankind (i.e., the innate goodness of people, the individual's role in coping with nature). In turn, Rokeach (1973) studied values as they pertained to individuals, including ambition, self-control, social recognition, and equality.

Finally, House et al. (1999) in the Global Leadership Organizational Behavior Effectiveness (GLOBE) project and Schwartz (1992) have looked at values as they appear on multiple levels. In GLOBE, respondent values were measured at the organizational and societal level, while Schwartz measured them at the individual and cultural (not necessarily national) level. While we subscribe to the multiple levels approach to values and conceptualize values at both the individual level (which the newcomer brings to the organization) and at the group level (those norms that the group possesses to govern behavior), for this chapter we will discuss values primarily at the individual level.

In summary, values are beliefs that have motivational power, serve a social entity, provide standards and norms against which to make judgments, and exist on several levels. Our interest in values centers on how the values that individuals have when they enter an organization interact with the values that the organization espouses. Thus in order to link values to subsequent performance, it is necessary to describe the process involved in how initial entry employees' and organizations' values become intertwined. However, before we begin to describe this process, we should first examine the terminus of this journey—performance.

Performance

> Try not to become a man of success but rather try to become a man of value.
>
> –Albert Einstein

Beginning in the early 1990s, personnel psychologists began to consider job performance as a multidimensional construct. Ilgen and Hollenbeck (1991) are early contributors to this shift to a multidimensional definition of performance by differentiating between jobs and roles. They argue that any model of performance must account for the constants provided by jobs and the flexibility provided by roles.

Campbell, McCloy, Oppler, and Sager (1992) extended this discussion by identifying additional dimensions of performance. Based upon prior work with the U.S. Army (Campbell, 1990), they identified eight possible job performance dimensions, some of which focused on more technical proficiency aspects of performance (e.g., *job specific task proficiency, written and oral communication task proficiency,* and *management/administration*) and some that focused on the more psycho-social aspects of performance (e.g., *demonstrating effort, maintaining personal discipline, and facilitating peer* and *team performance*). What is unique about this taxonomy as well as a later eight-dimensional model (Campbell et al., 1992) is that they expand the traditional model of job performance beyond the core technical proficiency requirements to elements that actually impact the social structure in which the performance is conducted. This expansion of the traditional view is also found in a growing body of literature that investigates contextual performance (Borman & Motowidlo, 1993).

In particular, Borman and Motowidlo proposed that individual performance can be categorized into either task performance or contextual performance. Task performance refers to those core technical functions of individual behavior within an organization. Contextual performance is defined as the elements of individual performance that serve to maintain the broad social, organizational, and psychological environment in which the core technical functions must operate.

In the intervening years since its conception, evidence grew for this task-contextual performance distinction. Notably much of this work has been conducted within a military setting. For example, Motowidlo and Van Scotter (1994) examined the factors related to the overall performance of junior grade Air Force mechanics. Using hierarchical regression, they found that contextual performance uniquely accounted for approximately 11 percent of the variance and task performance uniquely accounted for approximately 13 percent of the variance in supervisor evaluations.

Additionally, Borman, White, and Dorsey (1995) investigated supervisor and peer reports of 493 first-term Army soldiers. Using path analysis, they demonstrated that elements of contextual performance may be distinguished from task performance. Specifically, they showed that while task performance accounted for 13 percent of the variance in supervisor ratings of overall performance and 7 percent in peer ratings of overall performance, adding contextual performance into the model significantly increased the explained variance for supervisor ratings ($\Delta R2 = 15\%$) and peer ratings ($\Delta R2 = 12\%$). Again, support is provided that contextual performance coupled with task performance is a valid element of a multidomain construct of performance.

In summary, evidence supports the conclusion that while performance is a multidimensional domain, the clustering of these multiple dimensions into task and contextual performance is the most parsimonious way to conceptualize such performance. Indeed, the taxonomy of Campbell et al. (1992) and the identification of task and conceptual performance dimensions have served as organizing frameworks in recent studies of military performance and its precursors (Thomas et al., 2001; Thomas, Adler, & Castro, 2004).

We have identified the departure point of our journey—the values an individual possesses when joining an institution and the organizational values of said institution. We have also identified the terminus of this journey—job performance as characterized by the technical functions required by the organization (task) as well as performance that contributes to the social structure within which such task performance occurs (context). It is appropriate now to describe those intervening processes that we believe carry the traveler from start to finish. We begin with the process by which entrants first learn the values of their organization and begin to determine the fit with their own personal values—socialization.

Socialization

If the elders have no values, their children and grandchildren will turn out badly
                                                                    –Chinese proverb

Socialization has been defined in multiple ways, from "learning the ropes" (Schein, 1968, 1988) to the process by which employees are transformed from outsiders to insiders (Feldman, 1981). Louis (1980) provides a definition drawing upon multiple sources (e.g., Van Maanen, 1976; Van Maanen & Schein, 1979) that describes socialization as a change process through which individuals learn "the values, abilities, expected behaviors, and social knowledge essential for assuming an organizational role" (pp. 229–230).

It is this definition that first stipulates the role that socialization plays in the development of an organizationally specific self-concept. We subscribe to Louis's definition of socialization and contend that the process of socialization must address: (1) how a stable role identity within the organization is formed, as well as, (2) how it is then linked to appropriate values, behaviors, and performance. This last component of socialization is best thought of as the change mechanism for how an individual comes to understand the organizational culture, climate, and norms, embody its espoused values, and in turn, becomes a highly representative and highly performing employee. Other researchers have made this similar point by explicitly proposing a change mechanism when defining socialization (e.g., Feldman, 1981; Porter, Lawler, & Hackman, 1975; Van Maanen, 1975).

In general, socialization research can be roughly categorized into one of two approaches: investigation into the processes of socialization (e.g., stages, feedback-seeking, information processing) or the content of what is actually learned or acquired through socialization (Chao, O'Leary-Kelly, Wolf, Klein, & Gardner, 1994). While the content of socialization is critical, we have chosen to emphasize the processes involved because it is more generalizable across organizations than the specific content of what is learned or acquired through socialization.

Moreland and Levine (1988, 2001) suggest that there are three basic reciprocal processes that must occur during socialization: evaluation, commitment, and role transition—displayed in Figure 3.2.

During evaluation, the group and the individual appraise each other, in an ongoing process of gaining insight into the other's characteristics. This is essentially a process of understanding and sense-making. The process of commitment involves how strongly tied the individual is to the group and how strongly tied the group is

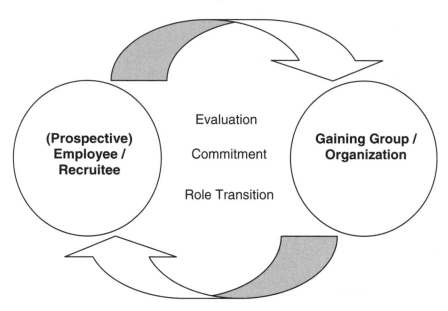

Figure 3.2
Reciprocal Processes Involved in Organizational Socialization

to its members. Finally, as each group member has a role within the group, the group and the individual negotiate the specifics of the role in the group. It is during role transition that the group and its group members negotiate the structure, composition, and positioning of these roles.

These reciprocal processes are thought to occur within a series of qualitatively different phases that employees undergo during the socialization process. There are many viewpoints as to the exact nature and timing of these stages, as is the case in much of stage-theory in general. We propose that the reciprocal processes highlighted above form the basis of continual judgments made by employees across all stages of socialization. For instance, both an initial entry employee and a seasoned veteran employee are likely to gauge their commitment to the organization and the organization's commitment to them on a continual basis.

We noted that socialization is typically thought of as occurring in stages. There is a fair degree of consensus among socialization researchers that a three-stage model of socialization is the most parsimonious (e.g., Feldman, 1976; Porter et al., 1975; Van Maanen, 1975). These stages are: (1) *anticipatory,* (2) *encounter,* and (3) *change/ acquisition,* presented with process variables per stage in Figure 3.3.

During the anticipatory stage, potential employees learn all they can about the organization. Potential employees are actively engaged in information gathering. They are trying to decide if the group fits their individual needs. There are a number of ways that potential employees can find out about a particular group; they can talk to current members, former members, or simply read any available literature on the

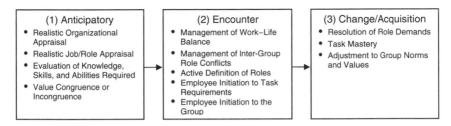

Figure 3.3
Stages of Organizational Socialization

group. From the group perspective, established members are engaged in recruitment, trying to decide which potential employee should be invited into the group. There are many possible recruitment techniques, such as: inviting potential employees in for an interview or talking to other group members who know the newcomers. If this stage is successful, the potential employee moves from a nonmember status to becoming a new member, or an initial entry employee. The endpoint of this stage is the entry point into the organization or conversely the exit point if a potential employee is not selected or self-selects not to join the group.

However, before moving on to the next stage of organizational socialization it is important to note that Feldman (1981) argues for the importance of four variables that may impact potential employees' perceptions of the gaining group/organization during the anticipatory phase. These are: possessing a realistic appraisal of the organization; possessing a realistic appraisal of the job; possessing the required knowledge, skills, and abilities; and possessing values congruent with the organization.

During the encounter stage the initial entry employee begins to see what the organization is truly like and shifts their values, skills, and attitudes (Feldman, 1981; Porter et al., 1975; Van Maanen, 1975). The encounter phase has its own set of process variables that determine how successful socialization has been. These are: (1) management of work–life balance, (2) management of inter-group role conflicts, (3) active definition of roles, (4) employee initiation to task requirements, and (5) employee initiation to the group. Through these variables, the encounter stage of socialization forms the framework for linking organizational values to role-specific behaviors. Our contention is that through these processes, the seeds for the stable role identity are first sown and an image of the job-specific role identity is formed, refined, and brought into close definition with the aid of proper organizational socialization.

It is in the third phase, change and acquisition, that role identity is internalized, and relatively long-lasting changes occur, and initial entry employees make a strong adjustment to organizational values (Chao et al., 1994) and master job-specific behaviors and skills (Feldman, 1981; Porter et al., 1975). As with the encounter stage, certain process variables impact the success of the change and acquisition stage as well (Feldman, 1981). These are: (1) resolution of role demands, (2) task mastery, and (3) adjustment to group norms and values. With the resolution of role demands, agreement occurs on what is expected and what is considered appropriate task/role behavior, including resolution strategies on how to deal with work–life and inter-group conflicts. Task mastery describes the individual's proficiency in learning and executing job tasks. Finally, the individual adjusts to the organization's values and norms. Within this adjustment, organizational values become encoded (salient and relevant) within the individual's role identity.

Looking at our model in Figure 3.1, it can be seen that our conceptualization of what qualifies as markers for successful completion of socialization differs some-what than Feldman's (1981). First, Feldman does not discuss performance as the endpoint and criterion for socialization as we do. Rather, Feldman identifies these process variables as indications that the employee has been successfully socialized. While we agree that these are markers for socialization, we think that they serve as behavioral antecedent conditions facilitating high performance as well. Second, we note that task mastery is represented in both Feldman's conceptualization as well as ours; however, we propose that there are three additional specific behaviors that serve as mediators within this class. These are: collective efficacy, cohesion, and commitment.

What we believe is missing from the socialization literature, however, is the psychological process that links successful socialization with such outcomes as task mastery, cohesion, collective efficacy, and commitment. We posit that the development of a role identity (or role-specific self-concept) that blends the individual's values with internalization of organizational values into a cogent and coherent structure is the likely end-state to a successful socialization program. Indeed, Lord, Brown, and Freidberg (1999) suggest that it is only when values and self-identities form coherent, interrelated patterns that powerful organizational effects will result (i.e., leadership impact). In the next section, we will discuss these concepts.

Role Identity

> All the world is a stage,
> And all the men and women merely players.
> They have their exits and entrances;
> Each man in his time plays many parts.
>
> —William Shakespeare

Theories of the self are the multiple hypotheses a person has about themselves that guide perceptions, thoughts, and actions. Markus and Cross (1990) suggest that the concept of the self refers to an "insider's view" of personality, and that the "work-ing self-concept is influential in the shaping and controlling of intrapersonal behavior (self-relevant information processing, affect regulation, and motivational processes) and interpersonal processes (social perception, social comparison, and social interaction)" (p. 578). While consensus has yet to be reached in the literature about the exact makeup of self-concept, there are three points that researchers tend to agree upon: (1) self-concept contains a stable aspect, (2) yet may change in differing situations, and (3) is closely linked to traits, values, and behavior (e.g., Donahue, 1994; Higgins, Klein, & Strauman, 1987; Roberts & Donahue, 1994).

These first two points generally dichotomize into identity consisting of a global and role-specific component. Individuals possess some sense of a stable self-concept that transcends situations, and may be referenced without a specific context. Leonard, Beauvais, and Scholl (1999) term this identity as a *global identity* while Markus and Nurius (1986) regard it as the *working self*. This global identity may be the one that is drawn upon when individuals are asked to describe themselves without a relevant context specified.

On the other hand, individuals also possess a potentially more useful construct in the representation of multiple and differing self-concepts. For example, an individual may be a soldier, a teacher, a mother, a wife, a runner, and a Red Cross volunteer. This individual possesses identities for each of these roles, which while probably correlated are still distinct. These *role-specific* identities carry information about what are considered proper behaviors, what value orientations are salient, and what attitudes are considered relevant for a particular situation (Leonard et al., 1999).

While the global identity provides a starting point for role-specific identities, it is the role specific identities that provide the relevant information that influence a role (e.g., traits, competencies, and values). Stryker and Serpe (1982) use the example of an individual who identifies him/herself as an academic at one level, a member of the business administration faculty at another, and a finance professor at yet another level of specificity. It is because of this level of specificity that role-specific identity is thought to have the greatest impact on one's attitudes, value orientations, and subsequent behavior.

We are aware of only one study that explicitly tests the link between self-concept and behavior. Grojean (2002) found that the relationships between values and contextual performance were moderated by the presence of a strong citizenship role identity. The critical values measured were Schwartz's (1992) continuum of *self-enhancement* and *self-transcendence*, which focuses on the individuals' pursuit of self-interests as opposed to the interests of those around them. It was hypothesized that individuals who possessed more self-transcendent values would be more likely to contribute to extra role behaviors as operationalized within contextual performance.

In this study, data were collected from military cadets preparing for commissioning regarding personality, values, and attitudes. Supervisors for these cadets provided ratings of the participants' citizenship performance. The predicted relationship between self-transcendent values and contextual performance was supported, albeit extremely weakly. However, this relationship was found to be moderated by the participants' citizenship role identity. Under conditions of a high (or strong) citizenship role identity, values possessed a strong and significant relationship to contextual performance (0.30 standardized beta), while in the low condition it remained insignificant.

Thus it appears that the argument for role identity's (self-concept) inclusion in our model is well based. It is then appropriate to investigate what we believe to be the next steps of the journey leading to performance, task mastery, cohesion, collective efficacy, and commitment.

Socialization and Identity Outcomes

What we must decide is perhaps how we are valuable, rather than how valuable we are.
                                                                    –Edgar Z. Friedenberg

At first glance, readers will notice a few things about the four identity and socialization outcome variables. First, each of these psychological constructs has a devoted and rather large literature (e.g., *task mastery,* Kammeyer-Mueller & Wanberg, 2003; *collective efficacy,* Bandura, 1997; *cohesion,* Festinger, 1950; *organizational commitment,* Meyer & Allen, 1997). Second, these constructs are likely to be interrelated both theoretically and practically. And third, these constructs reflect both individual and group levels in linking the socialization of values to performance within organizations. These variables are well reviewed in the literature, are likely to be interrelated, and reflect both individual and group level properties. This then underscores their importance as process variables, particularly in studying processes at work in organizations.

Task mastery has been operationally defined as "reflecting the self-appraisal of one's ability to successfully fulfill job responsibilities" (Kammeyer-Mueller & Wanberg, 2003, p. 781). Moreover, the general concept of task mastery has been identified as an integral component of other socialization models (e.g., Chao et al., 1994; Kammeyer-Mueller & Wanberg, 2003). It stands to reason that employees who possess mastery of the basic skills and tasks associated with their job will have a stronger sense of being integrated into the group or the organization and are, in all likelihood, higher performers as well. In a recent study, Kammeyer-Mueller and Wanberg found that this was exactly the case in their four-wave longitudinal study of seven organizations. Specifically, they found that task mastery was positively related to perceptions of group integration as well as organizational commitment, a construct that they conceptualized as a distal outcome of successful newcomer integration.

By mastering tasks and skill sets in their primary job, employees convey two things to the organization: (1) that at a more proximal level, they are contributing to the overall performance of the organization, and (2) that at a tacit level, they understand and support the overall organizational mission, goals, and values. Task mastery is closely related to another identity outcome, *efficacy expectations.* Having developed and mastered skills and tasks working their primary job, employees are very likely to be much more confident about their future chances of success or high performance concerning their job and also in how their mastery of the job supports the overall group.

Efficacy beliefs (Bandura, 1977, 1986) have generated a great deal of research in academic and organizational settings. Much of the focus of efficacy research in organizations that has been conducted has determined that it is a moderator of stressor–strain relationships (e.g., Chen & Bliese, 2002; Jex & Bliese, 1999; Schaurbroeck & Merritt, 1997) and that it also serves as an antecedent condition of performance (e.g., Eden & Zuk, 1995; Taylor, Locke, Lee, & Gist, 1984). Typically, efficacy is thought to be an individual level phenomenon, but Bandura (1997) also suggests that the concept of a group-level efficacy, or collective efficacy, is important when considering organizational or group-level phenomena. In fact, collective efficacy is generally viewed as an important aspect of group functioning (Bandura, 1986) and is thought to be required to overcome performance problems faced by groups, especially when involving interactive and interdependent tasks (Paskevich, Brawley, Dorsch, & Widmeyer, 1999).

Because of its implications for group, team, or organizational performance, we suggest that of the two efficacy types, collective efficacy plays a more vital role in how the socialization of organizational values is linked to performance because it represents a distinct marker for an individual's acculturation into a work group. In effect, the degree to which individual employees believe in the future success of their unit is linked to their socialization into the group, as successfully identified members are likely to have higher levels of self-efficacy. Military researchers, probably more than any other organizational researchers recently, have examined collective efficacy and its correlates (e.g., Chen & Bliese, 2002; Jex & Bliese, 1999; Sommers, Sinclair, & Thomas, in press) and have found that it is negatively related to individual role stress—the lack of role identity—and it is positively related to health and performance. Thus, we feel it serves as a good marker for the development of an employee's (soldier's) role identity and organizational socialization.

Group cohesion is one of the most researched constructs in the study of group dynamics. Despite the sheer volume of studies, group cohesion has remained an enigmatic construct because there has been a lack of consensus about how to define and measure it (Beale, Cohen, Burke, & McLendon, 2003). We subscribe to the definition provided by Carron (1982) that "cohesion is the dynamic process which is reflected in the tendency for a group to stick together and remain united in the pursuit of its goals and objectives" (p. 124). We also subscribe to the multidimensional conceptualization of cohesion, as have many researchers (e.g., Carron, Widmeyer, & Brawley, 1985; Cota, Evans, Dion, Kilik, & Longman, 1995; Festinger, 1950; Mullen & Copper, 1994). The three dimensions that most researchers agree upon suggest that cohesion is made up of (1) interpersonal attraction to other group members or the group itself, (2) a commitment to the group task or to the group dimension, and (3) group pride.

Cohesion is centrally linked to the development of one's role identity and one's organizational socialization. Hogg (1992) and Terry, Hogg, and Duck (1999) suggest that cohesion and solidarity within groups is hinged upon whether others perceive members' to be prototypical of the group. In other words, the more that members of the group are seen to embody the group's values, beliefs, and attitudes, the more likely that group will be cohesive.

Examining how cohesion is related to performance dimensions in our model is also necessary. As noted previously, performance can be generally broken down into two broad dimensions: task or contextual performance (Borman & Motowidlo, 1993). Griffith and Vaitkus (1999) provide a conceptual framework in an excellent review of the cohesion and performance literature in the military. They cite several meta-analytical studies that have shown low-to-moderate positive relations between cohesion and performance. For example, Oliver's meta-analyses (as cited in Griffith & Vaitkus, p.43) found a correlation of 0.20 for studies linking cohesion to individual performance and 0.40 for studies linking cohesion to group performance. These correlations are consistent with what is often found in the civilian meta-analyses (e.g., Mullen & Cooper, 1994).

Researchers interested in contextual performance see cohesion as an important antecedent condition (e.g., Van Dyne, Cummings, & Parks, 1995) as well. Moreover, a strong sense of cohesion and social identity may enhance group members' desires to help each other. This is argued to be the case because the stronger the bond between members of a group, the more pressure to conform to group norms exists (Kidwell, Mossholder, & Bennett, 1997). As such, group norms generally form around behavior that is important to group functioning such as demonstrating pro-social behavior and organizational citizenship. Research supports this contention. Kidwell et al., in a multilevel study that controlled for job satisfaction and organizational commitment, found that more pro-social behavior occurred in highly cohesive workgroups.

The final identity outcome that we specify is organizational commitment. Organizational commitment has been widely studied in the organizational sciences (see Meyer & Allen, 1997, for a review). Much of commitment research has focused on its relationship to employee intentions to leave an organization and to actual turnover (Hom & Griffeth, 1995; Mowday, Porter, & Steers, 1982; Somers, 1995; Whitener & Waltz, 1993). Commitment is also linked to organizational citizenship behavior (Jex, Adams, Bachrach, & Sorenson, 2003), workplace conflict (Leather, Lawrence, Beale, Cox & Dickson, 1998; Thomas, Bliese, & Jex, 2004), health (Frone, 2000; Spector & Jex, 1998), and role stress (Jex et al., 2003; Mathieu & Zajac, 1990). Thus, an abundance of recent research suggests that commitment serves as both a behavioral antecedent of performance and as a behavioral indicator of successful organizational socialization as indicated in our model.

Discussion

Coming together is a beginning. Keeping together is progress. Working together is success.

–Henry Ford

Perhaps the most significant implication of this chapter is that it reveals a means for values to relate to performance, where research-based evidence is introduced that links all the model's components. We have presented values as cognitive adaptations that one makes when being inculcated into a group/organization. During the initial entry of an employee into a group/organization, the individual's personal value orientations and organizational value orientations either become congruent and lead to a representative and high-performing employee, or they never reach congruence, and the initial entry employee is either a victim of attrition (either leaving outright or dismissed by the organization) or becomes a marginalized member who contributes little to the organization.

The mechanism that links values to performance has three parts: (1) development of a job-specific self-concept or role identity, (2) organizational socialization, and (3) behaviors that indicate that the employee has a well-developed identity and has been successfully socialized into the organization. Each of these can best be thought of as mediating variables, which set the stage for the next component of the model and so on, until values ultimately affect performance. We believe these mediating variables do just that and introduce them as the mechanism by which values and performance are related in the absence of no compelling direct link.

As an illustration, consider an Army soldier who endorses the U.S. Army core value of integrity. Soldiers who endorse the value of integrity as their own are not necessarily high performers unless they have progressed through the sequence of the three mediating variables reviewed above. They could be paying lip service to sharing this value, rather than believing it, or they could simply be reading it from a laminated card issued to them by their unit. But with proper role identity development and socialization experiences for being soldiers, they may come to believe in the organization and embody the values that the organization identifies as its own, such as integrity. It is a much more plausible way for values to be transmitted to the point at which they affect behavior in a manner significantly different than through rote memorization or familiarity. We suggest that this explains why there is often no direct link found between values and performance. In a nutshell, this chapter has proposed the missing links in this relationship.

The process we describe that links values and performance may have wide-reaching practical implications for how armed services ensure the values endorsed result in the performance desired. Consider the end result of the U.S. Army's Aberdeen Proving Ground Investigation in 1997. Several leaders within a training unit were tried and convicted on charges of sexual misconduct, inappropriate relationships, and violations of orders and regulations. These leaders were not confined to the noncommissioned officer ranks, but included the company commander as well. The Army's subsequent investigation into this incident uncovered hundreds of other allegations into similar misconduct, with some dating back to the Korean War (D. A. Ricketts, Department of the Army, Headquarters Equal Opportunity Office, personal communication, September 18, 2000). It was after this scandal that the U.S. Army invested a great deal of resources into the development and inculcation of institutional values in its members. The Army developed a campaign plan (Character

Development XXI) specifically designed to accomplish the strategic goal of conveying and acculturating the organization's values. For example, one of the critical elements of this plan expanded soldier basic training from eight to nine weeks to include 54 hours of instruction that stress the Army's values, while promoting teamwork, discipline, and heritage. This training specifically introduced the Army's organizational values and gave blocks of instructions with illustration for what each core value meant. Thus, the U.S. Army intentionally sought to inculcate a specific value set in each individual.

We admire the breadth, scope, and initiative of Character Development XXI, but we feel the U.S. Army simply focused on the wrong cognitive structure. The evidence to date has been that while soldiers are more aware of the institutional values of the Army, there appears to have been little appreciable change in incidents of violations of these values (e.g., misconduct of drill sergeants at Ft Leonard Wood in 1998, mistreatment of prisoners at the Abu Graib prison in 2003). Additionally, as stated earlier, there is no evidence at all that these values alone are directly linked to performance.

While we are in no way inferring that ethical violations are the norm within the Army, we hold that perhaps had the Army focused its attention on developing a clear role identity for soldiers (e.g., making the self-concept of soldiering salient) rather than the mere exposition of organizational values, incidents of violations of these values would be less likely. As we have discussed previously, values become significantly more relevant *when* they are embodied within a central and salient role identity. In addition, the development of this sense of identity should also provide more evidence for stronger unit cohesion, higher levels of commitment, a higher sense of task mastery in soldiers, and a stronger sense of collective efficacy about organizational success, and in the end, higher levels of task and contextual performance.

Socialization and Training

Following this train of thought, perhaps socialization plays a more crucial role to the long-term development and person–environment fit within individuals than previously assumed. To date, it appears that much of the literature concerning socialization has focused on group dynamics (e.g., Forsyth, 1990). We suggest that socialization should serve to define, develop, refine, and reinforce self-concepts, namely role identity within the organization. If self-concept plays such a crucial role in organizing values, beliefs, and attitudes, then it would appear that the period of socialization in which roles are shaped and values are transmitted and assimilated would be an ideal point in time to make certain that newcomers to an organization have formed the proper role identity that best serves the organization.

In the military, the basic training arena is the most likely venue where a recruit's role identity can be shaped in a very controlled socialization experience and where the inculcation of core organizational values has the best chance of success, as long as these values are tied to the self-concept of service and linked to the manifestation of these values in appropriate behaviors.

The U.S. Marines Corps uses this to the remarkable advantage of their organization. In the book *Making the Corps*, Tom Ricks describes his experiences with a marine platoon as it progresses through Marine Corps boot camp. Ricks's hypothesis, based upon official Marine Corps policies and numerous interviews with both trainers and trainees, is that the primary result of this training is the development and complete assimilation of *marine* as a persistent self-concept. As Marine Corps boot camp is the first and primary socialization event in a marine's career, it would appear that Ricks's case study further supports our contention that successful socialization results in a strong and stable role identity that links the values of the individual and organization to behavior. In the strongest cases, such as the Marine Corps, this role identity persists far after the formal association with the organization ceases.

The U.S. Army has a slightly similar process involved with its elite organizations, the Rangers, Special Forces, and Airborne forces. Taking the case of the Airborne, soldiers are sent through a three-week process of training that qualifies them as basic parachutists. During this period, in addition to learning the basics of parachuting, trainees are exposed to what it means to be *airborne*. In this instance, the process of socialization is not focusing on the whole organization's values, but rather on those of a subculture within it. In the past, the graduation to full member (receiving the airborne wings and maroon beret) involved a series of harsh initiations; such as *blood wings* where the unprotected back of the badge was pushed into the entrant's chest; and *prop blasts* where initiates drank heavily, were hazed, and in some cases criminally mistreated (such as mild electrocution with field radio generators).

The leadership of the Army recognized that this socialization process into the subculture of the Airborne was inconsistent with the mainstream Army values and made a massive reorganization of the manner entrants were socialized into the organization. Commanders were held responsible for conducting ceremonies that embraced the Army values of duty and honor, while severely prohibiting the self-abasement rituals that had previously occurred. The outcome was that the Airborne corps more closely fit the values of the parent organization, and its members consistently demonstrate the ideals of the organization (U.S. Army, 1997).

Future Directions

Values

The question then remains: where do we go from here? Well, certainly our model provides numerous testable hypotheses for researchers to pursue. To begin with, we would ask the question, are there consistent organizational values across military organizations? Certainly, we can conceive of similarities across the U.S. Armed Forces, such as duty, loyalty, honor, integrity, and selfless service. Our question would go further to test this consistency across military organizations from different societies.

Once a consistency in organizational values is established, it would then be useful to identify individual values that were most conducive to adopting an organizational endorsed role identity. The implications of this area of research could in turn affect the manner in which applicants are recruited and ultimately selected. By targeting specific types of individuals (rather than casting a wide net and throwing away a lot of fish), this may go a long way to reducing the first-term attrition experienced by several of the services. Thus from a purely recruitment and selection viewpoint, understanding this linkage between individual and organizational values would have significant payoff.

While this future direction addresses the congruence of the applicant pool's individual values with the organization, it might also be useful to investigate if individual values exist that are more conducive to the socialization process itself. Are individuals who possess high values of inclusion, affiliation, and service more likely to successfully navigate the socialization process and emerge as fully vested military members?

Socialization

The next area of research we see tremendous potential in is the area of deliberate socialization. As demonstrated in our illustration, the socialization process can be undermined by having the wrong people serve as the socialization agents. Further investigation is needed to identify just what process occurs within the entrant that encourages the adoption of the appropriate role identity, what factors in the socialization agent contribute to this adoption, and what environmental conditions support it. We believe the linkage between socialization and role identity formation is the crucial linkage between values and, ultimately, consistent performance.

It will be particularly useful to investigate the tactics that newcomers use to learn about their new organization as well as the tactics the organization uses to accomplish socialization. We might also ask, what are the most effective strategies the organization can use to accomplish its socialization (e.g., orientation, norms transmission, clarification of performance and role expectations, mutual acceptance, or transformational processes)?

Identity and Socialization Outcomes

We specify four outcomes that we believe to arise from the successful development and adoption of the organizationally appropriate role identity. We base these outcomes on previous research into socialization processes, yet wonder if there are not perhaps other outcomes that are equally as critical to military success?

What is the relationship between self-identity and cohesion and commitment? Hogg (1992) states that this relationship occurs through the interattractiveness of group members (e.g., in-group, out-group). Is it really this simple, or is there another factor in the military environment? As mutual trust and support are critical elements on the battlefield, could the degree to which an appropriate role identity has been adopted allow fellow group members to be able to predict likely behavior in times of crisis?

Performance

As with the previous section, we based our identified performance outcomes on classic performance literature. The question arises then, are there performance expectations that are more inherent within military performance than in other situations?

Above and beyond the call of duty behavior comes to mind. What is it that motivates a service member to potentially sacrifice all in the service of a greater ideal? What bonds a member to the other members around him or her, causing the acceptance of great risk and peril? In times of peace, what motivates service members to become as proficient in their trade as possible in order to be prepared when called upon? Ultimately, we believe that the heightened focus on values and their subsequent relationship with performance must give way to the acknowledgement and focus on the journey which members travel to reach this ultimate destination.

References

Bandura, A. (1977). Self-efficacy: Toward a unifying theory of behavioral change. *Psychological Review, 84*, 1919–215.

Bandura, A. (1986). *The social foundations of thought and action: A social cognitive theory.* Englewood Cliffs, NJ: Prentice Hall.

Bandura, A. (1997). *Self-efficacy: The exercise of control.* New York: Freeman.

Beale, D. J., Cohen, R. R., Burke, M. J., & McLendon, C. L. (2003). Cohesion and performance in groups: A meta-analytic clarification of construct relations. *Journal of Applied Psychology, 88*, 989–1004.

Borman, W. C., & Motowidlo, S. J. (1993). Expanding the criterion domain to include elements of contextual performance. In N. Schmitt & W.C. Borman (Eds.), *Personnel selection in organizations* (pp. 71–98). San Francisco: Jossey-Bass.

Borman, W. C., White, L. A., & Dorsey, D. W. (1995). Effects of rate task performance and interpersonal factors on supervisor and peer performance ratings. *Journal of Applied Psychology, 80*(1), 168–177.

Campbell, J. P. (1990). Modeling the performance prediction problem in industrial and organizational psychology. In M. D. Dunnette & L. M. Hough (Eds.), *Handbook of industrial and organizational psychology* (2nd ed., Vol. 1, pp. 687–732). Palo Alto, CA: Consulting Psychologists Press.

Campbell, J. P. (1999). The definition and measurement of performance in the new age. In D. R. Ilgen & E. D. Pulakos (Eds.), *The changing nature of performance: Implications for staffing, motivation, and development* (pp. 399–429). San Francisco: Jossey-Bass.

Campbell, J. P., McCloy, R., Oppler, S., & Sager, C. (1992). A theory of performance. In N. Schmitt & W. Borman (Eds.), *New developments in selection and placement.* San Francisco, CA: Jossey-Bass.

Carron, A. V. (1982). Cohesiveness in sports groups: Interpretations and considerations. *Journal of Sport Psychology, 4*, 123–138.

Carron, A. V., Widmeyer, W., & Brawley, L. (1985). The development of an instrument to assess cohesion in sports teams: The Group Environment Questionnaire. *Journal of Sports Psychology, 7*, 244–266.

Chao, G. T., O'Leary-Kelly, A. M., Wolf, S., Klein, H. J., & Gardner, P. D. (1994). Organizational socialization: Its content and consequences. *Journal of Applied Psychology, 79*, 730–743.

Chen, G., & Bliese, P.D. (2002). The role of levels of leadership in predicting self and collective efficacy: Evidence for discontinuity. *Journal of Applied Psychology, 87*, 549–556.

Cota, A. A., Evans, C. R., Dion, K. L., Kilik, L., & Longman, R. S. (1995). The structure of group cohesion. *Personality and Social Psychology Bulletin, 21*, 572–580.

Donahue, E. M. (1994). Do children use the Big Five, too? Content and structural form in personality description. *Journal of Personality, 62*, 45–66.

Eden, D., & Zuk, Y. (1995). Seasickness as a self-fulfilling prophecy: Raising self-efficacy to boost performance at sea. *Journal of Applied Psychology, 80*, 628–635.

Erez, M., & Earley, P.C. (1993). *Culture, self-identity and work.* New York and Oxford: Oxford University Press.

Feather, N. T. (1995). Values, valences, and choice: The influence of values and perceived attractiveness and choice of alternatives. *Journal of Personality and Social Psychology, 68*, 1135–1151.

Feldman, D. C. (1976). A contingency theory of socialization. *Administrative Science Quarterly, 21*, 433–452.

Feldman, D. C. (1981). The multiple socialization of organization members. *Academy of Management Review, 6*, 309–319.

Festinger, L. (1950). Informal social communication. *Psychological Review, 57*, 271–282.

Forsyth, D. R. (1990). *Group dynamics.* Pacific Grove, CA: Brooks/Cole.

Frone, M. R. (2000). Interpersonal conflict at work and psychological outcomes: Testing a model among young workers. *Journal of Occupational Health Psychology, 5*, 246–255.

Griffith, J. & Vaitkus, M. (1999). Relating cohesion to stress, strain, disintegration, and performance: An organizing framework. *Military Psychology, 11*, 27–45.

Grojean, M. (2002) Characteristic adaptation as a mediator between personality and contextual performance: A partial test of the McCrae and Costa (1996) model. *Dissertation Abstracts International: Section B: The Sciences & Engineering, 63*(6–B), 3053.

Higgins, E. T., Klein, R., & Strauman, T. (1987). Self-concept discrepancy theory: A psychological model for distinguishing among different aspects of depression and anxiety. *Social Cognition, 3*, 51–76.

Hofstede, G. (1980). *Culture's consequences: International differences in work-related values.* Beverly Hills, CA: Sage Publications.

Hogg, M. A. (1992). *The social psychology of group cohesiveness: From attraction to social identity.* New York: New York University Press.

Hom, P. W., & Griffeth, R. W. (1995). *Employee turnover.* Cincinnati, OH: South Western.

House, R. J., Hanges, P. J., Ruiz-Quintanilla, S. A., Dorfman, P., Javidan, M., & Dickson, et al. (1999). Cultural influences on leadership and organizations: Project GLOBE. In William H. Mobley (Ed.), *Advances in global leadership* (Vol. 1, pp. 215–254). Oxford, UK: Elsevier.

Ilgen, D. R., & Hollenbeck, J. R. (1991). The structure of work: Job design and roles. In M.D. Dunnette & L.M. Hough (Eds.), *Handbook of industrial and organizational psychology* (Vol. 2, 2nd ed., pp. 165–207). Palo Alto, CA: Consulting Psychologists Press.

Jex, S. M., Adams, G. A., Bachrach, D. G., & Sorenson, S. (2003). The impact of situational constraints, role stressors, and commitment on employee altruism. *Journal of Occupational Health Psychology, 8*, 171–180.

Jex, S. M., & Bliese, P. D. (1999). Efficacy beliefs as a moderator of the impact of work-related stressors: A multilevel study. *Journal of Applied Psychology, 84*, 349–361.

Kammeyer-Mueller, J. D., & Wanberg, C. R. (2003). Unwrapping the organizational entry process: Disentangling multiple antecedents and their pathways to adjustment. *Journal of Applied Psychology, 88*, 779–794.

Kidwell, R. E., Jr., Mossholder, K. W., & Bennett, N. (1997). Cohesiveness and organizational citizenship behavior: A multilevel analysis using work groups and individuals. *Journal of Management, 23*, 775–793.

Kluckhohn, F. R., & Strodtbeck, F. L. (1961). *Variations in value orientations.* Evanston, IL: Row, Peterson.

Leather, P., Lawrence, C., Beale, D., Cox, T., & Dickson, R. (1998). Exposure to occupational violence and the buffering effects of intra-organizational support. *Work and Stress, 12*(2), 161–178.

Leonard, N. H., Beauvais, L. L., & Scholl, R. W. (1999). Work motivation: The incorporation of self-concept-based processes. *Human Performance, 52*(8), 969–998.

Lord, R. G., Brown, D. J., & Freidberg, S. J. (1999). Understanding the dynamics of leadership: The role of follower self-concepts in the leader/follower relationship. *Organizational Behavior and Human Decision Processes, 78*, 167–203.

Louis, M. R. (1980). Surprise and sense making: What newcomers experience in entering unfamiliar organizational settings.*Administrative Science Quarterly, 25*, 226–251.

Markus, H. R., & Cross, S. E. (1990). The interpersonal self. In L. Pervin (Ed.), *Handbook of personality: Theory and research* (pp. 576–608). New York: Guilford Press.

Markus, H. R.,& Nurius, P. (1986). Possible selves. *American Psychologist, 41*, 954–969.

Mathieu, J. E., & Zajac, D. M. (1990). A review and meta-analysis of the antecedents, correlates, and consequences of organizational commitment. *Psychological Bulletin, 108*, 171–194.

McClelland, D. C., & Burnham, D. (1976, March–April). Power is the great motivator. *Harvard Business Review,*100–111.

Meyer, J. P. & Allen, N. J. (1997). *Commitment in the workplace: Theory, research, and application.* Thousand Oaks: Sage Publications.

Moreland, R. L., & Levine, J. M. (1988). Group dynamics over time: Development and socialization in small groups. In. J.E. McGrath (Ed.), *Social psychology of time: New perspectives* (pp. 151–181). Thousand Oaks, CA: Sage Publications.

Moreland, R. L., & Levine, J. M. (2001). Socialization in organizations and work groups. In M.E. Turner (Ed.), *Groups at work: Theory and research* (pp. 69–112). Mahwah, NJ: Erlbaum.

Motowidlo, S. J., & Van Scotter, J. R. (1994). Evidence that task performance should be distinguished from contextual performance. *Journal of Applied Psychology, 79*(4), 475–480.

Mowday, R. T., Porter, L. W., & Steers, R. M. (1982). *Employee-organizational linkages: The psychology of commitment, absenteeism, and turnover.* New York: Academic Press.

Mullen, B., & Cooper, C. (1994). The relation between group cohesion and performance: An integration. *Psychological Bulletin, 115*, 210–227.

Parsons, T., & Shils, E. A. (1951). *Toward a general theory of action.* Cambridge, MA: Harvard University Press.

Paskevich, D. M., Brawley, L. R., Dorsch, K. D., & Widmeyer, W. N. (1999). Relationship between collective efficacy and team cohesion: Conceptual and measurement issues. *Group Dynamics: Theory, Research, and Practice, 3*, 210–222.

Porter, L. W., Lawler, E. E., III, & Hackman, J. R. (1975). *Behavior in organizations.* New York: McGraw-Hill.

Roberts, B. W., & Donahue, E. M. (1994). One personality, multiple selves: Integrating personality and social roles. *Journal of Personality, 62,* 199–218.

Rokeach, M. (1973). *The nature of human values.* New York: Free Press.

Sagiv, L., & Schwartz, S. H. (1995). Value priorities and readiness for outgroup social contact. *Journal of Personality and Social Psychology, 69*(3), 437–448.

Schaubroeck, J., & Merritt, D. E. (1997). Divergent effects of job control on coping with work stressors: The key role of self-efficacy. *Academy of Management Journal, 40,* 738–754.

Schein, E. H. (1968). Organizational socialization and the profession of management. *Industrial Management Review, 9,* 1–16.

Schein, E. H. (1988). Organizational socialization and the profession of management. *Sloan Management Review, 30,* 53–65.

Schwartz, S. H. (1992). Universals in the content and structure of values: Theoretical advances and empirical tests in 20 countries. *Advances in Experimental Social Psychology, 25,* 1–65.

Schwartz, S. H. (1994). Are there universal aspects in the structure and contents of human values? *Journal of Social Issues, 50,* 19–45.

Schwartz, S. H., & Bilsky, W. (1990). Toward a theory of the universal content and structure of values: Extension and cross-cultural replications. *Journal of Personality and Social Psychology, 58,* 878–891.

Somers, M. J. (1995). Organizational commitment, turnover and absenteeism: An examination of direct and interaction effects. *Journal of Organizational Behavior, 15,* 535–547.

Sommers, J. A., Sinclair, R. R., & Thomas, J. L. (in press). The multilevel effects of occupational stressors on soldiers' well-being, organizational attachment, and readiness. *Journal of Occupational Health Psychology.*

Spector, P. E., & Jex, S. M. (1998). Development of four self report measures of job stressors and strain: Interpersonal conflict at work scale, organizational constraints scale, quantitative workload inventory, and physical symptoms inventory. *Journal of Occupational Health Psychology, 3,* 356–367.

Stryker, S., & Serpe, R. (1982). Commitment, identity salience, and role behavior: Theory and research example. In W. Ickes & E. Knowles (Eds.), *Personality, roles, and social behavior* (pp. 119–218). New York: Springer-Verlag.

Taylor, S., Locke, E., Lee, C., & Gist, M. (1984). Type A behavior and faculty research productivity: What are the mechanisms? *Organizational Behavior & Human Performance, 34* (3), 402–418.

Terry, D., Hogg, M., & Duck, J. M. (1999). Group membership, social identity, and attitudes. In D. Abrams & M. Hogg, (Eds.), *Social identity and social cognition* (pp. 280–314). Malden, MA: Blackwell.

Thomas, J. L., Adler, A. B., & Castro, C. A. (2004). *US Army OPTEMPO and performance: Differing effects for subjective and objective criteria.* Manuscript submitted for publication.

Thomas, J. L., Bliese, P. D., & Bullis, C. R. (2001). *Unit climate, leadership and performance: An aggregate-level investigation.* Defense Technical Information Center (DTIC Publication Number ADA401707). Alexandria, VA: DTIC.

Thomas, J. L., Bliese, P. D., & Jex, S. M. (2004). *Interpersonal conflict and organizational commitment: Examining two levels of supervisory support as multi-level moderators.* Manuscript submitted for publication.

Thomas, J. L., Dickson, M. W., & Bliese, P. D. (2001). Values predicting leader performance in the US Army Reserve Officer Training Corps Assessment Center: Evidence for a personality-mediated model. *Leadership Quarterly, 12*, 181–196.

U.S. Army. (1997). The Department of the Army human relations action plan: The human dimensions of combat readiness. Army G1, Pentagon, Arlington, VA: Author.

Van Dyne, L., Cummings, L. L., & Parks, J. M. (1995). Extra-role behaviors: In pursuit of construct and definitional clarity (a bridge over muddled waters). *Research in Organizational Behavior, 17*, 215–285.

Van Maanen, J. (1975). Police socialization: A longitudinal examination of job attitudes in an urban police department. *Administrative Science Quarterly, 20*, 207–228.

Van Maanen, J. (1976). Breaking in: Socialization to work. In R. Dubin (Ed.), *Handbook of work, organization, and society* (pp. 67–130). Chicago: Rand-McNally.

Van Maanen, J., & Schein, E. H. (1979). Toward a theory of organizational socialization. *Organizational Dynamics, 7*, 18–36.

Whitener, E. M., & Waltz, P. M. (1993). Exchange theory determinants of affective and continuance commitment and turnover. *Journal of Vocational Behavior, 42*, 265–281.

CHAPTER 4

MILITARY COURAGE

Carl Andrew Castro

Courage is rightly esteemed the first of human qualities because it is the quality which
guarantees all others.

–Winston Churchill

Within the pantheon of the great virtues, courage is always listed. Indeed, courage is
considered one of the cardinal virtues along with temperance (submission to authority) and wisdom (the intellect of the community) (Welton, 1922). Dr. Samuel
Johnson, the great eighteenth-century literary figure, viewed courage as first among
all the virtues because without courage there would be little opportunity to practice
the other virtues (Boswell, 1924). Indeed, emperors and generals alike have praised
the importance of courage. Marcus Aurelius (trans. 2002) saw courage as one of
the touchstones to goodness, while General Charles Krulak (1995), former Commandant of the U.S. Marine Corps, viewed courage as the touchstone to selfless love.
The U.S. Army also recognizes the significance of courage and includes it in a list of
seven foundational leadership values (see Grojean & Thomas, this volume).

Despite this universal celebration of courage, there is scant scientific literature on
the topic. Instead, the discussion and development of the importance of courage
remain within the domain of ethics (for example, Walton, 1986; Rorty, 1986) and
literature (Bloch, 1980; Fussell, 1989; O'Brien, 1987), most notably war memoirs
of those who experienced combat (Gole, 1997/98 for a literary review). The only
noteworthy exception is the work of Rachman (1976, 1977, 1978, 1984; but see

*The views expressed in this chapter are those of the authors and do not reflect the official policy or position of the
U.S. Department of Defense or the U.S. Government.*

Asarian, 1981; Evans & White, 1981). The reasons for this deficiency might be due to the general belief that the study of virtues such as courage lie outside the domain of science. Recently, however, there has been somewhat of a revival in the scientific study of courage, as the study of courage has moved into the field of psychology (Pury & Kowalski, 2004). This shift is undoubtedly influenced in part by the recent emphasis on the positive contributions that psychology makes to society at large (Peterson & Seligman, 2004; Seligman & Csikszentmihalyi, 2000). As a result, many investigators have begun to view concepts such as courage as ripe for scientific inquiry.

From a scientific perspective then we are surely in the emerging stages of the empirical study of courage. Yet, this does not mean we must necessarily proceed in our investigations of courage without a framework to guide us. The goal of this chapter is to provide such a framework. This chapter is organized into four parts. In the first part, a working definition of courage is provided. As will be seen, the working definition of courage presented deviates significantly from previous conceptions of courage, in that the concept of fear is omitted. In the second section, which comprises the bulk of this chapter, a process-based model of courage is provided, with the hope that this model will be useful for guiding future research on courage. In the third part, how courage can be developed and sustained is discussed. In the final section, a road map for future research on courage is presented. The chapter concludes with a test (or challenge if you prefer) that serves as a check point for each of us as we proceed on our road to the development and sustenance of courage and self-sacrifice.

Defining Courage

Tell me, if you can, what is courage?

—Plato

Courage can be defined as "the power to face unpleasant facts." Courage is a state of mind, a motivational force informed by the decision that unpleasant facts need to be faced in order for the morally correct behavior to be chosen. Thus, courage involves character, intellect, and effort. Courage is not a gift of nature; nor is it skill reserved for the lucky few. All of us have the power within us to be courageous. Courage involves intellect because unpleasant facts can only be faced if these facts are recognized and if the appropriate action is pursued. Courage requires effort; unpleasant facts must be confronted even when the obstacles seem insurmountable. As Moran (1945) noted nearly 60 years ago in his landmark analysis of courage, "It is a cold choice between two alternatives, the fixed resolve not to quit; an act of renunciation which must be made not once but many times by the power of the will" (p. 61). There are many unpleasant facts that may need to be faced. These facts include being killed or injured, losing your job or family, experiencing social disapproval or embarrassment, or bearing a long-term illness. All of these unpleasant facts require courage. Whether these different types of unpleasant facts might involve different types of courage is an issue itself and will be discussed below.

Noticeably absent from this definition of courage is the reference to fear. This omission is deliberate (but see Mowrer, 1939; 1960). Focusing on fear in courage is too narrow as there are many possible reactions to threats or unpleasant facts other than fear which require courage to overcome them. For example, while facing enemy fire in combat may result in fear, dealing with the death of a close team member in combat is more likely to induce anger or sadness; yet, the soldier is still expected to carry on with the mission. Together, fear, anger, and sadness represent the three basic emotions most frequently avoided, with love, joy, and surprise representing the three basic emotions most frequently sought (Parrott, 2001). Regardless of the emotional response elicited, courage is required to overcome the threat or unpleasant fact.

From a philosophical perspective, Plato (trans. 1961) maintained that men without courage are men without temperance or wisdom, just as without wisdom men are not truly courageous. In order for an action to be considered courageous, men must know what they do is courageous and must know it is right. Therefore, actions which are undertaken out of ignorance of what is right (lack of wisdom) are just as cowardly as knowing what is right yet being unable to do it (lack of courage) or knowing what is right and doing it, but not feeling and understanding the fear (i.e., risks) that must be overcome (lack of temperance). However, it is the unpleasant facts (or threats) which lead to fear, and courage enables us to face these unpleasant facts. As Aristotle (trans. 1977) notes, it is when man faces unpleasant facts that he is said to be brave. The focus on facing unpleasant facts or threats as opposed to overcoming fear has important implications for how courage is developed and sustained.

The Battlemind Model of Courage

> Courage born of passion or excitement should always be looked upon with suspicion. It may fail at the very moment it is most needed.
>
> —Horace Porter

The framework for understanding and predicting courage offered in this chapter is termed the *battlemind model of courage*. It should be stated from the outset that there is very little empirical support for the battlemind model of courage. The goal in presenting this model is not to provide an end point, but rather a starting point to begin the systematic investigation of courage. Before introducing the specific components of the battlemind model of courage, it is useful to quickly review how the seminal works in the field of courage have shaped current thinking about courage in order to identify key components that any model of courage must contain.

A good place to begin our discussion of courage is with Aristotle. Like his fellow Grecian thinkers Aristotle viewed courage as a quintessential attribute of the virtuous man. Moreover, courage was not limited to soldiers, but civilians too could possess this most important quality. While unquestionably accepted today that civilians too could possess courage, such an extension of who could evidence courage represented a significant advancement in the conceptualization of courage. Courage was no longer limited to performance on the battlefield but extended to conduct at work, at home, and in the community. The battlemind model of courage presented below follows this line of reasoning as well; and although focused on the military, the model is equally applicable to civilians. The Grecian philosophers also believed that courage could be developed; although how this was to be achieved was never satisfactorily answered. Indeed, how courage can be developed and sustained remains an important, yet unresolved, question today. Even though there is very little if any empirical data to guide us in determining the best means for developing and sustaining courage, the battlemind model of courage provides points of focus aimed at guiding us in our scientific investigations into this issue.

Aristotle's contribution to the study of courage is noteworthy because he went beyond the thinking of his fellow Grecians in two important respects. First, Aristotle defined courage as "a mean with respect to things that inspire confidence or fear" (p. 400). Second, Aristotle provided the conditions that must exist for an act to be considered courageous, most notably awareness that the action requires risk or self-sacrifice. Thus, from the Greeks, most notably Aristotle, we have the notion that courage can be developed, that courage is a virtue applicable to civilians as well as military personnel, and that courageous actions require knowledge that risk or self-sacrifice is required.

The next significant work to appear on courage is that of Horace Porter (1888). In his little known, but extremely insightful essay, Porter argued for separating courage "into the two grand divisions of moral courage and physical courage" (Porter, 1888, p. 246). Surprisingly, however, Porter refused to provide definitions for these two types of courage, although he did conclude that moral courage is superior to that of physical courage because moral courage is a daily necessity, while physical courage is required only in times of emergencies. The distinction between moral and physical courage remains with us today, with the U.S. Army also recognizing a distinction between moral and physical courage. While the battlemind model of courage presented below acknowledges that there may be various types of courage, there is nothing explicit or implicit in the processes of developing or sustaining courage that differentiates these types of courage.

The most important work to appear on courage since the Greeks is that of Charles Moran (Moran, 1945). Moran presented a reservoir model of courage, in which he argued that courage is finite, that it can be used up, and that it needed to be constantly replenished. Moran argued that a man can perform courageously and without fear one day, and then the next day behave as a coward; conversely, a man can be a coward one day and be brave the next. For Moran, cowardly behavior occurs when the reservoir of courage runs low, while acts of courage occur when the reservoir is high. Interestingly, the level of courage in the reservoir can change significantly from one day to the next, or even during the course of a battle, resulting in seemingly unpredictable acts of courage (or cowardice). Indeed, war memoirs of combat veterans are replete with examples that conform to this pattern of courage–cowardice or cowardice–courage behavior change (Gole, 1997/98).

Moran, however, went on to state that courageous behavior could be predicted. "Courage can be judged apart from danger only if the social significance and meaning of courage is known to us, namely that a man of character in peace becomes a man of courage in war" (p. 160). Moran argued that if you are a man of courage in peacetime than you are a man of courage in war. Conversely, if you are a coward in peacetime, then you will be a coward during war. It is this unpleasant fact that we don't want to face. To my knowledge, Moran's was the first claim that courageous behaviors in combat can be predicted based on courageous actions in peacetime. Moran's view that courage reflected character meant that it was not a virtue that could be turned on and off at a whim as many supposed, because courage takes time to develop. As Moran (1945) observed,

> It is altogether a most comfortable doctrine. They would have the best of both worlds. They believe that while there is yet peace a man must do the best for himself; it is the only rational thing to do. He must live for himself, his standards are naturally self and mammon. Suddenly, there is a war and as suddenly human nature is transfigured. The stir and fervour and exhilaration of the social atmosphere in times of excitement bring out qualities which in peace are dormant. They would imply those sleek citizens, that beneath a coat of selfishness in peace lay all the qualities we have learnt to prize in war. (p. 159)

Moran's views on courage appear paradoxical. At first, he states that the level of courage in the reservoir can change (often suddenly), but then states that courageous actions in one situation can predict courageous actions in another. It is difficult to see how Moran's reservoir model of courage can reconcile these two views, unless one proposes that environmental events or contexts also impact the level of courage in the reservoir. The battlemind model of courage does exactly this by proposing a three component model of courage in which the three components interact. According to the battlemind model of courage, engaging in courageous behaviors leads to character development, which is mediated through a sustaining forces component, resulting in future courageous behaviors. Thus, the level of courage, and therefore the predictability of courageous actions, is determined by the interaction between the sustaining forces and the resulting character development.

Moran (1945) also deviates from Porter (1888), and current U.S. Army doctrine, by asserting for the first time that the distinction between moral and physical courage is artificial. General Krulak (1995) reaffirmed Moran's position by explicitly stating that the distinction between moral and physical courage is erroneous,

> I used to think that there was no linkage between them [physical and moral courage], that's incorrect. I believe now that physical and moral courage are inextricably linked...physical courage is only a small part of the totality of what you and I call moral courage.

The battlemind model of courage adopts a similar view.

Finally, the work of Finfgeld (1999) must be considered. Finfgeld presented a process model of courage based on qualitative research conducted among individuals with long-term health problems or illnesses. In an environment of an ongoing struggle, being courageous involved accepting and understanding a situation as threatening, and then pushing beyond the struggle. Being courageous leads to the development of the courageous self, defined by an increase in personal integrity and thriving; where the individual becomes someone other than he or she was in the beginning. In essence, the courageous self represents a form of character development. The courageous self contributes significantly to the sustaining forces that allow the individual to continue to be courageous. As will be seen, I have drawn heavily upon Finfgeld's model in the development of the battlemind model of courage.

As shown in Figure 4.1, the battlemind model of courage consists of three primary components: (1) *courageous actions*, (2) *battlemind*, and (3) *sustaining forces*. The three components of the battlemind model of courage all interact. Engaging in courageous actions leads to the development and sustenance of battlemind. As battlemind is strengthened, interpersonal and intrapersonal forces are fortified. And finally, as the sustaining forces are strengthened, courageous actions become more likely as a result of stronger courage. We will now discuss each of these components in more detail.

Courageous Actions

The first component of the battlemind model of courage is courageous actions. This component of the model attempts to explain the relationships between threats or unpleasant facts, adverse emotional responses, and courageous actions. The battlemind model of courage views courageous actions as synonymous with bravery and valor. The objective of all courageous actions is to overcome the threat or unpleasant fact. As noted earlier, the emphasis on overcoming the threat or unpleasant fact represents a significant shift from other conceptualizations of courage. Indeed, early theories of courage focused exclusively on overcoming the fear (e.g., Rachman, 1976), with little or no attention placed on the threat or unpleasant facts. For example, Mowrer (1960), a leading theoretician on emotion, explicitly linked fearlessness with courage. "May it not be that courage is simply the absence of fear in a situation where it might be expected to be present?" (p. 435). Even today, the U.S. Army equates courage with facing fear. As argued earlier, however, fear is only one of many possible responses to unpleasant facts or threats. The battlemind model of courage conceptualizes courage as the bridge between threats or unpleasant facts and actions that are viewed as brave or courageous.

Threat-Adverse Emotional Response Process

Imbedded within the courageous actions component is the threat-adverse emotional response process. The threat-adverse response process begins with the threat or unpleasant fact, resulting in an adverse emotional response. Fear, anger, and sadness are the three primary emotional responses that arise in the presence of threats

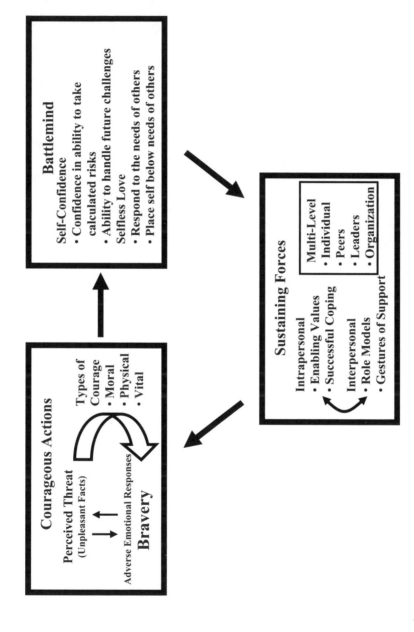

Figure 4.1
The Battlemind Model of Courage

or unpleasant facts (Ortony & Turner, 1990; Parrott, 2001). The threat-adverse emotional response sub-process is recursive, regardless if the emotional response that ensues from the threat involves fear, anger, or sadness. For example, the perception of a threat that leads to fear will in turn lead to an increase in the perceived threat, which in turn will lead to an increase in fear, which will lead to an increase in the perceived threat, and so on. Notice in this example that it is not the unpleasant fact or threat per se that induces fear, but the outcomes that one expects to result due to the threat or unpleasant fact. Often though, what one expects to occur in the presence of threats, particularly fear, is very unlikely, and sometimes even irrational. Many adverse emotional responses such as fear are often able to grab us, causing us to believe and do things that we otherwise would not. It is this aspect of the threat-adverse emotional response process which makes it so treacherous, and why we must end the cycle as soon as possible.

The adverse emotional responses elicited by perceived threats or unpleasant facts are reflexive. That is, no learning takes place. In the presence of the threat the emotional response follows without any action on the part of the affected individual required. Certainly, such reflexive responses can be adaptive. For example, in combat when the enemy is trying to kill you, fear can serve to increase your awareness of the environment around you such as identifying places where you can obtain cover and concealment from the enemy's fire, thereby increasing your likelihood of surviving. In this case, the fear response could be said to be a good thing. However, if your fear causes you to freeze, thereby exposing you to enemy fire, or results in your refusal to assist a wounded team member because you are afraid of being wounded or killed yourself, then fear in this case would be seen as a bad thing, and you would be seen as a coward. It is because of these latter reasons that emotional responses such as fear, anger, and sadness are typically viewed as aversive or undesirable. However, by learning to correctly identify which emotional responses are likely to occur in specific threatening situations we can develop ahead of time the appropriate actions to take when the threatening event actually does occur. Further, anticipating how others might respond in threatening situations can help us be more conscious of the need to act because others are not likely to do so. These remedies for responding to adverse emotional responses, however, are only possible if the emotion is brought to the level of consciousness.

The threat-adverse emotional response process may be terminated in one of three ways. The threat is ignored, the threat ends, or the threat is confronted. Perceiving an event as threatening or unpleasant, yet ignoring it or failing to take action is cowardice. This is a particularly damning indictment if the situation involves a leader failing to defend a subordinate from unjust punishment or accusations. As should be obvious, one can commit a terrible injustice by doing nothing.

The threat might also end without any action being taken. For example, imagine you are on a combat patrol when your squad comes under machine gun attack. Without prompt action, every member of the squad will be killed. While you are formulating your plan of action, the grenadier in your squad locates the machine gun nest, lobs several grenades at the machine gun site, killing all the enemy combatants.

In this example, the threat was eliminated by the courageous action of someone else. However, waiting for someone else to act so you don't have to assume any risks is a form of cowardice.

Confronting unpleasant facts is bravery. Bravery represents the behaviors that are referred to as courageous actions. Thus, bravery requires action directed toward overcoming the threat, and it is courage that provides the basis for the action. The greater the threat or unpleasant facts that must be surmounted, the greater the bravery. That is why risking one's life to save a fellow soldier in combat is typically viewed as a braver act than risking one's social standing in the community by defending an unpopular politician. Whether one is successful or not in overcoming the threat is never the issue, as there can be no doubt that assuming risks to do the right thing involves courage.

It is possible that the threat-adverse emotional response process is never activated because the threat or unpleasant fact is not perceived as threatening or harmful. That is, one can refuse to acknowledge that the unpleasant fact exists even after having been appraised of the situation. This is a form of denial, which is also a form of cowardice.

Types of Courage

The battlemind model of courage acknowledges that there are at least three major classes of courage: moral, physical, and vital. The idea that there are multiple forms of courage was also articulated by Porter (1888), who argued that there were two major types of courage, physical and moral. The inclusion of vital courage as the third type of courage is a fairly recent development (Lopez, O'Byrne, & Peterson, 2003). The distinctions among these three types of courage appear to be based on the threat to be overcome, as opposed to differences in the adverse emotional reactions each type induces or the processes by which the courageous actions operate.

Typically, moral courage is defined as the carrying out of some action despite intense social disapproval (e.g., Rachman, 1978). Examples of moral courage include persistence in carrying out courses of action despite threats of disapproval, unpopularity, and loss of office (Kennedy, 1963). For instance, refusing to commit atrocities against prisoners of war or detainees when pressured by other unit members to do so represents an act of moral courage. Mackenzie traces the motivating source of moral courage to the social abstractions of a pursuit of justice and truth, to feelings of compassion, and finally to self-respect (Mackenzie, 1962).

Physical courage is usually defined as the carrying out of some action despite risk of injury or death. Examples of physical courage include exposing oneself to enemy fire on the battlefield or simply enduring the misery and privations of war (Kahalani, 1984; Kellett, 1982; MacDonald, 1962; McDonough, 1985; Stouffer, et al., 1949). As Hynes (1997) notes in his description of soldiers during World War I,

> most men dread going under fire, and especially returning to it. Once there, however, they no longer tremble....The courageous act here is not some extreme individual gesture...but simply going back to the trenches and standing there, enduring the shells, the misery, and the privation. It is a passive courage, a stoic endurance where there is

nothing else to be done. Such courage doesn't win medals, but it is a fine and difficult virtue, as old soldiers know. (p. 58)

From this perspective then, physical courage certainly appears widespread.

Vital courage may be defined as carrying on with life while enduring a long-term illness or injury such as dealing with a leg amputation resulting from combat. Finfgeld (1999) refers to the chronically ill as engaging in an ongoing, never-ending struggle. Yet, in many ways this ongoing struggle with life-long injuries is synonymous with the courage of endurance by which men at war survive, albeit on a much shorter timeline, when they are called upon time and time again to risk their lives in service of their country (Hynes, 1997). Similarly, moral courage too may be viewed as an ongoing struggle as numerous decisions in our daily lives require actions that may be viewed as unpopular or threatening to our jobs or livelihood. It is this aspect of moral courage, that it is constant and ongoing, that have led many to claim it as the superior form of courage.

Whether there are really important distinctions among moral, physical, or vital courage is currently unknown. While Moran (1945) and Krulak (1995) have argued that there is no distinction between physical and moral courage, others have countered that there is a big difference between risking your job for something you believe in compared to your life in the service of your country (Gole, 1997/98). Without doubt this is true, as risking one's life has a sense of finality to it that risking one's popularity certainly lacks. Despite this distinction, however, even Porter (1888) argued for the primacy of moral courage over that of physical courage. How vital courage fits into this debate is unknown. For the present, it is useful to acknowledge that these three main classifications of courage exist (Miller, 2000).

Battlemind

Engaging in courageous actions leads directly to personal growth and professional development. Similar to Finfgeld's (1999) notion of *courageous self*, the battlemind model of courage denotes that as individuals live courageously (i.e., engage in courageous actions) they experience the emergence of self-confidence and selfless love, and they are fundamentally different from the persons they used to be. In many respects this is what we mean when we speak of character development: that the person has changed, that personal growth has occurred.

The term battlemind was coined by Dedlak, and formalized by General Crosbie Saint (1992), when he was the Commanding General of the U.S. Army in Europe. Battlemind refers to one's inner strength to endure hardship and adversity with confidence and resolution. For a soldier, it is the will to persevere and win in combat. The inclusion of this component in the model recognizes the fact that courageous actions lead directly to personal development. The two main factors of the battlemind component are *self-confidence* and *selfless love*.

Self-Confidence

Self-confidence involves the ability to take calculated risks and to handle future challenges when confronted with threats or unpleasant facts. Calculated decision making requires intellect and maturity. It means forgoing rash and impetuous actions in favor of thoughtful, directed behaviors that are designed to eliminate (or even reduce) the threat or unpleasant fact. It involves the ability to develop multiple courses of action, and selecting the right one. Like any skill, the capacity to develop and identify the best course of action to pursue to overcome threats requires practice and effort. As General Krulak said, "You need to reach back to your moral touchstone to ensure that who you are and what you stand for is as large a part of your professional reputation as your ability to drive tanks, lead troops, fly helicopters or draft an overlay" (Krulak, 1995).

Selfless Love

Selfless love involves two key elements: placing personal needs below the needs of others and responding to the needs of others. Selfless love requires subordinating personal desires and wishes. This type of self-sacrificing love might correctly be viewed as the moral touchstone of selflessness (Krulak, 1995). "When we choose the more difficult path because we know it's the right path to choose then we stoke the fires of self-sacrificing love" (Krulak, 1995). It takes courage to place values above yourself.

It is important to appreciate that the development of one's battlemind depends on the presence of both self-confidence and selfless love. For instance, it is easy to imagine numerous threatening or unpleasant situations in combat in which you know what needs to be done and you are capable of doing it, yet you refuse to act, not because you lack self-confidence but because you see no need in placing your personal welfare at risk to help a team member; you lack selfless love. Similarly, it is also possible given the same situation that you know what needs to be done; you truly want to help your team member (your selfless love is high), yet you don't act (or you act in a foolish manner) because you lack the necessary skills to act appropriately (your self-confidence is low). It is only when self-confidence and selfless love are both high that the appropriate courageous action takes place. However, the courageous action occurs not because of the direct effects of self-confidence and selfless love on courage but because self-confidence and selfless love strengthen the sustaining forces, which directly influence whether the courageous action occurs.

Sustaining Forces

There are numerous factors which sustain courageous actions. These factors are located within the sustaining forces component of the battlemind model of courage. The two broad categories of sustaining forces include intrapersonal and interpersonal variables (Finfgeld, 1999).

Intrapersonal

Intrapersonal variables include *enabling values* and experiences of *successful coping* in the face of threats and unpleasant facts. The idea that there are values that ensure courageous actions is not new. As noted earlier, wisdom and temperance have been associated with courage. Within a military milieu, enabling values such as intellect, subordination, fairness, brotherhood, and trust are probably a good place to begin a systematic investigation into the roles values play in sustaining courageous actions.

Successfully confronting unpleasant facts is also a sustaining force for engaging in courageous actions in the future. As Porter (1888) stated, "The moral influence of the prestige which comes from past success does much toward developing courage" (p. 253). Past success with coping strategies directed at the unpleasant fact provides support for future courageous behavior, not strategies involving ignoring or avoiding the unpleasant fact. In fact, overcoming past failures of courage is just as important for sustaining future courageous actions because failures in courage can serve to decrease self-confidence, and increase the likelihood to fail to act courageously in the future.

Interpersonal

Interpersonal variables include role models and gestures of support. Role models are critical for sustaining courageous actions. As Finfgeld (1999) noted, role models serve to validate and affirm courageous actions because they provide a clear demonstration that courageous actions can lead to success. Role models provide the observer concrete behaviors that leaders and the organization find courage valuable and worthy of emulation. Role models also give the real-world proof that the desired virtues such as courage are in fact esteemed and respected. Without role models, courage is likely to remain an abstract concept with little practical significance.

Gestures of support are extremely helpful when we are confronted with threatening situations or unpleasant facts. Although gestures of support are not absolutely necessary for courageous actions to occur, they are certainly necessary for the creation of an environment that fosters courageous behaviors. What absolutely needs to be avoided is an environment in which courageous actions are ridiculed or minimized. Gestures of support should communicate a sense of respect and admiration for the individual confronting the threat. Oftentimes, courageous actions require personal sacrifices, and these sacrifices should be acknowledged publicly (and privately). Courageous actions should be rewarded. In the military this typically involves the awarding of medals or promotions. The objective of these types of recognition is to encourage other unit members to also engage in courageous actions. Courage is contagious.

Intrapersonal and interpersonal sustaining forces can influence each other to either facilitate or hinder courageous actions from happening. Role models and gestures of support can facilitate the development of enabling values and the formation of successful coping strategies even in the absence of prior courageous behavior. Conversely, the absence of role models and a supportive unit climate that encourages and rewards courageous behaviors can cause the extinction of courageous actions. It is for this latter reason that prior courageous actions are not sufficient by themselves to ensure future courageous actions. For example, when a soldier fails to act courageously on the battlefield his self-confidence and self-esteem are without doubt adversely impacted, especially if he is a member of a unit where courageous behaviors are highly esteemed. However, supportive leadership can provide the shamed soldier another opportunity to redeem himself. In this case, supportive leadership can right the negative consequences of previous cowardly behavior.

Multilevel Forces

The battlemind model of courage loops from the courageous actions component where bravery occurs to the battlemind component where character development takes place, to the sustaining forces component, and so on. The overall flow of the model is unidirectional and circular. However, the interpersonal forces that sustain courageous behavior are found at numerous levels that are mutually reinforcing. This makes the battlemind model of courage dynamic in that there are external factors which can influence courageous actions. At the individual level, unit members foster a courageous environment by recognizing and praising all courageous actions that they observe. Leaders also foster an environment where courageous behaviors occur by serving as role models and by directly rewarding those unit members who display courageous behaviors. The military organization fosters a courageous environment by clearly communicating the importance of courage, and how courageous behaviors will be recognized, rewarded, and inculcated into the military culture.

The Development of Courage and Self-sacrifice

Courage is a quality so necessary for maintaining virtue, that it is always respected, even when it is associated with vice.

–James Boswell

The practical questions discussed in this section are, can courage be taught or developed, and, if so, what are the best ways for doing so? These are by no means easy questions to answer, yet the answers are vital for any program or initiative designed to facilitate courage.

The first step toward the development of courage and self-sacrifice is to start talking about it. Discussions of courage must be held at every level within the military and within society. We must think about courage, and wonder enough about courage to talk to others about it. We must care about being brave. General Krulak noted that early in his career he heard and talked a lot about courage, however, the more senior he became the less and less he heard about courage, until he reached the rank of colonel and general, when nobody talked about courage (Krulak, 1995). Courage must be a common topic of conversation at every level within the military and the Department of Defense. Military leaders must demand courage in their subordinates. Nations must expect it of their citizens.

Courage must be seen as an active force in character development that becomes progressively organized into the makeup of our personality, in combination with other virtues such as intellect and subordination, which defines who we are and what we stand for as service members in the military. Goldman (1998) argued that character development must not be done in "ideological isolation." The approach must be unified. There must be agreement on what courage is and what we want to achieve. The outcomes should be measurable. In short, a "cultural change" is required. According to Goldman, the solution requires three things: (1) a stated vision for the kind of environment the military wants, (2) a strategy, and (3) collective will to pursue it.

Character development must go beyond being a top priority rigorously pursued in all professional training and development courses. Courage must be dwelt upon as the saving virtue. We must recognize that the courage it takes to turn in a superior officer for falsifying a unit readiness report takes priority over showing loyalty toward that same superior officer. We must recognize that the courage it takes to defend those who cannot defend themselves takes priority over military orders. Phrases such as "duty, honor, and country" mean nothing without the courage to act. Courage is indeed the virtue that guarantees all others. As Aristotle noted about courage, "it is by habituating ourselves to make light of alarming situations and to face them that we become brave, and it is when we become brave that we shall be most able to face an alarming situation" (p. 95). Courageous actions beget courageous actions.

Rachman (1976, 1977, 1978, and 1984) proposed that training for courage include the gradual and graduated practice of the dangerous tasks likely to be encountered utilizing the well established clinical method of reducing fear associated with phobias, namely desensitization. Notice that Rachman emphasizes focusing on the fear. Paradoxically, the problem with applying a pathological model involving phobias to the development of courage lies in the peculiarity of cases involving phobias in which the dangers were mainly unreal, and all the mind required was to be assured of the harmlessness of the objects that had inspired its fears. If the dangers had been real and their effects had been destructive the desensitization training by which the fear was expected to be overcome would not have been so effective. For example, in combat, the fear of being shot at would not necessarily be lessened by exposing the soldier to combat. When sent into combat the soldier would find his apprehensions realized, seeing that combat can be fatal and that there is actual destruction. The soldier's worst fears would have been realized. No doubt this type of desensitization training would not have been very effective for either reducing fear or developing courage (Porter, 1888). Instead, the development of courage must be treated as a socialization process where one learns how to accustom oneself to recognizing and responding to threatening situations with a calm and sound temperament, thereby developing the capacity to cope in all circumstances. Such an approach for confronting threatening situations or unpleasant facts seems much more profitable as it is likely to generalize to broader and more pertinent situations requiring courageous behavior.

Today the call for courage in individual life is to typically face difficulties of a physical or moral character. However, even the call to face physical danger is occasional. Yet, a man who keenly realizes the pain and danger he is called upon to face may train himself to face them. And while fear may be present, the only fear he need know is the fear of being afraid. It is this courage of deliberate purpose which has moral excellence. The courageous person pursues what he or she judges right in spite of obstacles of every kind (Welton, 1922). It is one's assessment of the unpleasant fact that is really the central issue. You might ask yourself the question, "What would I do if I wasn't afraid?" Perhaps the highest form of courage is to confront impending threats, to be unrecognized, and to stand alone (Hsün, 1963).

Future Research and Direction

The central assumption outlined in this chapter is that the study of courage is within the purview of science. The battlemind model of courage contains many areas requiring scientific examination. The first among these is how courage should be assessed. That is, should courage be viewed from the perspective of the threat or unpleasant fact (that is, the risk), the adverse emotional response, or the specific action required to overcome either the threat or adverse emotional response? The battlemind model of courage argues that the focus should be on actions directed at overcoming the unpleasant facts or threats. Thus, courageous actions (or bravery) are appraised from the standpoint of the observer, which includes peers, leaders, the military organization, and even society.

The reasoning for this approach is that behaviors can be observed, measured, and developed. Paradoxically, frequently those recognized for their courageous actions feel that they did nothing deserving special attention, that they simply did their job. These courageous souls are genuinely embarrassed to be so publicly identified. Thus, relying on the testimonies of those who have acted bravely would invariably lead us to a dead end in terms of identifying those behaviors that represent courage, although we would most certainly learn a great deal from them regarding their motivation for their actions and how other sustaining forces such as role models and gestures of support facilitated their courageous actions (Pury & Kowalski, 2004).

Focusing on threats and actions to overcome those threats means that we must identify those threats or unpleasant facts that we believe require courageous actions. While a definitive list of threats or unpleasant facts requiring courage probably does not exist, threats that the majority of us would agree require courage most certainly do exist. For example, most of us would agree that risking your life by entering a burning building to rescue a young child represents a significant threat to self that requires courage to act. Similarly, most of us would also acknowledge that risking your job to turn in your supervisor for falsifying accounts requires a certain degree of courage. Once we have identified those threats or unpleasant facts requiring courageous actions we can then develop a set of actions that we expect all service members to take when confronted with those or similar threats or unpleasant facts.

The battlemind model of courage proposes that threats or unpleasant facts elicit adverse emotional responses, namely, fear, anger, or sadness. However, which threats or unpleasant facts produce which adverse emotional response is not known, and certainly represents an ideal area for scientific inquiry. Moreover, fear, anger, and sadness only represent the primary emotions, secondary and tertiary emotions also need to be considered. For example, the secondary emotions associated with fear include horror and nervousness, with the tertiary emotions associated with horror being alarm, shock, fear, fright, terror, panic, and hysteria, while the tertiary emotions associated with nervousness include anxiety, tenseness, apprehension, worry, distress, and dread (see Parrott, 2001, for a complete taxonomy). Whether these basic, secondary, and tertiary emotions can be linked to specific threats or unpleasant facts or to clusters of threats or unpleasant facts would significantly advance our understanding of the threat-adverse emotional response process.

Closely related to the idea that there are numerous adverse emotional responses that can result from a threat or an unpleasant fact is the notion that there exists more than one type of courage. While the battlemind model of courage acknowledges that physical, moral, and vital courage differ in terms of the threat or unpleasant fact that must be overcome, there is no evidence to indicate that the processes by which they operate differ. Parsimony would mandate that in order for different types of courage to exist, it must be demonstrated that the different types of courage postulated can be dissociated. The strongest evidence for supporting the hypothesis that different types of courage exist would be to demonstrate that different processes or structures underlie the various types of courage postulated. Demonstrating that physical, moral, and vital courage elicit different adverse emotional responses would support the notion that they represent different types of courage. It should also be noted that there might exist sub-types of courage. For example, physical courage involves risks involving death, injury, disease, privation, suffering, torture, and imprisonment; moral courage comprises risks of job loss, family estrangement, public embarrassment, or humiliation; and vital courage includes long-term illnesses and/or injuries, loss of sight, and loss of limb. That these sub-types of courage can be linked to adverse emotional responses remains to be explored.

Additional support for the proposition that there exist multiple forms of courage would be to demonstrate that a person can have one type of courage and not the others. For instance, if it could be demonstrated that a soldier who has displayed physical courage on the battlefield lacks moral courage to protect subordinates from unfair punishment, then this would support the idea that these two types of courage are indeed different. Along similar lines, if superiors or subordinates never report the presence of physical courage in service members without also reporting the presence of moral courage, then this would support the hypothesis that these two types of courage are similar.

The battlemind model of courage postulates that there are three primary components to courage and that these three components interact. The existence of the primary components and the nature of how the components interact require scientific verification. First among these predictions is that engaging in courageous actions leads directly to the development of battlemind, represented by increases in self-confidence and selfless love. However, it is possible that personal growth can occur in other areas as well as a result of behaving bravely. Certainly, this proposal too merits further exploration. Next, the battlemind model of courage predicts that as battlemind develops other intrapersonal forces will be strengthened, which in turn serve to sustain future courageous actions.

These intrapersonal forces were termed enabling values and successful coping. These enabling values include intellect, subordination, fairness, trust, and brotherhood, but others might also exist. It is also important to determine precisely how successful coping leads to future courageous behavior. Finally, the battlemind model of courage predicts that intrapersonal and interpersonal forces (role models and gestures of support) drive future courageous behavior. How intrapersonal and interpersonal forces interact to sustain courageous actions also merits investigation.

The systematic study of courage will require longitudinal and cross-sectional studies, using both civilian and military populations, depending on the type of courage or unpleasant fact that is of interest. For example, questions regarding vital courage involving long-term illnesses are perhaps best conducted with cancer patients, while inquiries into vital courage involving permanent physical injuries might include combat amputees. Similarly, research involving physical courage might involve the study of soldiers in combat or the study of firefighters during forest fire season. The study of moral courage may comprise any population, including elected officials or senior military officers who have most likely confronted numerous ethical dilemmas requiring moral courage. In studies examining the development and sustenance of courage both senior and junior members of the organization should be included. Indeed, there might be important differences not only among differing populations in how they perceive courage, but there might also be important cultural differences as well. To date, none of these areas have been explored.

The Test

General Krulak describes the defining moment that at one time or another we all face when confronted with unpleasant facts. Amongst the smoke and noise, and ambiguity, and chaos inherent in all decisions involving courage there is always a moment of silence when you know what to do, Krulak contends. The only real issue is what will you do? As General Krulak observes, "Your character will be defined each time you come out of that moment of silence and make your decision."

References

Aristotle (1977). *The ethics of Aristotle: The Nicomachean ethics* (J.A.K. Thomson, Trans. H. Tredennick, Ed.). Middlesex, England: Penguin.
Asarian, R. D. (1981). The psychology of courage: A human scientific investigation (Doctoral dissertation, Duquesne University), *Dissertation Abstracts International, 42*, 2023B.
Aurelius, M. (2002). *Meditations*. G. Hays, Trans. New York: The Modern Library.

Bloch, M. (1980). *Memoirs of war,* 1914 – 15. Ithaca, New York: Cambridge University Press.

Boswell, J. (1924). *The Life of Samuel Johnson.* London: The Navarre Society. (Original work published in 1838.)

Evans, P. D. & White, D. G. (1981). Toward an empirical definition of courage. *Behavior Research and Therapy, 19,* 419–424.

Finfgeld, D. L. (1999). Courage as a process of pushing beyond the struggle. *Qualitative Health Research, 9,* 803–814.

Fussell, P. (1989). *Wartime: Understanding and behavior in the Second World War.* New York: Oxford University Press.

Goldman, W. D. (1998). The wrong road to character development? *Military Review,* January–February, 62–68.

Gole, H. G. (1997/98). Reflections on courage. *Parameters,* Winter 1997/98, 147–157.

Hsün, T. (1963). *Hsün Tzu: Basic writings.* Translated by Burton Watson. New York: Columbia University Press.

Hynes, S. (1997). *The soldiers' tale.* New York: The Penguin Press.

Kahalani, A. (1984). *The heights of courage: A tank leaders war on the Golan.* Westport, CT: Greenwood Press.

Kellett, A. (1982). *Combat motivation: The behavior of soldiers in battle.* Boston: Kluwer-Nijhoff.

Kennedy, J. F. (1963). *Profiles in courage.* New York: Pocket Books.

Krulak, C. (1995). Speech presented at the Command and General Staff College, Fort Leavenworth, Kansas.

Lopez, S. J., O'Byrne, K. K., & Peterson, S. (2003). Profiling courage. In S. J. Lopez & C. R. Snyder (Eds.). *Positive psychological assessment: A handbook of models and measures* (pp. 185–197). Washington DC: American Psychological Association.

MacDonald, C. B. (1947). *Company commander.* Washington, DC: Infantry Journal Press.

Mackenzie, C. (1962). *Certain aspects of moral courage.* New York: Doubleday.

McDonough, J. (1985). *Platoon leader.* Novato, CA: Presido.

Miller, W. I. (2000). *The mystery of courage.* Cambridge, MA: Harvard University Press.

Moran, L. (1945). *The anatomy of courage.* Boston: Houghton Mifflin Company.

Mowrer, O. H. (1939). Stimulus response theory of anxiety. *Psychological Review, 46,* 553–565.

Mowrer, O. H. (1960). *Learning theory and behavior.* New York: Wiley.

O'Brien, T. (1987). *If I die in a combat zone.* New York: Laurel.

Ortony, A., & Turner, T. J. (1990). What's basic about basic emotions? *Psychological Review, 97,* 315–331.

Parrott, W. (2001), Emotions in social psychology. Philadelphia: Psychology Press.

Peterson, C. & Seligman, M. (2004). *Character strengths and virtues: A handbook and classification.* Oxford: Oxford University Press.

Plato. (1961). *The collected dialogues of Plato: Laches.* B. Jowett, Trans. Princeton, NJ: Princeton University Press.

Porter, H. (1888). The philosophy of courage. *Century Magazine,* June, 246–254.

Pury, C. L. S., & Kowalski, R. M. (2004, 30 September – 3 October). *Prototypes of courage.* Paper presented at the 3rd International Positive Psychology Summit, Washington, DC.

Rachman, S. J. (1976). Courage, fearlessness and fear. *New Scientist, 44,* 271–273.

Rachman, S. J. (1977). The conditioning theory of fear acquisition. *Behaviour Research and Therapy, 15,* 375–387.

Rachman, S. J. (1978). *Fear and courage*. San Francisco: Freeman and Company.

Rachman, S. J. (1984). Fear and courage. *Behavior Therapy, 15*, 109–120.

Rorty, A. O. (1986). The two faces of courage. *Philosophy, 61*, 151–171.

Saint, C. E. (1992). Battlemind guidelines for battalion commanders. *United States Army, Europe, and Seventh Army Training Manual*. Heidelberg, Germany: U.S. Army Europe.

Seligman, M. E. P., & Csikszentmihalyi, M. (2000). Positive psychology: An introduction. *American Psychologist, 55*, 5–14.

Stouffer, S., Lumsdaine, A., Williams, R., Smith, M., Janis, I., Star, S., & Cottrell, L. (1949). *The American soldier: Combat and its aftermath*. Princeton, NJ: Princeton University Press.

Walton, D. N. (1986). *Courage: A philosophical investigation*. Berkeley: University of California Press.

Welton, J. (1922). *Groundwork of ethics*. London: W.B. Clive.

PART III

DIVERSE GROUPS

CHAPTER 5

THE U.S. RESERVE COMPONENT: TRAINING STRATEGIES FOR ADAPTING TO DEPLOYMENT

Robert A. Wisher and Michael W. Freeman

Reservists have always played a vital role in the U.S. military, and this role has widened with the decades-long drawdown in the active force (Duncan, 1997). Reservists are military personnel who do not ordinarily serve in the nation's active military but can be summoned to assist civilian authorities with local emergencies and natural disasters (Doubler & Listman, 1993) and to supplement active forces when needed as specified in United States Code 10 USC §10102. For example, reservists can be called on short notice to bolster a military operation overseas. When called to active duty, reservists can experience sudden shifts in responsibilities, job demands, living arrangements, and compensation. Personal adjustments can be hard.

Due to the irregular nature and limited preparation time for reserve deployments, training strategies to prepare reservists and reserve units are driven by time and mission requirements. Ideally, training strategies incorporate the refreshment of certain individual military skills as well as the learning of new tasks and procedures that apply to a specific upcoming mission (Evans, 1992). In addition, training should also incorporate time for the rehearsal of collective tasks and missions while shaping unit cohesion. These training demands test the units responsible for the training: how can the citizen-soldier be prepared for activation with a constrained number of training days? Furthermore, this training should ideally aid the citizen-soldier in preparing for the psychological realities and stressors of deployment, separation from family, and the potential horrors of warfare. Thus, from basic military skills to specialized occupation skills, from the development of a group identity to

The views expressed in this chapter are those of the authors and do not reflect the official policy or position of the U.S. Department of Defense or the U.S. Government.

the preparation for the stress of deployments, both the reservist and the trainers face a difficult challenge.

This chapter reviews considerations for developing such training strategies. To understand the task of preparing a reservist for military operations, it reviews the structure, organization, and mobilization of reservists. Examples of current training practices and the demands and consequences of recent deployments are then presented. A review of the scientific and medical literature discusses the psychological adjustments of reservists documented during and after deployments. Finally, the chapter considers the potential of technology to help shape a training strategy for the reserve component.

Organizational Perspectives

The concept of the citizen-soldier traces to the Roman Empire, when, in times of emergency, the army relied on part-time soldiers living along its extensive borders and at its vast frontiers (Sumner, 1997). These remotely positioned auxiliary forces supplemented soldiers from the large, permanent camps, holding off opponents until the nearest legion could march from its camp and cut off the insurgent's retreat (Connolly, 1975). Today, the reserve forces may be called to respond to local emergencies, as is the case with the National Guard under the command of a governor. But unlike the locally bound auxiliary forces of Roman times, today's reservist may deploy to distant sites around the globe (Jacobs, 1994).

Statutory tools are available to activate all or part of the reserve component to meet Department of Defense requirements as specified in United States Code 10 USC §12301(a). Activation is the administrative aspect of the reserve component, preparation another. Members of the reserve component must be ready to face an enemy in combat, and they must be prepared to provide a rapid response to the consequences of a weapon of mass destruction. The readiness challenge to develop and sustain forces prepared to engage under uncertain threat conditions requires a training strategy that is adaptive, agile, and achievable.

Organization of Reserve Forces

The reserve component of the United States Armed Forces is organized into two groups, each with two major categories. The first group is comprised of the reserve counterparts of each service (U.S. Army Reserve, U.S. Marine Corps Reserve, etc.). The second group is the National Guard, which is normally under the control of the governor of each state or territory until federalized or "called up" to active service. The two major categories are Active Reserve and Individual Ready Reserve (IRR). The Active Reserve is made up of service members assigned to positions in specific units. These members are obligated to attend paid monthly drills, maintain their occupational skill qualifications, and train full time two weeks each year with the unit to which they are assigned. The unit provides leadership and administrative support to these members while integrating them into the collective mission of the unit (Office of the Assistant Secretary of Defense for Reserve Affairs, 2000).

The IRR is made up of service members not assigned to specific units. The IRR is primarily composed of service members who have recently completed active duty service but have not yet fulfilled their service commitment. This provides a pool of individual replacements qualified in their occupational specialty with recent operational experience. IRR members do not normally affiliate with specific units or train/maintain their skills.

Organization of Units

The Active Reserve is further organized into units that augment each of the services. Since the National Guard is subject to the control of each state, in peacetime National Guard units fall outside of the formal Department of Defense military command structure. State governors serve as the commanders in chief. In contrast, the IRRs, such as the Army Reserve, are always federal and are subject to the direct control of the military command structure. Reserve component organizations are organized to reflect the organization of their active component counterparts.

Most of the service members in the organization are trained in military occupational specialties (MOS) that reflect the core capability of the organization. For example, an engineer unit would have mostly combat engineer specialties. This simplifies career management and training for those individuals since they have a ready-made community of practice with a progression of skill levels and mentors. However, most organizations also have positions for individuals with skills different from the majority, usually in the administrative and logistics areas. These are often referred to as low-density MOSs since they each make up a small percentage of the unit strength. The low number of individuals and the specialized nature of these MOSs also mean the organization can usually ill afford to send them to external training or provide dedicated time for skills development (Shanley, Leonard, & Winkler, 2001).

Mobilization Policy

The activation and mobilization of the Ready Reserve is governed by policy directives and instructions (Department of Defense, 2004a). These policy instruments concern the call or ordering of units and individual members of the reserve component in support of operational missions and contingency operations, during a national emergency, or in time of war. The policy calls for the maximum utilization of the core capabilities of reserve units throughout the duration of active service. Core capabilities are those that reserve units possess through their normal, peacetime training and assignments. With a Ready Reserve in excess of 1.2 million members (as of 2002), the capabilities are tremendous. However, core capabilities are not necessarily the immediate focus in certain deployments. The need to respond quickly, and to emerging events, calls for a need to prepare beyond the core capability.

There are certain core military capabilities that are handled mostly by reservists. For example, 100 percent of continental U.S. air defense interceptors derive from a selected reserve capability and 97 percent of the Army's civil affairs units are based in the reserves. There are numerous other core capabilities, including sealift, port security, and psychological operations, that reside primarily in the reserve component. In time of national emergency and war, a host of additional capabilities can be supplied through a mobilization of the reserve component.

Mobilizations encompass a spectrum of participation levels and durations, from short-term selective mobilizations and volunteers to a total mobilization. In between are levels such as the Presidential Selective Reserve Call-up, which allows the President to activate up to 200,000 reservists for 90 days with an option for a second 90-day period. The net effect of a mobilization is to bring to a combatant command a force that is trained and ready for its mission. (The United States has five regional combatant commands spanning every corner of the globe with the exception of Antarctica, which by treaty prohibits any military measures.)

A training strategy, then, is constrained by time limitations imposed by statutory factors and the urgency required to bring a trained capability to an operation. There is not the luxury of time to prepare for all contingencies and for all possible tasks that may be encountered. Expectations are established and priority is given to training on tasks that are likely to be encountered or are otherwise critical. These tasks are then trained during a predeployment phase, after mobilization has occurred. A case study of how a training strategy is implemented for a peacekeeping operation is reviewed by Wisher (2003). The training strategy in this study called for dividing the predeployment training into three phases, geared to the timeline of forming a unit for deployment to a peacekeeping mission in Egypt. Key leaders were trained initially, followed by the leadership cadre, and finally the bulk of junior enlisted for the battalion-sized unit. A certification exercise tested qualifications on all tasks related to the peacekeeping operation prior to deployment. In this specific case, there was ample time to plan and prepare for the mission, which was well-understood due to many prior rotations.

The IRR represents an interesting condition for understanding training strategies during a mobilization. Many members had served on active duty for years. However, since their departure from active duty service their proficiency on many military-relevant tasks has naturally declined. On the other hand, these same members may have developed useful skills in the civilian economy. If relevant, how can these skills be identified and applied? Beyond the question of skill proficiency rests the issue of personal stress that comes from suddenly being called back to serve in the military after having been ensconced in civilian life. The IRR has been subject to previous mobilizations, so there are lessons to be learned on training practices from these experiences that can apply to future training strategies.

IRR and Skill Decay

An example of IRR mobilization and changes in skill proficiency is reported in Wisher, Sabol, Sukenik and Kern (1991), in their investigation of the preparation of the IRR for Operation Desert Storm. Although since surpassed by the mobilizations following the terrorist attacks of 9/11, Operation Desert Storm prompted what was to that point the largest mobilization of reserve component forces since World War II. In January 2001, the Army authorized the activation of 20,277 soldiers in the IRR who had been separated for up to one year. In a comprehensive analysis of more than 17,000 members of the IRR who were called up, hands-on performance, written, and weapons qualifications scores were merged with data from personnel files and responses to a questionnaire on attitudes, job experience, and personal impact of the call-up. Skill decay was contrasted between those who had recently completed their active duty assignments (six months or less) to those who had separated between six and twelve months. The principal findings related to skill decay were:

1. Skill decay was evident in written diagnostic and certification tests and weapons qualification scores.

2. The picture on skill recertification was mixed. Skills were in general adequately refreshed, but skill decay deficits were not completely eliminated.

3. Skills assessed in written tests decayed mostly within the first six months since separation; weapon qualification skills decay mostly after ten months.

4. Scores on the most recent skills qualification test were the strongest predictor of skill and knowledge retention, followed by scores on the Armed Forces Qualification Test, a measure of aptitude.

5. Skill retention was higher for those who entered the IRR directly from active duty.

6. Pay grade (i.e., rank) had little effect on degree of skill loss.

In a follow-on study of skill reacquisition by combat engineers from the IRR who volunteered for a mobilization training exercise, Kern, Wisher, Sabol, and Farr (1994) reported that the increase in task knowledge during a five-day rapid train-up was strongly related to prior active-duty status (full-tour versus initial-entry training only). Furthermore, the mobilization exercise afforded a more extensive separation period in which to examine skill decay and reacquisition. Operation Desert Storm was limited to a 12-month separation interval; for the mobilization exercise, the separation interval was up to five years since having left active duty. Kern et al. provided evidence that the rate of skill reacquisition during the rapid train-up was stable for up to 36 months after separation from service. That is, despite greater skill decay, the training time needed to re-acquire skills was independent of time away from service, up to 36 months. Sabol and Wisher (2001) describe this finding in technical detail.

Taken together, the findings from these mobilization studies provide useful input for the development of more effective predeployment training strategies. For example, similarity of civilian occupation and military occupational specialty, such as combat medic and nursing, mitigate the degree of skill decay and reduce the retraining time. Thus, an assessment of civilian occupation can shorten the predeployment training for certain individuals.

IRR Attitudes and Motivation

In parallel with the Wisher et al. (1991) report on the call-up of the IRR for Operation Desert Storm, Steinberg (1991) reported on attitudes toward the call-up and identified areas of concern relating to the call-up. The results suggest extremely high levels of dissatisfaction with the process, which reduced the time available for critical task training and increased stress, which could reduce the effectiveness of training. The majority of members of the IRR had a negative attitude toward being called up. They were dissatisfied with the way processing was conducted, and complained about disorganization, long lines, incorrect or missing records, and finance problems. Specifically, they indicated that the in-processing center was not organized to handle so many people at once, and given the large number of people, did not adapt their procedures to handle them efficiently.

Other concerns reported by Steinberg (1991) were related to the disruption of their lives, specifically its impact on their jobs, income, schooling, and families. This could be a significant source of stress, leading to reduced attention during training. The variables that differentiated positive and negative attitudes included how they felt about active Army service when they left (i.e., those that liked the Army upon separation were more positive about the call-up), how well they liked their primary military occupational specialty during their last duty (i.e., those who liked their most recent Army job were positive about the call-up), and how confident they were in performing well as a soldier in a combat situation. Variables that did not differentiate positive and negative attitudes included marital status, drop in personal income, and age.

Sequence of Training

To meet these challenges, the Reserve operates in a *train-mobilize-complete training-deploy-redeploy-demobilize cycle* (see Figure 5.1). In the *train* phase of the cycle, individuals qualify in their occupational specialties and are assigned to units. Under the direction of their chain of command, units maintain the qualifications of the individuals and train on their collective tasks to the highest level they are able to in their allocated one weekend per month and a full two weeks per year. Since time is the limiting factor, priority is given to those tasks that are most critical to accomplishment of the most probable mission and to maintaining the safety of the individuals and that provide the fundamentals necessary for collective performance.

Upon *mobilization*, military units pass through an administrative process to bring soldiers onto full-time active duty. Soldiers and units then enter the *complete training* phase of the cycle where they finish the training necessary for their assigned

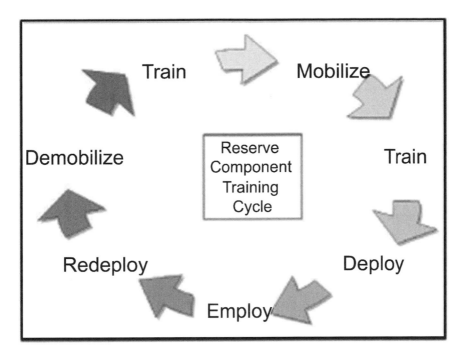

Figure 5.1
Reserve Component Operations Cycle

missions along with all required administrative actions. The units then *deploy* by moving to the mission location where they complete any final training requirements that may have emerged in response to last-minute changes in the mission situation.

At the end of the deployment the units and soldiers *redeploy* to a *demobilization* station and engage in an administrative process to return them to reserve status. Depending on the nature of the deployment and mission, this phase also includes psychological counseling and training on coping skills to assist in the transition back to their civilian lives. Afterwards, the process recycles with maintenance of individual qualifications and priority training on critical collective tasks to prepare for the next mobilization.

This cycle is the same for all types of call-ups. However, the number and categories of tasks vary by unit's mission and the security threat. The more critical the mission and dangerous the environment, the longer and more detailed the training in the complete training phase prior to deployment. This necessarily prolongs the activation period for reservists called-up for missions with a high chance of direct combat. Comparatively, training for peacekeeping missions in less threatening environments would be shorter. Regardless of the kind of mission, however, the post-mobilization training phase culminates in certification by the military service that the unit and individuals are prepared to complete their assigned missions and survive in the environment into which they will deploy.

Training for the IRR differs from training other reservists. Because the IRR is made up of individuals with prior active duty experience, they are fully qualified in their occupational specialty at the time they transition to the IRR pool but they usually do not participate in training unless mobilized. Unlike the regular reservists, members of the IRR do not attend monthly training. Thus, any training program for the IRR needs to consider time and resources available at mobilization, the critical skills necessary, and cost concerns associated with training activated IRR service members (Bodilly, Fernandez, Kimbrough, & Purnell, 1986). Typically, after an initial period of refresher training, IRR service members report to their assigned units and complete the remainder of the training process with that unit.

Psychological Adjustments

Among other factors such as deficient equipment, shortages of supply, and inadequate training, unhealthy personnel can compromise the ability of a unit to accomplish its mission. Stressors from the threat of death and wounding, witnessing carnage, violence, and human degradation, and exposure to other traumatic events can contribute to the fitness of personnel to perform their duties (Wright, Huffman, Adler, & Castro, 2002). Exposure to combat stressors has been linked to serious psychological (e.g., Hoge, Castro, Messer, McGurk, Cotting, & Koffman, 2004) and physiological health problems (e.g., Boscarino, 1997). Stressors can also come about during peacekeeping missions. For example, Adler, Dolan, and Castro (2000) established linkages between exposure to traumatic events in Kosovo and an increase in physical symptoms indicative of stress, such as reduced sleep, and an increase in alcohol consumption.

The Impact of Deployment on Reservists

For reservists, deployment stressors have similarities and differences to those stressors faced by their active duty counterparts. The stressors associated with threat of harm, exposure to dead bodies, and the harsh environmental conditions are faced by both the active duty and reserve forces deployed on the same mission. Differences in stressors are more likely to emerge when considering the context of the deployment. For reservists, the disruption of their civilian life may be a significantly greater stressor than for their active-duty counterparts because activation signifies profound changes in employment and the routine of family and civilian life. Furthermore, the question of whether reservists are as ready to take on the tasks of activated military personnel is less clear, as outlined in the section on task degradation. Besides the issue of stressors, reservists, depending on reserve category, may experience the typical moderators of deployment stress differently, such as group cohesion. For those reservists activated from the IRR, they may be less likely to have time to establish a cohesive working relationship with their unit. For members of National Guard units, cohesion may be relatively strong because everyone comes from one geographical region and they may have had time to develop a sense of cohesion.

An important question is whether as a result of their reserve status, reservists are more at risk for developing psychological symptoms than their active-duty counterparts. In one of the few studies to address this question directly, Stretch, Marlowe, Wright, Bliese, Knudson, and Hoover (1996) examined various units from Pennsylvania and Hawaii that participated in the Persian Gulf War. Comparisons between 766 reserve veterans who deployed and 948 reserve veterans who did not deploy were made. The results of the study indicated that a subset of personnel was scored as at risk for development of posttraumatic stress disorder (PTSD). Overall, the deployed individuals exhibited significantly higher levels of psychological distress than did individuals from the same units who did not deploy. In addition, the prevalence rate for PTSD symptoms was slightly higher for reserve veterans than for active duty veterans. Stretch et al. (1996) considered lack of psychological preparation as a possible factor that explained the elevation of rates among the reservists. In a study of reservists from Iowa who were veterans of the Persian Gulf War, most of the symptoms reported, such as PTSD and anxiety, were comparable with those reported by their active duty counterparts but rates of chronic fatigue and alcohol abuse were higher in the reservist sample (Iowa Persian Gulf Study Group, 1997).

In another study of the psychological effects of activation on reserve veterans, Stuart and Bliese (1998) assessed the long-term psychological health of those who served during the Persian Gulf War. The focus in this study was whether stressors related to activation were related to the psychological distress of reservists who returned to civilian life. Subjects were 1,156 members of the Army National Guard and 739 members of the Army Reserve who served either in the Persian Gulf region, the United States, or Germany during a set period. A questionnaire measured psychological distress, including items from the Brief Symptom Survey which yielded a Global Severity Index (GSI). For the total sample, elevated and significant GSI scores were found in the Persian Gulf subgroup but not in the group serving in Germany or the United States. This analysis controlled for current stressors as well as military and demographic characteristics.

Taken together with research on stress in the reserve component during deployment (Perconte, Wilson, Pontius, Dietrick, & Spiro, 1993), it appears that reservists may encounter more difficulty in terms of the psychological effects of deployments when compared to their active duty counterparts. This difference in psychological outcomes is not due to activation alone (e.g., Stuart & Bliese, 1998). It may be that because reservists face a quick adjustment to military life, their predeployment training does not provide them with the same capability to cope with deployment that the active duty force may possess as a result of their day-to-day experiences with military life. Predeployment training alone may be too short a period for effective adaptation to a deployment.

Prevention and Intervention Programs

A strategy for training the reserve component, then, must consider prevention programs designed to minimize the mental health impact of activation prior to deployment. These programs should factor in information regarding the interpersonal, occupational, and potentially traumatic stressors that may emerge during a deployment (Dobson & Marshall, 1997). Evidence has accumulated to support the concept that life stressors are directly related to a wide array of mental and physical health outcomes (de Jong, Timmerman, & Emmelkamp, 1996). Stress management techniques are an important component of preventive training.

Studies have demonstrated positive effects of worksite stress-management interventions on health. For example, in a critical review of 64 articles published between 1974 and 1994, civilian intervention programs such as meditation, biofeedback, cognitive-behavioral strategies, and combinations of these and other techniques were assessed against health-outcome measures, such as somatic complaints, physiological, cognitive, job, and organization measures (Murphy, 1996). The effectiveness of interventions varied. Meditation produced the most consistent results and biofeedback was the least effective, and least frequently used, intervention. In general, combinations of techniques rather than single techniques were more effective across measures. Furthermore, research on the trainers of stress-management intervention showed that training does not have to be given by clinical psychologists but instead may be provided by individuals from other professional backgrounds with equally effective health outcomes (de Jong & Emmelkamp, 2000). Perhaps these interventions can be adapted for use with military reservists as part of an integrated effort to prepare them psychologically for the demands of deployment.

Considerations for Training Strategies

The strategies to train a reservist, or a reserve unit, must take into account a multitude of planning factors. First, how much time is available to prepare? Second, what are the critical tasks that the reservist must master? Third, what information regarding culture or history must the reservist learn? Fourth, how much of task-related and deployment-related information does the reservist already know and what are the performance and knowledge gaps? Fifth, how can psychological adjustment, before and after a deployment, be accommodated in a training strategy? Related questions concern what resources are available to provide the training in terms of instructors, ranges, and other infrastructure facilities. Furthermore, can technology be applied as a means to improve training proficiency? Answers to these and other questions, taken together, frame a training strategy.

One way to deal with potentially limited resources of staff, training sites, and time is to capitalize on existing civilian institutes of learning. The use of civilian institutions, such as accredited universities, junior colleges, community technical schools, and other recognized training institutions, is a strategic consideration for the delivery of training to reservists. There are cost incentives and advantages to accessing subject matter expertise that reside at such institutions. In the United States, a policy has been issued that authorizes such use when it is demonstrated that such training fulfills a military requirement and is less costly (Department of Defense, 2004b). For subject matter not readily available in the military service school system (due perhaps to an unforeseen threat) or in cases that training slots are not available (due perhaps to a surge in personnel) the use of civilian institutions is a practical alternative to military training infrastructure. Examples of training for an infantryman that could be provided in a civilian institution include cultural awareness, languages, and information technology. Those that should remain in the military setting include marksmanship and any tasks requiring the use of specific military equipment.

Technology Applications

Technology offers significant opportunities, although it is not a substitute for training reservists in all areas. Training technologies, such as simulations and games, can help overcome some of the significant training challenges facing reserve units and individuals. Empirical studies suggest that use of interactive technologies can reduce the costs of instruction by about one third. Further, the studies provide evidence that either achievement can be increased by about one third while holding time constant, or time needed can be reduced by about one third while achieving the same, targeted instructional objectives (Wisher & Fletcher, 2004).

Team building and rehearsals are especially challenging for geographically dispersed reserve units with extremely limited time to train. This kind of training can be assisted using distributed simulations and collaborative learning technologies such as video teletraining and application sharing (Freeman, Wisher, Curnow, & Morris, 1999). Collaborative technologies are best for premobilization phases of the operations cycle, especially for staffs and others that already use collaborative technologies to accomplish their tasks. Participation in collaborative environments helps build a common understanding of goals and interdependence with other members of the team (Bonk, Wisher, & Nigrelli, 2004). Such collaborative environments also provide a foundation for advanced team building, including the deep trust necessary to conduct dangerous missions as a member of a team, during the mobilization and deployment phases.

On a social level, interpersonal interactions have been shown to be widespread in virtual, collaborative learning environments used by reservists for advanced career training (Orvis et al. 2002). This level of interpersonal interaction allows unit cohesion to begin forming even before face-to-face predeployment training is conducted. An engaging form of simulation being pursued for military training is represented by multiplayer online games. Participation in these games can motivate reservists through interdependent roles and the social bonds and cohesion that are formed between players (Sellers, 2002). Whether such electronically mediated cohesion has the same stress-reducing effects is yet to be empirically tested. Thus, there is a gap in research on this question in a military context.

Herz and Macedonia (2002) note that simulations have been an integral part of military training for decades, though such use has been growing somewhat separately from the commercial gaming industry. They note that the military is finally exploiting advances in the commercial simulation and gaming industry to advance its training and education. The U.S. Army, for instance, has distributed video games at no cost as part of its recruitment efforts. Millions of potential recruits have gone through "basic training" in *America's Army* (Belanich, Sibley, & Orvis, 2004). Soon millions more will likely be playing *Full Spectrum Warrior* on an Xbox (Institute for Creative Technologies, 2004).

Simulations can also provide training experience on unique equipment while avoiding wear and tear on actual equipment and limiting operations costs. On an operational level, many items of military equipment, especially combat vehicles like tanks and fighting vehicles, have very large costs of operation. For example, total costs of operating M1A2 tanks are over $430 per mile (McDonald, Bahr, & Abate, 2000).

Increased emphasis on virtual simulations can make up for difficult-to-access training facilities and resources such as ranges and ammunition for gunnery. Limited access to the ranges and facilities necessary for safe and effective training on their assigned weapons and equipment is especially troublesome to reservists. Modern weapons are lethal at extended distances and require large tracts of land to provide for realistic training while reducing the danger to surrounding communities. Additionally, these large tracts of land are subject to environmental concerns associated with the operation of heavy equipment and lethal weapons (Sortor, 1994).

Advanced Distributed Learning

The U.S. reserve component has already begun working with technology-based initiatives to augment its tight training schedule. When the U.S. Department of Defense launched the Advanced Distributed Learning (ADL) initiative in November 1997, the National Guard Bureau was an early partner. ADL is the most visible in a long campaign of initiatives to incorporate into practice the benefits of technology-based instruction and performance aiding (Wisher & Fletcher, 2004). These technologies can be delivered over the Web in a manner that takes advantage of emerging specifications and standards related to online instruction. The ADL initiative is the Department of Defense proponent for these standards, with the aim of global interoperability of online learning content.

The goal of the ADL initiative is to ensure access to high quality education and training, tailored to individual needs, developed and delivered cost-effectively, available anytime and anywhere. This goal is viewed as something that can be achieved affordably, and thereby made feasible, only through the use of computer and online technologies. ADL is preparing for a world where communications networks and personal delivery devices are pervasive and inexpensive, and straightforward to the users in terms of ease of use, bandwidth, and portability. It is appropriate for instruction on technical skills, collective tasks, and to some extent training related to psychological adjustment and coping.

The use of technologies such as ADL for training the reserve component should be included in any contemporary training strategy. The National Guard Bureau offers a great example of the integration of technology with training through the Distributive Training Technology Project (Wisher, Moorash, Kronholm, & Gelosh, 2004). This is a state-of-the-art communications and learning-delivery system designed to support the National Guard's traditional and expanding missions. Using these resources, soldiers can study foreign languages and improve skills in critical thinking, information technology, and cultural awareness. There are more than 350 specially designed multimedia classrooms throughout the country, linked by a high-bandwidth network. The total training capability, though sizable, is not currently able to accommodate a national training surge when considering the overall size of the National Guard.

The Distributive Training Technology Project provides the National Guard with a significant opportunity to maintain the required readiness, and offset the cost of the program. The advantages of the program in terms of readiness include increasing the number of soldiers that can be trained at the same time, thus lowering the cost of instructors and transportation. The program also reduces the amount of time it might take to deliver requisite training to multiple large groups while broadening the scope of education, making more information available to more people at the same time. Such technologies provide the reserve component with groundbreaking methods of training their citizen-soldiers but, of course, reservists still need face-to-face training in order to prepare more fully for the demands of combat and other deployments.

Future Directions

Reservists face the challenge of being prepared for activation in terms of both task mastery and psychological readiness. Reservists can be expected to be deeply concerned about the unexpected disruption caused by a call-up and need time to settle their affairs at home (Steinberg, 1991). They need information that can help them cope with their financial concerns and support services for families. Fortunately, U.S. Defense officials have recognized the vital role that families play in support of the readiness of the armed forces. Because of lessons learned from Operation Desert Storm and deployments since, family programs are being enhanced, partnerships are being formed, and programs that directly support family readiness are being resourced. The degree to which these programs are indeed effective and address the needs of reservists and their families remains under investigation.

The impact of the call-up of reservists for Operation Iraqi Freedom and Operation Enduring Freedom has also had a profound impact on the reserve component. Since 9/11, half of the Army's reservists have been mobilized, and between 12,000 and 15,000 have been mobilized twice (Kennedy, 2004). The high rate of activation of reservists for deployment on six-month peacekeeping and twelve-month combat rotations has led to a shift in training priorities and reorganization of the reserve component. Training is increasingly focused on combat skills such as marksmanship, weapons maintenance, and fitness. The weekend drills are now called *battle assemblies* to signify this increased emphasis on combat readiness.

Efforts are also underway to create more certainty for reservists by developing a five-year activation cycle, and to minimize the chance of a reservist being called up repeatedly within a short period of time (Kennedy, 2004). The impact of these changes on Army reservists and their families, and the impact of these changes on the optimal way to organize training of the reserve component have yet to be assessed.

The aim of this chapter is to frame the necessary elements of a reserve component training strategy. It is particularly oriented to the needs of reservists, from both an individual skill and psychological perspective, who are called to active duty. This chapter has also focused exclusively on the experience of reservists in the United States. It is unknown the degree to which these experiences are relevant to the reservists in other nations, but it would be useful to examine the issues facing reservists in other nations and to share training technologies to support interoperability.

The development of a model predicting the health, retention, and performance outcomes of reservists will no doubt have to take into account a multitude of the factors mentioned here. Training, expectations, family readiness, employer attitudes, the emergence of group cohesion, and the effectiveness of leaders are just some of the variables that should be considered in developing a model of reserve readiness. The context of such variables, including military policies toward reservists, and the type, length, and intensity of deployments are also likely to influence reserve outcomes.

One useful area for future research could focus on time efficiencies gained with integrated distributed technologies into the call-up process. These changes can be beneficial not only for training, as outlined in the current chapter, but also for the many time-consuming administrative procedures. Such technologies could also potentially be adapted for intervention programs to reduce the performance and psychological effects of stressors, especially among those individuals who demobilize and return to civilian communities without accessible military health care assets. Training strategies must consider all of these factors to be an effective means of readying members of the reserve component for the missions that loom ahead.

References

Adler, A. B., Dolan, C. A., & Castro, C. A. (2000). U.S. soldier peacekeeping experiences and well-being after returning from deployment to Kosovo. *Proceedings of the 36th International Applied Military Psychological Symposium* (pp. 30–34), Split, Croatia.

Belanich, J., Sibley, D. E., & Orvis, K. L. (2004). *Instructional characteristics and motivational features of a PC-based game* (Research Report No. 1822). Alexandria, VA: U.S. Army Research Institute for the Behavioral and Social Sciences.

Bodilly, S., Fernandez, J., Kimbrough, J., & Purnell, S. (1986). *Individual Ready Reserve skill retention and refresher training options* (Report Number RAND/N-2535-RA). Santa Monica, CA: RAND Corporation.

Bonk, C. J., Wisher, R. A., & Nigrelli, M. L. (2004). Learning communities, communities of practice: Principles, technologies, and examples. In K. Littleton, D. Miell, & D. Faulkner (Eds.), *Learning to collaborate, collaborating to learn* (pp. 199–219). Hauppauge, NY: Nova Science.

Boscarino, J. A. (1997). Diseases among men 20 years after exposure to severe stress: Implications for clinical research and medical care. *Psychosomatic Medicine, 59,* 605–614.

Connolly, P. (1975). *The Roman Army.* London: Macmillan Educational Press.

de Jong, G. M., & Emmelkamp, P. M. G. (2000). Implementing a stress management training: Comparative trainer effectiveness. *Journal of Occupational Health Psychology, 5*(2), 309–320.

de Jong, G. M., Timmerman, I. H. G., & Emmelkamp, P. M. G. (1996). The Survey of Recent Life Experiences: A psychometric evaluation. *Journal of Behavioral Medicine, 19,* 525–538.

Department of Defense (2004a). Department of Defense Directive Number 1235.10 "Activation, Mobilization, and Demobilization of the Ready Reserve." September 23, 2004. Washington, DC.

Department of Defense (2004b). Department of Defense Directive Number 1200.16 "Contracted Civilian-Acquired Training for Reserve Components." March 20, 2004. Washington, DC.

Dobson, M., & Marshall, R. P. (1997). Surviving the war zone experience: Preventing psychiatric casualties. *Military Medicine, 162,* 283–287.

Doubler, M. D., & Listman, J. W. (1993). The National Guard: An illustrated history of America's citizen-soldiers. Dulles, VA: Potomac Books.

Evans, K. L. (1992). The mobilization of the Individual Ready Reserve Infantrymen during Operation Desert Storm: Training Performance Analysis (Research Report 1621). Alexandria, VA: U.S. Army Research Institute for the Behavioral and Social Sciences.

Freeman, M., Wisher, R., Curnow, C., & Morris, K. (1999). Down the digital dirt roads: Increasing access to distance learning with hybrid audiographics. *Proceedings of the 1999 Interservice/Industry Training Simulations and Education Conference.* Arlington, VA: National Training Systems Association.

Herz, J. C., & Macedonia, M. R. (2002). Computer games and the military: Two views. *Defense Horizons, 11.* Washington, DC: National Defense University.

Hoge, C. W., Castro, C. A., Messer, S. C., McGurk, D., Cotting, D., & Koffman, R. L. (2004). Combat duty in Iraq and Afghanistan, mental health problems, and barriers to care. *New England Journal of Medicine, 351,* 1–10.

Institute for Creative Technologies. (2004). *Full Spectrum Warrior* offers troops digital training. *Selective Focus, 3*(1), 27–34. Los Angeles, CA: Institute for Creative Technology.

Iowa Persian Gulf Study Group (1997). Self-reported illness and health status among Gulf War veterans: A population-based study. The Iowa Persian Gulf Study Group. *Journal of the American Medical Association, 277,* 259–261.

Jacobs, J. A. (1994). *The future of the citizen-soldier force.* Lexington, KY: The University of Kentucky Press.

Kennedy, H. (2004). Army reserve seeks to toughen up training for part-time soldiers. *National Defense, 91,* 52. Retrieved August 26, 2005, from http://www.nationaldefensemagazine.org/issues/2004/Dec/ArmyReserveSeeks.htm

Kern, R., Wisher, R., Sabol, M., and Farr, B. (1993). *Reacquisition of skill by combat engineers mobilized from the Individual Ready Reserve* (Research Report 1667). Alexandria, VA: U.S. Army Research Institute for the Behavioral and Social Sciences.

McDonald, L. B., Bahr, H., & Abate, C. (2000). Cost-effectiveness of embedded training in army ground vehicles. *Proceedings of the 2000 Interservice/Industry Training, Simulation and Education Conference.* Orlando, Florida.

Orvis, K. L., Wisher, R. A., Bonk, C. J., & Olson, T. M. (2002). Communication patterns during synchronous web-based military training in problem solving. *Computers in Human Behavior, 18,* 783–795.

Perconte, S. T., Wilson, A. T., Pontius, E. B., Dietrick, A. L., & Spiro, K. J. (1993). Psychological and war stress symptoms among deployed and nondeployed reservists following the Persian Gulf War. *Military Medicine, 158,* 516–521.

Sabol, M. A., & Wisher, R. A. (2001). The retention and reacquisition of military skills. *Military Operations Research, 6*(1), 59–80.

Sellers, M. (2002). Creating effective groups and group roles in MMP games. *Gamasutra.* Retrieved February 15, 2005, from http://www.gamasutra.com/resource_guide/20020916/sellers_01.htm

Shanley, M. G., Leonard, H., & Winkler, J. D. (2001). *Army Distance Learning: Potential for Reducing Shortages in Enlisted Occupations.* Santa Monica, CA: RAND.

Sortor, R. E. (1994). *Training Readiness in the Army Reserve Components.* Santa Monica, CA: RAND.

Steinberg, A. G. (1991). *Individual Ready Reserve (IRR) call-up: Attitudes, motivation, and concerns.* (Research Report 1594) Alexandria, VA: U.S. Army Research Institute for the Behavioral and Social Sciences.

Stretch, R. H., Marlowe, D. H., Wright, K. M., Bliese, P. D., Knudson, K. H., & Hoover, C. H. (1996). Post-traumatic stress disorder symptoms among Gulf War veterans. *Military Medicine, 161,* 407–410.

Stuart, J., & Bliese, P. D. (1998). The long term effects of Operation Desert Storm on the psychological well-being of U.S. Army Reserve and National Guard Veterans. *Journal of Applied Social Psychology, 28,* 1–22.

Sumner, G. (1997). *Roman Army: Wars of the Empire.* London: Brassey's.

Wisher, R. A. (2003). Task identification and skill deterioration in peacekeeping operations. In T. W. Britt and A. B. Adler (Eds.), *The psychology of the peacekeeper: Lessons from the field* (pp. 92–109). Westport, CT: Praeger.

Wisher, R. A., & Fletcher, J. D. (2004). The case for advanced distributed learning. *Information and Security: An International Journal, 14,* 17–25.

Wisher, R. A., Moorash, A., Kronholm, E., & Gelosh, D. (2004). Distance learning in the military: Trends, benefits and challenges. Published in the *Proceedings of the 20ᵗʰ Annual Conference on Distance Teaching and Education.* Madison, WI.

Wisher, R. A., Sabol, M., Sukenik, H., & Kern, R. (1991). *Individual Ready Reserve (IRR) call up: Skill decay.* (Research Report 1595) Alexandria, VA: U.S. Army Research Institute for the Behavioral and Social Sciences.

Wright, K. M., Huffman, A. H., Adler, A. B., & Castro, C. A. (2002). Psychological screening program overview. *Military Medicine, 167,* 853–861.

CHAPTER 6

THE ROLE OF WOMEN IN THE MILITARY

Penny F. Pierce

On a mission just south of Baghdad over the winter, a young soldier jumped into the gunner's turret of an armored Humvee and took control of the menacing .50-caliber machine gun. She was 19 years old, weighed barely 100 pounds, and had a blond pony-tail hanging out from under her Kevlar helmet.

"This is what is different about this war," Lt. Col. Richard Rael, commander of the 515th Corps Support Battalion, said of the scene at the time. "Women are fighting it. Women under my command have confirmed kills. These little wisps of things are stronger than anyone could ever imagine and taking on more than most Americans could ever know." (Scharnberg, 2005)

The mission described above in a 2005 news report illustrates the extent to which women service members may find themselves embroiled in combat operations. Despite U.S. military regulations that limit women to noncombat arms units, modern military operations may require them to engage in combat. This reality is just one step in a series of changes that have occurred throughout the history of women's military service in the United States. The purpose of this chapter is to bring to light major contemporary issues regarding women in the military and to provide direction for future research. Following a brief historical review of women's role in the U.S. military, the gender issues associated with job performance evaluations and retention decisions are examined, as are gender issues that affect the military job environment. The health implications of women's service in the military are also assessed with a focus on the impact of deployment on the psychological well-being of women. Throughout, the socio-cultural context of the military organization is highlighted in order to address issues associated with being female in a predominantly male-dominated institution.

Perspectives on Women in the Military

Historical Background

In her historical review of women's participation in U.S. military operations, Hoiberg (1991) summarized the recurrent role women have played in the military since revolutionary days. During America's War for Independence, women served as nurses and also served on the front lines, preparing weapons, dressed as men, and otherwise involved in military action. Women's participation in the military continued during the U.S. Civil War when women served again as nurses and even as scouts and spies (De Pauw, 1981). In the Spanish-American War, the U.S. government contracted with more than 1,000 women to provide nursing care to the troops. Subsequently, the U.S. Army Nurse Corps was established in 1901. The creation of the Corps provided formal recognition to women's military service but women still had no rank or benefits. The formalization of women's involvement in the U.S. military continued with the start of World War I. During the war, tens of thousands of U.S. women served both in the United States and overseas. Many served as nurses in the Army and Navy, and many enlisted in the Navy and Marines performing clerk, telephone operator, translator, and other support jobs. Societal ambivalence toward women's participation in the military was epitomized by the fact that women were permitted to serve on active duty but without rank, and women were not permitted to join the Army in non-nursing jobs (although the other services permitted them). Despite this societal ambivalence about the role women should play in the U.S. military, thousands of women performed military jobs, at times serving under combat conditions (History and Collections, n.d.).

Following the end of World War I, women were removed from wartime jobs. The aim of returning women to traditional roles at home is described by Cooke (1993) as a kind of "cultural amnesia" in which "women's military activities...are reconstructed as minor (or even nonexistent), allowing the culture to maintain the myth 'of men in arms and women at home'" (p. 178).

The need for women in the U.S. military, however, reemerged when the United States entered World War II. Despite remaining societal ambivalence toward women serving in the military, their successful contributions during World War I set the stage for their further acceptance during World War II. About 400,000 women served in the military during the war. Not only did women serve in the Army and Navy Nurse Corps, but also in the Women's Army Corps (WAC), Army Air Forces, the Navy's Women Accepted for Volunteer Emergency Service (WAVES), Marine Corps Women's Reserve, and Coast Guard. By the end of the war, women had served in a wide range of noncombatant jobs, and yet, as in previous wars, even some of those in noncombatant jobs were in fact exposed to combat and more than 400 were killed by hostile fire (Dienstfrey, 1988).

At the end of World War II, the role of women in the military was the subject of renewed debate (Hoiberg, 1991) but in 1948, the U.S. Congress passed a measure ensuring permanent status for women in all branches of the U.S. military. Following this milestone, women service members were deployed to the Korean and Vietnam conflicts, where more than 80 percent served as nurses (Enloe, 1993). The expansion of women's participation in the U.S. military was spurred when an all-volunteer force was initiated in 1973 and the military met with personnel shortfalls. A year later, all occupational specialties were opened to women except those directly related to combat. Since that time, women's participation in military operations has reflected a significant expansion in role assignments (see Hoiberg, 1991 for a review).

Laws prohibiting discrimination based on gender have also been a driving force increasing women's representation and full participation in most occupations in the military. Despite these advances, the question of women's role in combat and combat units has remained an issue. In 1988, a *risk rule* was established stating that exposure to hostile fire or capture were a proper basis for excluding women from certain jobs (Center for Military Readiness, 2004).

The Persian Gulf War was a critical turning point for women in the military because of the large number of women who deployed (40,793 served in the theater of operations). The number of female recruits increased from 2 percent to 9 percent during the Persian Gulf War, while relentless media attention showed tearful separations from small children and photographs of women loading sidewinder missiles on combat aircraft. Extensive media coverage brought to light the fact that women were deployed in large numbers and many of them were parents of dependent children. Although the attention was unsolicited by the women themselves, it stirred social debate regarding the role of women in combat and the readiness of the American people to see their daughters wounded, taken prisoner of war, or killed (see Schneider & Schneider, 1992).

Since the end of the Gulf War, there have been increasing concerns and debate regarding the role of women in combat (Center for Military Readiness, 2004; Scarborough, 2001). The 1992 Presidential Commission on the Assignment of Women in the Armed Forces addressed many controversial and sensitive issues and voted to retain the exemption of women from close combat units that directly engage the enemy on land, sea, and in the air. However, the 1948 law prohibiting women in combat aircraft was repealed, opening the way for both cultural and structural trends toward gender equality and competition for top leadership positions. In 1991, on the heels of the Persian Gulf War, Congress revoked sections of the federal code to permit Air Force and Navy women to fly in combat aircraft, an action that was influenced by their demonstrated capable performance and ability to withstand stress. This change was then followed in 1994 by then-Secretary of Defense Les Aspin's publication of a policy memorandum that rescinded the *risk rule*. By eliminating "substantial risk of capture" as a factor in assigning female soldiers, many additional positions were open to women, including nontraditional occupations. The new assignment policy for women in the military provided a definition of "direct ground combat" as "exposure to hostile fire well forward on the battlefield with a high probability of physical contact with the enemy" (Assignment Policy for Women in the Military).

Between 1993 and 1996, the Department of Defense removed obstacles to the recruitment, training, and assignments to over 260,000 positions previously closed to women. More than 80 percent of all jobs and over 90 percent of all career fields are now open to both men and women. Nevertheless, most positions below brigade level that engage in direct combat on the ground (i.e., armor, infantry, and field artillery in the Army and Marine Corps) are closed to women. Further, women are restricted from assignment to the Special Forces (e.g., Navy Seals) including Special Forces aircraft and submarine duty. Despite these restrictions, women make up over 14 percent of active duty military personnel, serving in all branches of the military (Department of Defense, 2004).

When President George W. Bush announced the initiation of military actions in Iraq on March 19, 2003, this time, in contrast to the first Persian Gulf War, women were more readily accepted in nontraditional positions and they had vigorously trained for those more directly engaged in combat. Women were flying Kiowa scout helicopters, repairing mechanized vehicles, opening supply lines, leading the assault for an engineer support battalion, and for the first time, flying a B-2 in a combat mission. The risk to women service members was also dramatized by the capture of three enlisted women from the 507th Transportation Unit of the 3rd Infantry Division in northern Iraq. The wounding and subsequent capture of Private Jessica Lynch and Specialist Shoshana Johnson, followed by the death of Private Lori Piestawa, a young single mother, put a female face on the American soldier in combat.

As in prior wars, contradictions between policy and practice were played out in everyday operations. Despite the fact that the Army's combat arms, infantry, armor, and artillery remain closed to women by regulation, many women service members come under fire, and some are subject to combat conditions and participate in combat missions ("Female MPs ride into combat," 2005).

The emergence and ultimate integration of women into combat roles has been controversial as well as an area of concern for the public, policy makers, and military planners. Debate continues regarding the ability of women to perform on military missions despite a growing recognition of their performance in a variety of roles in both peacetime and wartime scenarios. Skeptics persist in their concerns regarding women's lack of physical strength, psychological ability to deal with the stressors of deployment and combat, as well as the strain of separation from their children (Katzenstein, 1998; Mitchell, 1989; Peach, 1996; Sasson-Levy, 2003). To the extent that historical events and societal shifts have driven the armed forces to increasingly include women, the debate is becoming largely academic.

Social Models of Gender Roles

The inclusion of women in the military directly confronts traditional socially constructed meanings of gender with respect to capacity to do the job, the willingness to engage in dangerous duty and opportunity to progress through the leadership chain to the top. The meaning of gender is socially constructed. As Segal (1995) wrote,

> The cultural contradictions and ideological ambivalence involved in women's participation can be seen in the reactions of both those who favor maintenance of patriarchal

values and radical feminists (Chapkis, 1981; Elshtain & Tobias, 1990; Enloe, 1980). Those at both ends of the ideological spectrum on gender roles oppose having women serve in armed forces. (p. 768)

An emerging feminist discourse regarding the history and role of women in the military is informative from a sociological perspective. The divergence of positions on women's participation in a predominantly male institution was best articulated by Sasson-Levy (2003), when she stated that "while liberal feminists endorse equal service as a venue for equal citizenship, radical feminists see women's service as a reification of martial citizenship and cooperation with a hierarchical and sexist institution" (p. 440).

Others object to women's participation in the military because of alternative social constructions of femininity. Femininity is perceived as antithetical to the military, which is viewed as the epitome of male institutions. Herbert (1998) suggests that in an effort to gain acceptance within the military organization, some women engage in "masculine" practices, accepting the masculine as the norm for soldiering. The term *combat, masculine-warrior*, was coined by Dunivin (2000), illustrating the link between military service and masculinity.

Despite the sociological debate regarding women's presence and activities in the military, an indisputable fact is that women serve in uniform alongside their male counterparts. Unlike men, however, women have always been volunteers in military service. The decision to become a soldier, sailor, or marine has always been one of choice. The impact of this choice has challenged notions of masculinity and femininity (Enloe, 1993). The media attention on the performance, accomplishments, and even the capture, injury, and death of women service members, has brought the public face-to-face with the reality that women serve in the U.S. military. The degree to which social constructions of the meaning of gender will change as a result of women's participation in the military, or women's participation in the military mirrors the shifts in gender roles experienced in civilian settings, is unknown. Regardless, women are participating in the U.S. military in increasing numbers and while restrictions have been lifted, gender differences remain in experiences on-the-job, job satisfaction, retention trends, and health outcomes following deployment.

Gender Issues: Job Performance, Retention, and Sexual Harassment

Job Performance and Leadership

Stereotypical perceptions of women influence evaluations of job performance as well as the selection process for increased rank and leadership positions. A study conducted by Looney, Robinson-Kurpius, and Lucart (2004) assessed the effects of gender on leader performance on military evaluations. In comparing female and male leaders in the military, there were no differential evaluations although more emotion-based characteristics were attributed to the women. Such emotion-based characteristics (e.g., empathy) are not as highly valued in measuring leadership capacity as are stereotypic masculine leadership characteristics (e.g., stoicism). In fact, men leaders who were perceived as emotional were rated as demonstrating fewer leadership characteristics. Appearing too emotional, an equivalent of appearing feminine, is considered negative for leaders whether men or women. Indeed, O'Neil (1981) discussed the *masculine mystique*, where emotionality, vulnerability, and expressing feelings were viewed as feminine and considered something that should be avoided by men. Consistent with the negative association between stereotypical feminine characteristics and leadership, Hartman, Griffeth, Crino, and Harris (1992) found that female leaders with masculine characteristics were evaluated as most promotable regardless of the gender stereotype of the job or the sex of the rater.

Performance reports biased by gender stereotypes may also negatively affect women's career progression in the military and may account, in part, for the lack of women in higher ranks. Career progression and attainment of rank depends in large measure on supervisory evaluations of performance and an estimation of one's potential for additional responsibility. It has been known for some time that personal characteristics of both the evaluator and rater can bias evaluations (Rice, Yoker, Adams, Priest, & Prince, 1984). In one study of performance evaluations across organizations, only the military yielded findings that significantly favored male over female leaders (Eagley, Karau, & Makhijani, 1995).

Perhaps in part because of this negative association between femininity and leadership, there is an underrepresentation of women at the highest levels of military leadership. Other factors may also contribute to the small number of women that is even eligible to assume top level responsibilities. First, a minority of women who begin a military career actually progress through the ranks far enough to be in a position to compete for top jobs, due to time devoted early in the career to childbearing. Second, specific career fields that "breed" future leaders such as combat aviation and commanding naval vessels were closed to women until recently. Certainly, as more women participate in deployments and have an opportunity to demonstrate leadership capabilities under stressful and demanding circumstances, there will be greater recognition and support of promotion to command positions.

In the absence of gender-biased evaluations, equal rates of promotion could be used as an indicator of whether men and women are performing similarly at similar military tasks. Given the reality of such bias, it is difficult to assess the nature of women's performance in military jobs. Yet this critical variable may best be determined not so much by individual evaluation as by group functioning. The military functions as part of small units accomplishing tasks for the benefit of larger groups, and this may well be the focus for future research on military job performance and gender. Besides performance, another area of critical importance to the military organization is retention.

Retention

Retention of a trained and ready force is a priority for all branches of military service. In military terms, "retention" refers to the voluntary continuation in military service after completing the initial obligation (U.S. General Accounting Office,

1990). Significant funds are expended in the accession and training process that are designed to be returned with years of committed and faithful service. Attrition in the military is costly and with the increasing number of women in the military, it is important to identify retention issues related to gender (U.S. General Accounting Office, 2001).

One of the key reasons why gender is an important consideration in the analysis of retention rates is that women leave the service at higher rates than men. In 2001, for example, the overall attrition loss for enlisted women was 48.6 percent, or 4.5 percentage points higher than the 44.1 percent rate for men (U.S. GAO, 2001). *Attrition* here refers to the voluntary and involuntary loss of military personnel prior to completion of the first term of enlistment or obligated duty (U.S. GAO, 1990). About 30 to 35 percent of enlisted personnel separate before completing their first term of service, and the estimated cost of recruiting, training, and screening for basic skills is $20,000 per person (Clark et al., 1999). With advanced technical training, the cost can reach a three- to fourfold figure.

Gender differences are associated with a range of variables that, in turn, may influence this gender difference in retention rates. One such variable is the way in which the job itself is perceived. Previous studies have found that those with high job satisfaction are more likely to stay in the military (Becker & Billings, 1993; Kocher & Thomas, 1994; Lakhani, 1991; Prevosto, 2001). In civilian organizational studies, job satisfaction has also been consistently shown to be related to turnover and the intention to leave (Arnold & Feldman, 1982; Cotton & Tuttle, 1986; Hiller & Dyehouse, 1987; Mobley, 1982; Steel & Ovalle, 1984). Dissatisfaction with work conditions and lack of career progression lead to attrition in the early years of a military career. Although both men and women report a link between job satisfaction and retention, the determinants of job satisfaction differ by gender. While Miller and Wheeler (1992) found no gender differences in satisfaction with meaningful work, women were more responsive to this variable in their intention to leave. That is, women showed a greater link between lack of meaningful work and decisions to leave the military than did men. This result is consistent with what other researchers have reported (e.g., Lacy, Bokemeier, & Shepard, 1983), which indicates that relative to men, women place more emphasis on the importance of meaningful work. Yet, none of the civilian studies adequately capture the unique demands of a military career with extended training, deployments, geographic mobility, and ever-increasing family separations. Only when multiple health, work, family, and deployment factors are considered together can we begin to understand the complexity of the decision to leave or stay in military service.

Deployments are an example of a factor that has a complex relationship to retention decision making. Previous research suggests that deployment may not necessarily be linked to higher rates of leaving the service. In a study conducted with service members deployed to the Persian Gulf War (Pierce, 1998), women who were deployed to the theater of operations were more likely to stay in military service than those who were deployed elsewhere. Nevertheless, those serving in the theater also had a significantly higher rate of posttraumatic stress disorder (PTSD), and those who left the service were more likely to report PTSD symptoms and other psycho-logical symptoms than those remaining in the military. Pierce (1997) also found that among those women who left the military following service during the Persian Gulf War, those who served in the theater of operations reported symptoms frequently (79 percent of symptoms were endorsed) in contrast to those who were deployed but who served in another location (52 percent of symptoms were endorsed). In addi-tion, independent of location, nearly half of the women in the all-female sample left the military following deployment to the Persian Gulf War, raising concerns about the impact of both mental and physical health on retention following deployment. Such results suggest that while deployment experience alone does not result in increased departures from military service, deployment experience coupled with psy-chological problems may increase departures.

In general, however, family-related factors have been found to be significant predictors of retention decisions, and being in a committed relationship may in-crease the likelihood that a woman leaves military service. For example, in a regres-sion analysis controlling for age, women living with a husband or partner were 1.78 times more likely to leave military service than women who were single (Pierce, 1998).

The influence of family on retention decisions is particularly strong among per-sonnel in the reserve components (Schumm, Bell & Gade, 2000; Schumm, Bell & Resnick, 2001), but it is not known how the dynamics of deployments for the Iraq war will affect couples' decisions to accept a lifestyle that requires frequent deploy-ment-related sacrifices. Deployments are very stressful on the functioning of the fam-ily system. In more recent deployments, in early reports of those who completed their tour during Operation Enduring Freedom (OEF) in Afghanistan, 26 percent (n=1,883) reported that the process of reunion and reintegration with their family was stressful (Core Capability Program Overview, 2003). Despite the recognition of these psychological stressors, data is are still limited on the association of deploy-ment stress and combat with the decision to remain in military service. Further, there is no evidence regarding the ways in which the repeated and extended deployments characteristic of current operations will influence family functioning, which in turn, will influence retention, particularly among women with children or the intent to have children.

Reasons women leave military service relate most directly to the motherhood/mili-tary-career problem described by Schneider and Schneider (1992). As early as 1949, Rear Admiral Clifford Swanson recognized pregnancy as a normal biological phe-nomenon in the age group of most military women and suggested that women should be allowed to have families and remain in service (Holm, 1982). However, an executive order signed by President Truman in 1951 permitted the services to ter-minate women from service if they gave birth to, or assumed responsibility for, a child. The justification for this widespread paternalistic discrimination was that preg-nancy and subsequent childrearing responsibilities would jeopardize mission capabil-ity, worldwide deployment, and also create an unsafe work environment for women in the reproductive years of life.

Litigation led to a Supreme Court ruling in 1973 to order the military services to provide servicewomen with family benefits equivalent to the benefits received by servicemen (Frantiero v. Richardson). It was only when faced with further litigation that in 1975 the Department of Defense discontinued the policy of discharging women when pregnant or responsible for dependent children. The Second Circuit Court held, in Crawford v. Cushman, that the Marine Corps' regulation requiring the discharge of a pregnant marine as soon as pregnancy is discovered violated the Fifth Amendment (Crawford v. Cushman, 531 F. 2nd 114 [2nd Cir., 1976]). When the law was changed to allow women to serve in the military once they became pregnant and later when women were permitted to remain in service as a single parent, concerns emerged regarding the impact these personnel decisions would have on the readiness and mobility of the forces. For example, voluntary separations for pregnancy have been a major contributor to higher female attrition (U.S. GAO, 2001). Still, many women remain in the military when they become pregnant.

When the destroyer tender Acadia docked in April 1991 in San Diego after seven months of Gulf duty with a tenth of its female crew pregnant, it caught the attention and concern of the media as well as military planners concerned about wartime readiness. Yet, on closer analysis, the Navy described the finding as "consistent with the pregnancy rate of military women in peacetime, and consistent with the rate of pregnancy of civilian women in the 20–to–24 age group" (Schneider & Schneider, 1992, p. 263). The majority of military women are of childbearing age, yet pregnancy, especially unplanned pregnancy, raises particular concerns and creates a unique set of circumstances for the military and these service members.

Although the laws have changed to provide for women to remain in military service through the childbearing years, concerns persist regarding the impact on individual performance as well as military readiness. Despite the fact that women service members remain in the workplace through pregnancy, stereotypes persist regarding negative job performance, lost work hours, and questions about whether or not pregnancy is a deliberate evasion of service. Thomas and Thomas (1994) examined the effects of parental status on absenteeism among Navy enlisted personnel, and found the pregnancy rate of Navy women to be comparable to their civilian age cohorts; the military is not unique. Only medical absences resulted in a significant sex difference and this difference between men and women could be accounted for by women taking time off for pregnancy. In fact, Olson and Stumpf (1978) reported that women missed fewer days of work than men, even when hospitalization for childbirth was included. Army studies have revealed that there were differences in women's and men's lost work time (Savell, Rigby, & Zbikowski, 1982), but there were no differences in absence from work between men and women once pregnancy was taken into account (Brown, 1993). Concerning absenteeism, the military is not different from other organizations that include young women of childbearing and childrearing age.

Still, studies have found that personnel turnover was 3 to 4 times greater for women than men primarily due to pregnancy and family child care issues (Center for Military Readiness, 2004). It is not clear what leads to this lower rate of retention among women. It may be that women leave military service because of childrearing

demands or, in part, because of the way supervisors and colleagues respond to pregnancy in the workplace. For example, there are reports of negative and hostile reactions toward pregnant women, a devaluation of their competence compared to non-
pregnant women and men (Butensky, 1984), and reports of pregnancy leading to
bias in performance reports (Halpert, Wilson, & Hickman, 1993). These negative
reactions were found to be most pronounced if the pregnancy was unplanned, resulting in an additional source of stress for pregnant service members (Forrest, 1994;
Kruger, 1979).

To the extent that armed forces are increasingly composed of older career personnel, especially in the reserve forces, other family variables, such as the number of children, become more important for the retention of female military personnel (Segal
& Harris, 1993). Demographically, women's participation in the military is positively associated with later age at first marriage, later age at birth of first child, and
fewer children. In nations such as the United States and Canada, where there has
been a delaying of family formation, there has also been an increase in women's representation in the military (Stanley & Segal, 1988). In Western societies, the social
construction of the family associates women's roles with reproduction and child rear-
ing and less with the role as warrior. Segal (1995) states,

> the greater the movement away from traditional family forms, especially those based on
> the nuclear family, the greater the representation of women in the military. This does not
> mean the demise of family values, but a transformation in the structures that support
> such values. (p. 769)

The military has made great advances in recent years to provide increased emphasis
on the family by enhancing childcare services and other family-friendly policies in
an effort to attract and retain qualified personnel.

The relationship of gender to performance evaluations and retention reviewed
above are only some of the outcomes of interest to military women. Beyond these
two outcomes, however, is the question of what kind of job environment women
service members' experience. One key factor that influences the job environment
for those engaging in nontraditional job fields is the presence of sexual harassment.
While job environment influences job performance and retention decisions, the contextual job factor of sexual harassment is considered in a separate section below
because of its potential for having a multilayered impact on women serving in the
military.

Sexual Harassment

Approximately 50 percent of women will experience sexual harassment at some
point during their working lives (Fitzgerald & Shullman, 1993). Specific characteristics of work environments have been associated with the increased likelihood of
being subjected to sexually harassing behavior. These characteristics include high
male-to-female ratios, traditionally male environments, and the predominance of
male supervisors (Gutek, 1985; U.S. Merit Systems Protection Board, 1995). The

military provides just such an environment and studies of military personnel suggest that military settings are conducive to increased sexual aggression toward women (Martindale, 1991; Wolfe et al., 1998). The most likely victims of sexual harassment are women with low socio-cultural and organizational power (Harned, Ormerod, Palmieri, Collingsworth, & Reed, 2002). In the military organization, junior enlisted women are therefore the most vulnerable to harassment as well as the most reluctant to report unwanted sexual behavior for fear of reprisal, not being taken seriously, or ridicule.

Theories that view sexual harassment as a psychological process consider the following to be central to the determination of harm: the victim's appraisal of the behavior as offensive, exceeding personal resources, or threatening personal well-being (Fitzgerald, Swan, & Magley, 1997). Being subjected to sexual harassment has also been linked to various negative outcomes for the individual both in terms of psychological well-being and job performance. A study by Magley, Hulin, Fitzgerald, and DeNardo (1999) suggested that women who experience sexual harassment report negative outcomes that include: poor job consequences, (Munson, Miner, & Hulin, 2001; Schneider, Swan, & Fitzgerald, 1997), psychological distress and post-traumatic stress disorder (Wolfe et al., 1998), and a variety of other consequences (Fitzgerald, Drasgow, Hulin, Gelfand, & Magley et al., 1997; Glomb, Munson, Hulin, Bergman, & Drasgow, 1999; Munson, Hulin, & Drasgow, 2000; Schneider et al., 1997) including their physical health (Koss & Heslet, 1992; Koss, Koss, & Woodruff, 1991; Wolfe, Brown & Bucsela, 1992). Indeed, given the link between individual and unit levels of depression (see Bliese, Volume 2 of this set), high rates of sexual harassment and their concomitant effects on individual service members are likely to detrimentally affect unit morale and functioning as well.

Sexual assault is also a problem that a substantial number of working women face. The lifetime prevalence rates of sexual assault among women range from 14 percent to 25 percent (Koss, 1993). Again the rate of sexual assault is highest among those with the least socio-cultural and organizational power, placing junior enlisted women at particular risk. Sexual assault has been closely linked to subsequent psychological symptomatology including posttraumatic stress disorder (National Victims Center, 1992; Resnick, Kilpatrick, Dansky, Saunders, & Best, 1993; Rothbaum, Foa, Riggs, Murdock, & Walsh, 1992; Wolfe et al., 1998).

Sexual misconduct has been a focus of U.S. Department of Defense inquiry during the global war on terrorism. Women in the U.S. Central Command deployed to Iraq, Kuwait, and Afghanistan reported being sexually assaulted or raped in such numbers as to prompt Defense Secretary Donald H. Rumsfeld to order a senior-level inquiry into 112 incidents. This inquiry included exploration into how the armed services treat victims of sexual attack. Victim concerns go beyond the attack itself to its aftermath, including a lack of emergency medical care and rape kits, incomplete criminal investigations, and retaliation by peers for reporting the assault ("Military women reporting rapes," 2004).

Labeling or marginalizing the victim is a concern for many of those who have been subjected to harassment or sexual assault as they decide whether or not to report the incident. Others may respond to the individual victim by attributing the complaint to the individual's oversensitivity, misunderstanding, or complicity (Loy & Stewart, 1984). Both the fear of retribution or being labeled a troublemaker may prohibit women from reporting unwanted sexual advances or sexual assault. The military, like other hierarchal organizations, may respond to such complaints defensively or inappropriately or may fail to respond altogether (Gutek & Koss, 1993). Sexual harassment, or in the extreme, sexual assault, is likely to significantly impair women's psychological health, job performance, career progression, and ultimate retention decision.

The Impact of Military Operations on Women's Health

Women's health may be affected not only by being subjected to sexual harassment and sexual assault but also by other aspects of the military environment. Stressors women experience include discrimination (e.g., Brown & Fielding, 1993) and work–family conflict (Cinamon & Rich, 2002; Gutek, Searle, & Klepa, 1991; Vinokur, Pierce, & Buck, 1999). Balancing multiple roles such as service member, spouse, and parent may result in both role-specific stress and role overload (Radloff, 1977; Stephens et al., 1994). Negative spillover across roles has been shown to negatively affect mental and physical health (Bolger, DeLongis, Kessler & Wethington, 1989; Bromet, Dew, & Parkinson, 1990; Small & Riley, 1990; Tiedje et al., 1990). Work/life stress is also a major predictor of military women's health. The link between work stress and health has been found to be most pronounced among junior enlisted women, younger women, and reserve and guard members.

Women's performance during the recent operations in Afghanistan and Iraq have highlighted issues related to the risk of sexual harassment and assault. Evidence from previous deployments has demonstrated other unique health risks encountered by women service members. There are gender-specific considerations regarding women's psychological health both during and following wartime service.

The perception of stressors and the response to stressors may differ by gender. For example, there is evidence that women perceive stressors differently than men (e.g., Spielberger & Reheiser, 1994), respond to stressors differently (e.g., Jick & Mitz, 1985), and there is evidence of differences in coping styles (Lutzky & Knight, 1994; Soderstrom, Dolbier, Leiferman, & Steinhardt, 2000). Yet there is little systematic research regarding gender with respect to deployment stressors, stress responses, and readjustment (Adler, Huffman, Bliese, & Castro, in press; Pierce, 1997, 1998, in press; Wolfe, Brown & Kelley, 1993). Little is known about the general health effects of combat exposure on women's health despite the increasing number of women in military service and their integration into nontraditional roles taking them closer and closer to the danger and devastation of war.

Recent research suggests that military women do perceive wartime stressors differently than do military men (Wolfe, Brown, Furey, & Levin, 1993) and that there are gender differences in the response to stressors including posttraumatic stress disorder and physical and emotional health. Although there is much less rigorous research on military women than men, there is suggestive evidence that there are distinctive characteristics of PTSD in women (e.g., Breslau & Davis, 1992; Breslau, Davis, Andreski, & Peterson, 1991; Koss, Woodruff, & Koss, 1990; Resnick, Kilpatrick, Best, & Kramer, 1992). It is not known however, if the intensity and length of wartime stressors and other factors (e.g., prior traumatic events) affect men and women differently.

Deployment experiences are associated with increased rates of various psychological problems. The Centers for Disease Control's Vietnam veterans study (1988) identified a 15–40 percent lifetime rate of posttraumatic stress disorder among Vietnam veterans and other studies have identified psychological and adjustment problems associated with combat deployment including depression, job loss, divorce, and severe spousal abuse (Bell & Resnick, 2001; McCarroll, 2000; Prigerson, Maciejewski, & Rosenheck, 2001; Prigerson, Maciejewski, & Rosenheck, 2002). Posttraumatic stress disorder has also been frequently reported among Gulf War veterans (Blair & Hildreth, 1991; Persian Gulf Veterans Coordinating Board, 1994; Pierce, 1997; Rundell, 1990), although it is believed that female Gulf War veterans may be under-diagnosed with combat-related posttraumatic stress disorder (Pereira, 2002).

There is substantial evidence that exposure to a traumatic event (e.g., sexual assault, combat exposure) and posttraumatic stress disorder are also associated with complaints of poor physical health (Baker, Menard, & Johns; Centers for Disease Control, 1988; Decoufle, Holmgreen, Boyle, & Stroup, 1992; Eisen, Goldberg, Tru, & Henderson, 1991; Kulka et al., 1988; Kulka et al., 1990; LeDonne, 1988; Litz, Keane, Fisher, Marx, & Monaco, 1992; Pierce, 1997; Shalev, Bleich, & Ursano, 1990; Sibai, Armenian, & Alam, 1989).

War-related stress is hypothesized to be a major contributor to mental and physical health problems. Numerous studies have found that traumatic stress affects physical health; however the mechanism through which this occurs remains unclear (Pierce & Sonnega, submitted for publication; Wolfe et al., 1993). Previous studies of Air Force women mobilized during the Persian Gulf War (Pierce, Vinokur, & Buck, 1998; Vinokur et al., 1999) found significantly more physical and mental health problems were self-reported by women who were deployed to the theater, in comparison to women deployed elsewhere during the same period of time. A presidential commission and other oversight panels have consistently recommended further research investigating the physical effects of stress (Presidential Advisory Committee, 1996) to address this issue.

Again, there is little research regarding gender differences regarding postdeployment physical health, psychological recovery, and well-being. Adler et al. (in press) examined stressor duration (i.e., deployment length) and stressor novelty (i.e., no prior deployment experience) on the psychological health of male and female military personnel returning from a peacekeeping deployment. It is important to note that this is one of the first studies to include gender as an important consideration in understanding the ways in which men and women might respond to the stressors. Interestingly, the link between deployment length and increased distress was noted only for male soldiers. One explanation for this result is suggested by the *tend-and-befriend* model (Taylor et al., 2000) in that women's coping strategy of seeking social support may protect them from chronic stressors involved in lengthy deployments. This model may explain why men respond with greater rates of distress to extended deployments whereas women's rates of distress remain stable over time. Male service members may be more vulnerable to environmental factors such as a lack of social support.

Such results dispel the myth that women are more vulnerable to stress than men at least after prolonged exposure to a stressful environment (Adler et al. in press). Perhaps military training, indoctrination, and preparation for stressful deployments bolster the capacity to withstand a range of stressors that preserves psychological integrity and well-being. The coping strategies may be different for men and women as suggested in this emerging body of research but it is significant that when exposed to the stressors of a prolonged peacekeeping deployment there were no gender differences in psychological outcomes. Building on this work, we need similar studies examining postdeployment recovery following combat when men and women are exposed to extraordinarily high levels of threat for extended periods.

War is one of the greatest stressors known to humankind (Hobfoll et al., 1991). Understanding the factors that contribute to both successful and problematic responses to war exposure is essential before we can learn how best to provide clinically sensitive predeployment screening and preparation, design preventive measures for the period of deployment, and increase postdeployment vigilance and health care.

There is a need for research on the patterns of illness following deployments so preventive measures can be taken in a timely manner in the future (Pierce, 1997, 2005). Interest in postdeployment health began in earnest following the Persian Gulf War when complaints of an unexplained illness brought about an unprecedented exploration of the impact of environmental and combat exposure (Cotton, 1994; Pierce, 1997; Steele, 2001). Surveillance capability has been addressed since then but we still need improvements and comparative analyses between and among deployments to help us differentiate gender-related responses to various wartime scenarios, environments, and stressors.

There are a number of important women's health issues requiring further long-term surveillance and attention among women who deploy to high-threat conditions whether on combat, peacekeeping, or domestic terrorism missions. Specifically, attention needs to be directed toward studying the occupational, environmental, and psychological hazards that may affect women in unique ways using statistical modeling that incorporates all these factors. Only when multiple health, work, family, and deployment factors unique to women are considered together can we begin to understand the complexity of the response to deployment and wartime stressors.

Although the 1.6 million women veterans made up only 6 percent of the total veteran population in 2000, (U.S. Census, 2000) their numbers are rising with U.S. operations in Afghanistan and Iraq and their roles are extending even further. With great concern, the Veteran's Administration is reporting that women are the fastest-growing segment of the veteran population; by 2010 more than 10 percent of veterans will be women. Thus the need for such research is urgent in order to meet unique health care needs of women veterans.

Future Directions

There is considerable theoretical work to be completed in order to better understand gender differences within the military and how those differences can be addressed to enhance the performance, stature, and professionalism of all who serve. Segal (1995) suggested "We need systematic theories covering, for example, how military women construct identities (including how they deal with inconsistencies in role expectations) and under what conditions the presence of women changes the masculine culture of the military organization" (p. 772).

We have much more to learn about styles of leadership that maximize the strengths of women so they can have legitimate opportunities for top leadership positions.

Policy makers can benefit from research that provides evidence regarding issues of gender so traditional stereotypes of feminine and masculine traits and behavior can either be dispelled or addressed head-on to better meet the challenges of today's military. Physiological and psychological evidence has shown us that women are not just a smaller, shorter, weaker version of men, but that women have unique features that might prove advantageous in certain circumstances such as fine motor movement or multitasking. It is also important to learn more about gender differences that may exist in responding to military stressors so that interventions can be tailored to support adaptive coping responses. In addition, evidence is needed to support family-friendly policies that support lower ranking women through the childbearing years where the demands of job and family may exceed their resources, resulting in the decision to leave military service.

The debate and controversy regarding the role of women in the military among psychologists, sociologists, legislators, journalists, and feminists, does not take into account the most critical stakeholder and that is the experienced women themselves. Military women do not seek, nor do they particularly enjoy the attention that has only served to at times disconnect them from their fellow soldiers, sailors, airmen, and marines. The earnest desire of both men and women in uniform is to have the opportunity to do what they have been trained to do and that is to serve their country with pride and to experience personal satisfaction for a tough job well done.

References

Adler, A. B., Huffman, A. H., Bliese, P. D., & Castro, C. A. (in press). The impact of deployment length and deployment experience on the well-being of male and female military personnel. *Journal of Occupational Health Psychology*.

Arnold, H. F., & Feldman, D. C. (1982). A multivariate analysis of the determinants of job turnover. *Journal of Applied Psychology, 67*, 350–360.

Assignment Policy for Women in the Military. Women in Military Service for America Memorial. Available from http://www.womensmemorial.org

Baker, R. R., Menard, S. W., & Johns, L. A. (1989). The military nurse experience in Vietnam: Stress and impact. *Journal of Clinical Psychology, 45*, 736–744.

Becker, T. E., & Billings, R. S. (1993). Profiles of commitment: An empirical test. *Journal of Organizational Behavior, 14*, 59–65.

Bell, D. B., & Resnick, G. (2001). Recent research on family factors and readiness: Implications for military leaders. *Psychological Reports, 89*(1), 153–165.

Blair, D. T., & Hildreth, N. A. (1991). PTSD and the Vietnam veteran: The battle for treatment. *Journal of Psychosocial Nursing, 29*(10), 15–20.

Bolger, N., DeLongis, A., Kessler, R. C., & Wethington, E. (1989). The contagion of stress across multiple roles. *Journal of Marriage and the Family, 51*, 175–183.

Breslau, N., & Davis, G. C. (1992). Posttraumatic stress disorder in an urban population of young adults: Risk factors for chronicity. *American Journal of Psychiatry, 149*(5), 671–675.

Breslau, N., Davis, G. C., Andreski, P. & Peterson, E. (1991). Traumatic events and posttraumatic stress disorder in an urban population of young adults. *Archives of General Psychiatry, 48*, 216–222.

Bromet, E. J., Dew, M. A., & Parkinson, D. K. (1990). Spillover between work and family. In Eckenrode, J. & Gore, S. (Eds.), *Stress between work and family* (pp. 133–151). New York: Plenum Press.

Brown, N. (1993). *Women in combat in tomorrow's Navy* (Rep. A264531). Washington, DC: Defense Technical Information Center.

Brown, J., & Fielding, J. (1993). Qualitative differences and women police officers' experience of occupational stress. *Work and Stress, 7*(4), 327–340.

Butensky, M. (1984). Devaluation of the competence of pregnant women: Does the spread phenomenon that operates with disabilities also occur with pregnancy? *Dissertation Abstracts International, 45*(02), 718B.

Center for Military Readiness. (2004). Risk, recruiting, retention and readiness. CR04.

Centers for Disease Control. (1988). Health status of Vietnam veterans: II. Physical health. *Journal of the American Medical Association, 259*, 2708–2714.

Chapkis, W. (1981). *Loaded questions: Women in the military.* Amsterdam: Transnational Institute.

Cinamon, R. G., & Rich, Y. (2002). Gender differences in the importance of work and family roles: Implications for work-family conflict. *Sex Roles, 47*, 531–541.

Clark, K. L., Mahmoud, R. A., Krauss, M. R., Kelley, P. W., Grubb, L. K., & Ostroski, M. R. (1999). Reducing medical attrition: The role of the accession medical standards analysis and research activity. *Military Medicine, 164*, 485–487.

Cooke, M. (1993). Wo-man, retelling the war myth. In M. Cooke & A. Woollacott, (Eds.), *Gendering War Talk.* Princeton, NJ: Princeton University Press.

Core Capability Program Overview (2003, October 19–23).*Interventions to Enhance Psychological Resilience and Prevent Psychiatric Casualties.* Presentation by Colonel C.W. Hoge, MD, at the Joint Military Technical Workshop.

Cotton, P. (1994). Military declassifies some Gulf War documents. *Journal of the American Medical Association, 272*(5), 341.

Cotton, J. L., & Tuttle, J. M. (1986). Employee turnover: A meta-analysis and review with implications for research. *Academy of Management Review, 11*(1), 55–70.

Decoufle, P., Holmgreen, P., Boyle, C. A., & Stroup, N. E. (1992). Self-reported health status of Vietnam veterans in relation to perceived exposure to herbicides and combat. *American Journal of Epidemiology, 135*(3), 312–326.

De Pauw, L. G. (1981). Women in combat: The revolutionary war experience. *Armed Forces and Society, 7*, 209–226.

Department of Defense (2004, September). Retrieved March 30, 2005 from http://web1.whs.osd.mil/mmid/military/RG0409.pdf

Dienstfrey, S. J. (1988). Women veterans' exposure to combat. *Armed Forces and Society, 14*, 43–54.

Dunivin, K. O. (2000). Military culture: Change and continuity. In R. L. Taylor & W. E. Rosenbach (Eds.), *Military leadership: In pursuit of excellence.* Boulder, CO: Westview Press.

Eagley, A. H., Karau, S. J., & Makhijani, M. G. (1995). Gender and the effectiveness of leaders: A metaanalysis. *Psychological Bulletin, 117*, 125–145.

Eisen, S. A., Goldberg, J., True, W. R., & Henderson, W. G. (1991). A co-twin control study of the effects of the Vietnam War on the self-reported physical health of veterans. *American Journal of Epidemiology, 134*, 49–58.

Elshtain, J. B., & Tobias, S. (Eds.). (1990). *Women, militarism, and war: Essays in history, politics, and social theory.* Savage, MD: Rowman & Littlefield.

Enloe, C. (1980). Women: The reserve army of Army labor. *The Review of Radical Political Economics, 12*, 42–52.

Enloe, C. (1993). *The morning after: Sexual politics at the end of the Cold War.* Berkeley, CA: University of California Press.

Female MPs ride into combat. (2005, February 16). *Boston Herald*, p. 006.

Fitzgerald, L. F., Drasgow, F., Hulin, C. L., Gelfand, M. J., & Magley, V. J. (1997). The antecedents and consequences of sexual harassment in organizations: A test of an integrated model. *Journal of Applied Psychology, 82*, 578–589.

Fitzgerald, L. F., & Shullman, S. (1993). Sexual harassment: A research analysis and agenda for the 1990s. *Journal of Vocational Behavior, 42*, 5–27.

Fitzgerald, L. F., Shullman, S., Bailey, N., Richards, M., Swecker, J., Gold, Y., Ormerod, M., & Weitzman, L. (1988). The incidence and dimensions of sexual harassment in academia and the workplace. *Journal of Vocational Behavior, 32*, 152–175.

Fitzgerald, L. F., Swan, S., & Magley, V. N. (1997). But was it really sexual harassment? Legal, behavioral, and psychological definitions of the workplace victimization of women. In W. O'Donohue (Ed.), *Sexual harassment: Theory, research, and treatment* (pp. 5–28). Boston: Allyn & Bacon.

Forrest, J. (1994). Epidemiology of unintended pregnancy and contraceptive use. *American Journal of Obstetrics, 170*, 1485–1488.

Glomb, T. M., Munson, L. J., Hulin, C. L., Bergman, M. E., & Drasgow, F. (1999). Structural equations models of sexual harassment: Cross section generalizations and longitudinal explorations. *Journal of Applied Psychology, 84*, 14–28.

Gutek, B. (1985). *Sex and the workplace.* San Francisco: Jossey-Bass.

Gutek, B. A., & Koss, M. P. (1993). Changed women and changed organizations: Consequences of and coping with sexual harassment. *Journal of Vocational Behavior, 42*, 28–48.

Gutek, B. A., Searle, S., & Klepa, L. (1991). Rational versus gender role explanations for work-family conflict. *Journal of Applied Psychology, 76*, 560–568.

Halpert, J. U., Wilson, M., & Hickman, J. U. (1993). Pregnancy as a source of bias in performance appraisals. *Journal of Organizational Behavior, 14*, 649–663.

Harned, M. S., Ormerod, A. J., Palmieri, P. A., Collingsworth, L. L., & Reed, M. (2002). Sexual assault and other types of sexual harassment by workplace personnel: A comparison of antecedents and consequences. *Journal of Occupational Health Psychology, 7*(2), 174–188.

Hartman, S. J., Griffeth, R. W., Crino, M. D., & Harris, O. J. (1992). Gender-based influences: The promotion recommendation. *Sex Roles, 25*, 285–300.

Herbert, M. S. (1998). *Camouflage isn't only for combat.* New York: New York University Press.

Hiller, D. V., & Dyehouse, J. (1987). A case for banishing "dual career marriages" from the research literature, *Journal of Marriage and Family, 49*, 787–795.

History and Collections: World War I (n.d.). Retrieved March 30, 2005 from http://www.womensmemorial.org/historyandcollections/history/lrnmrewwi.html

Hobfoll, S. E., Spielberger, C. D., Breznitz, S., Figley, C., Folkman, C., Lepper-Green, B., Meichenbaum, D., Milgram, N. A., Sandler, I., Sarason, I., & van der Kulk, B. (1991). War-related stress: Addressing the stress of war and other traumatic events. *American Psychologist, 46*(8), 848–855.

Hoiberg, A. (1991). Military psychology and women's role in the military. In R. Gal and A.D. Mangelsdorff (Eds.). *Handbook of Military Psychology* (pp. 725 – 739). New York: Wiley and Sons.

Holm, J. (1982). *Women in the Military.* Novado, CA: Presidio Press.

Jick, T. D., & Mitz, L. F. (1985). Sex differences in work stress. *Academy of Management Review, 10*, 408–420.

Katzenstein, M. F. (1998). *Faithful and fearless: Moving feminist protest inside the church and the military.* Princeton, NJ: Princeton University Press.

Kocher, K. M., & Thomas, G. W. (1994). Retaining Army nurses: A longitudinal model. *Research in Nursing and Health, 17*, 59–65.

Koss, M. P. (1993). Rape: Scope, impact, interventions, and public policy responses. *American Psychologist, 48*, 1062–1069.

Koss, M. P., & Heslet, L. (1992). Somatic consequences of violence against women. *Archives of Family Medicine, 1*, 53–59.

Koss, M. P., Koss, P. G., & Woodruff, J. (1991). Deleterious effects of criminal victimization on women's health and medical utilization. *Archives of Internal Medicine, 151*, 342–347.

Koss, M. P., Woodruff, W. J., & Koss, P. G. (1990). Relation of criminal victimization to health perceptions among women medical patients. *Journal of Consulting and Clinical Psychology, 58*, 147–152.

Kruger, P. (1979). Risk factors and pregnancy outcome among Air Force women. *Military Medicine, 9*, 788–791.

Kulka, R. A., Schlenger, W. E., Fairbank, J. A., Hough, R. L., Jordan, K. B., Marmar, C. R., & Weiss, D. S. (1988). *Contractual report of findings from the National Vietnam Veterans Readjustment Study.* Research Triangle Park, NC: Research Triangle Institute.

Kulka, R. A., Schlenger, W. E., Fairbank, J. A., Hough, R. L., Jordan, K. B., Marmar, C. R., Weiss, D. S., & Grady, D. A. (1990). *Trauma and the Vietnam War generation.* New York: Brunner/Mazel.

Lacy, W. B., Bokemeier, J. L., and Shepard, J. M. (1983). Job attribute preferences and work commitment for men and women in the United States. *Personnel Psychology, 36*, 315–329.

Lakhani, H. (1991). Retention cost-benefit analysis of U.S. Army junior officers: A multidisciplinary analysis. *Journal of Political and Military Sociology, 19*, 1–17.

LeDonne, D. M. (1988, May–June). Trends in morbidity and use of health services by women veterans of Vietnam. *Navy Medicine, 79*, 22–25.

Litz, B. T., Keane, T. M., Fisher, L., Marx, B., & Monaco, V. (1992). Physical health complaints in combat-related post-traumatic stress disorder: A preliminary report. *Journal of Traumatic Stress, 5*, 131–141.

Looney, J., Robinson-Kurpius, S. E., & Lucart, L. (2004). Military leadership evaluations: Effects of evaluator sex, leader sex, and gender role attitudes. *Consulting Psychology Journal: Practice and Research, 56*(2), 104–118.

Loy, P. H., & Stewart, L. P. (1984). The extent and effects of sexual harassment of working women. *Sociological Focus, 17*, 31–43.

Lutzky, A. M., & Knight, B. G. (1994). Explaining gender differences in caregiver distress. The roles of emotional attentiveness and coping styles. *Psychology and Aging, 9*, 513–519.

Magley, V. J., Hulin, C., Fitzgerald, L. F., & DeNardo, J. (1999). Outcomes of self-labeling sexual harassment. *Journal of Applied Psychology, 84*, 390–402.

McCarroll, J. E. (2000). Deployment and the probability of spousal aggression by U.S. Army soldiers. *Military Medicine, 165*, 41–44.

Military women reporting rapes by U.S. soldiers. (2004, February 26). *New York Times*, p. A1.

Miller, J. G., & Wheeler, K. G. (1992). Unraveling the mysteries of gender differences in intentions to leave the organization. *Journal of Organizational Behavior, 13*(5), 465–478.

Martindale, S. (1991). Sexual harassment in the military: 1988. *Sociological Practice Review, 2*, 200–216.

Mitchell, B. (1989). *Weak Link: The Feminization of the American Military.* Washington, DC: Regency Gateway.

Mobley, W. H. (1982). Supervisor and employee race and sex effects on performance appraisals: A field study of adverse impact and generalizability. *Academy of Management Journal, 25*, 598–606.

Munson, L. J., Hulin, C., & Drasgow, F. (2000). Longitudinal analysis of dispositional influences and sexual harassment: Effects on job and psychological outcomes. *Personnel Psychology, 53*, 21–46.

Munson, L. J., Miner, A. G., & Hulin, C. (2001). Labeling sexual harassment in the military: An extension and replication. *Journal of Applied Psychology, 86*(2), 293–303.

National Victims Center (NVS). (1992). *Rape in America: A report to the nation.* Arlington, VA.

O'Neil, J. M. (1981). Patterns of gender-role conflict and strain: Sexism and fear of femininity in men's lives. *Personnel and Guidance Journal, 60*, 203–210.

Olson, M. S., & Stumpf, S. S. (1978). *Pregnancy in the Navy: Impact on absenteeism, attrition, and work group morale.* TR 78-35. San Diego, CA: Navy Personnel Research and Development Center.

Peach, L. J. (1996). Gender ideology in the ethics of women in combat. In J. H. Stiehm (Ed.), *It's Our Military Too!* (pp. 156 – 94). Philadelphia, PA: Temple University Press.

Pereira, A. (2002). Combat trauma and the diagnosis of post-traumatic stress disorder in female and male veterans. *Military Medicine, 167*(1), 23–27.

Persian Gulf Veterans Coordinating Board (1994). *Summary of the issues impacting upon the health of Persian Gulf veterans.* Washington, DC: Support Office of the Persian Gulf Veterans Coordinating Board.

Pierce, P. (1997). Physical and emotional health of Gulf War veteran women. *Aviation, Space, and Environmental Medicine, 68*(3), 1–5.

Pierce, P. (1998). Retention among Air Force women serving during Desert Shield/Storm. *Military Psychology, 28*(14), 1287–1312.

Pierce, P. (2005). Monitoring the health of Persian Gulf War Veteran Women. *Military Medicine, 170*(5), 349–354.

Pierce, P., & Sonnega, A. (submitted for publication). Correlates and sequaela of post-traumatic stress disorder in Gulf War veteran women.

Pierce, P. F., Vinokur, A. D., & Buck, C. (1998). Effects of war-induced maternal separation on children's adjustment during the Gulf War and two years later. *Journal of Applied Social Psychology, 28*(14), 1286–1311.

Presidential Advisory Committee on Gulf War Veterans' Illnesses: Final Report. (1996). Washington, DC: U.S. Government Printing Office.

Prevosto, P. (2001). The effect of "mentored" relationships on satisfaction and intent to stay of company-grade U.S. Army Reserve nurses. *Military Medicine, 166*, 21–26.

Prigerson, H. G., Maciejewski, P. K., & Rosenheck, R. A. (2001). Combat trauma: trauma with highest risk of deployed onset and unresolved posttraumatic stress disorder symptoms, unemployment, and abuse among men. *Journal of Nervous and Mental Disorders, 189*(2), 98–108.

Prigerson, H. G., Maciejewski, P. K., & Rosenheck, R. A. (2002). Population attributable fractions of psychiatric disorders and behavioral outcomes associated with combat exposure among U.S. men. *American Journal of Public Health, 92*, 59–63.

Radloff, L. S. (1977). The CES-D scale: A self-report depression scale for research in the general population. *Applied Psychological Measurement, 1*, 385–401.

Resnick, H. S., Kilpatrick, D. G., Best, C. L., & Kramer, T. L. (1992). Vulnerability-stress factors in development of posttraumatic stress disorder. *Journal of Nervous and Mental Disease, 180*, 424–430.

Resnick, H. S., Kilpatrick, D. G., Dansky, B. S., Saunders, B. E., & Best, C. L. (1993). Prevalence of civilian trauma and posttraumatic stress disorder in a representative national sample of women (1993). *Journal of Consulting and Clinical Psychology, 61*(6), 984–991.

Rice, R. W., Yoder, J. D., Adams, J., Priest, R. F., & Prince, H. T. (1984). Leadership ratings for male and female military cadets. *Sex Roles, 10*, 885–901.

Rothbaum, B. O., Foa, E. B., Riggs, D. S., Murdock, T., & Walsh, W. (1992). A prospective examination of post-traumatic stress disorder in rape victims. *Journal of Traumatic Stress, 1*, 79–107.

Rundell, J. R. (1990). Combat stress disorders and the U.S. Air Force. *Military Medicine, 155* (11), 515–518.

Sasson-Levy (2003). Feminism and military gender practices: Israeli women soldiers in "masculine" roles. *Sociological Inquiry, 73*(3), 440–465.

Savell, J. M., Rigby, C. K., & Zbikowski, A. A. (1982). *An investigation of lost time and utilization in a sample of first-time male and female soldiers.* U.S. Army Research Institute for the Behavioral and Social Sciences; Leadership and Management Technical Area. Alexandria, VA.

Scarborough, R. (2001, July 5). Panel queries Army's plans for women—fears change in combat rules. *Washington Times*, p. A1.

Scharnberg, K. (2005, March 20). Stresses of battle hit female GIs hard: VA study hopes to find treatment for disorder. *Chicago Tribune*, p. 1.

Schneider, D., & Schneider, C. J. (1992). *Sound Off! American Military Women Speak Out.* New York: Paragon House.

Schneider, K. T., & Swan, S., & Fitzgerald, L. F. (1997). Job-related and psychological effects of sexual harassment in the workplace: Empirical evidence from two organizations. *Journal of Applied Psychology, 82*, 401–415.

Schumm, W. R., Bell, D. B., & Gade, P. A. (2000). Effects of a military overseas peacekeeping deployment on marital quality, satisfaction, and stability. *Psychological Reports, 87*, 815–821.

Schumm, W. R., Bell, D. B., & Resnick, G. (2001). Recent research on family factors and readiness implications for military leaders. *Psychological Reports, 89*(1), 153–165.

Segal, M. W. (1995). Women's military roles cross-nationally: Past, present, and future. *Gender and Society, 9*(6), 757–775.

Segal, M., & Harris, J. J. (1993). *What we know about Army families.* (Special Report 21). Alexandria, VA: U.S. Army Research Institute for the Behavioral and Social Sciences.

Shalev, A., Bleich, A., & Ursano, R. J. (1990). Posttraumatic stress disorder: Somatic comorbidity and effort tolerance. *Psychosomatics, 31*, 197–203.

Sibai, A. M., Armenian, H. K. & Alam, S. (1989). Wartime determinants of arteriographically confirmed coronary artery disease in Beirut. *American Journal of Epidemiology, 130*, 623–631.

Small, S. A., & Riley, D. (1990). Towards a multidimensional assessment of work spillover into family life. *Journal of Marriage and the Family, 52*, 51–61.

Soderstrom, M., Dolbier, C., Leiferman, J., & Steinhardt, M. (2000). The relationship of hardiness, coping strategies, and perceived stress to symptoms of illness. *Journal of Behavioral Medicine, 23*, 311–327.

Spielberger, C. D., & Reheiser, E. C. (1994). The Job Stress Survey: Measuring gender differences in occupational stress. *Journal of Social Behavior and Personality, 9*, 199–218.

Stanley, S. C. & Segal, M. W. (1988). Military women in NATO: An update. *Armed Forces and Society, 14*, 559–585.

Steel, R. P., & Ovalle, N. K. (1984). A review and meta-analysis of research on the relationship between behavioral intentions and employee turnover. *Journal of Applied Psychology, 69*(4), 673–686.

Steele, L. (2001). Invited commentary: Unexplained health problems after Gulf War service— finding answers to complex questions. *American Journal of Epidemiology, 154*(5), 406–409.

Stephens, M. A. P., Franks, M. M., & Townsend, A. L. (1994). Stress and rewards in women's multiple roles: The case of women in the middle. *Psychology and Aging, 9*(1), 45–52.

Taylor, S. E., Klein, L. C., Lewis, B. P., Gruenewald, T. L., Gurung, R. A. R., & Updegraff, J. A. (2000). Biobehavioral responses to stress in females—Tend-and-befriend, not fight-or-flight. *Psychological Review, 107*, 411–429.

Thomas, P. J., & Thomas, M. D. (1994). Marital status and parental status on absenteeism among Navy enlisted personnel. Special Issue on Women in the Navy. *Military Psychology, 6*(2), 95–108.

Tiedje, L. B., Wortman, C. B., Downey, G., Emmons, C., Biernat, M., & Lang, E. (1990). Women with multiple roles: Role compatibility perceptions, satisfaction, and mental health. *Journal of Marriage and the Family, 52*, 63–72.

U.S. Census. (2000) U.S. Census Bureau.

U.S. General Accounting Office. (1990). *Women in the military: Attrition and retention* (GAO rep. B230552). Washington, DC: U.S. Government Printing Office.

U.S. General Accounting Office. (2001). *Military Personnel: First-term personnel less satisfied with military life than those in mid-career* (Report No. GAO-02-200). Washington, DC: U.S. Government Printing Office.

U.S. Merit Systems Protection Board. (1995). *Sexual harassment in the federal workplace: Trends, progress, continuing challenges.* Washington, DC: U.S. Government Printing Office.

Wolfe, J., Brown, P. J., & Bucsela, M. L. (1992). Symptom responses of female Vietnam veterans to Operation Desert Storm. *American Journal of Psychiatry, 149,* 676–679.

Wolfe, J., Brown, P. J., Furey, J., & Levin, K. B. (1993). Development of a wartime stressor scale for women. *Psychological Assessment, 5,* 330–335.

Wolfe, J., Brown, P. J. & Kelley, J. M. (1993). Reassessing war stress: Exposure and the Persian Gulf War. *Journal of Social Issues, 49*(4), 15–31.

Wolfe, J., Schnurr, P. P., & Brown, P. J. (1994). Posttraumatic stress disorder and war-zone exposure as correlates of perceived health in female Vietnam War veterans. *Journal of Consulting and Clinical Psychology, 62*(6), 1235–1240.

Wolfe, J., Sharkansky, E. J., Read, J. P., Dawson, R., Martin, J. A., & Ouimette, P. C. (1998). Sexual harassment and assault as predictors of PTSD symptomatology among U.S. female Persian Gulf War military personnel. *Journal of Interpersonal Violence, 13*(1), 40–57.

Vinokur, A. D., Pierce, P. F., & Buck, C. L. (1999). Work-family conflicts of women in the Air Force: Their influence on mental health and functioning. *Journal of Organizational Behavior, 20,* 865–878.

CHAPTER 7

SEXUAL ORIENTATION AND MILITARY SERVICE: PROSPECTS FOR ORGANIZATIONAL AND INDIVIDUAL CHANGE IN THE UNITED STATES

Gregory M. Herek and Aaron Belkin[1]

The question of whether gay men and lesbians should be allowed to serve openly in the military has sparked some of the most emotionally charged public policy debates in the United States in the past two decades. Whereas most Western industrialized societies have made provisions for allowing gay people to serve with varying degrees of openness (e.g., Belkin & Levitt, 2001; Belkin & McNichol, 2001; Gade, Segal, & Johnson, 1996), the United States has not. Consequently, discussion in the United States has focused primarily on whether allowing openly gay and lesbian personnel to serve would undermine the military's ability to accomplish its mission and, to a lesser extent, how a policy change might be implemented.

This chapter addresses the issue of sexual orientation and military service. To provide a context for considering current policies, we begin with an historical overview of how homosexuality has been understood in the United States and its armed forces. We then discuss and critique contemporary rationales for excluding gay men and lesbians from the military, focusing on the issues of unit cohesion and privacy. Next, we discuss social psychological issues relevant to the organizational and individual changes that might follow from eliminating the ban on gay and lesbian personnel. We conclude the chapter by offering suggestions for future research directions.

The Historical Context of Modern Military Policies toward Homosexuality

Whereas homosexual and heterosexual behaviors are ubiquitous among human societies, modern notions of homosexuality and heterosexuality, and indeed the very concept of sexual orientation, have developed only since the latter part of the 19th century. It is not surprising, then, that religious and secular authorities traditionally sought to regulate sexual *behaviors* rather than *identities* or *orientations*. For much of the history of the United States, laws prescribed penalties for various forms of non-procreative and extramarital sex (including homosexual acts) which were referred to collectively as sodomy. Many of the early American colonies, for example, enacted stiff criminal penalties for sodomy (which the statutes often described only in Latin or with oblique phrases such as "the unmentionable vice" or "wickedness not to be named"), and the purview of these laws included homosexual conduct. Men were executed for sodomy in colonial Virginia in 1624 and in New Haven and New Netherland (later to become New York) in 1646 (Katz, 1976). In 1778, Lieutenant Gotthold Frederick Enslin became the first soldier to be drummed out of the Continental Army for sodomy (Katz). Except for a brief period when the New Haven colony penalized "women lying with women," sodomy laws in the American colonies applied exclusively to acts initiated by men—whether with another man, a woman, a girl, a boy, or an animal. The colonial laws gave rise to sodomy statutes throughout the states in the 1700s and 1800s, some of which survived into the 21st century.[2]

The U.S. military did not maintain regulations concerning sodomy until the 1917 revision of the Articles of War. Two years later, in 1919, one of the earliest recorded controversies surrounding homosexual conduct in the military occurred in Newport, Rhode Island, where U.S. sailors and male civilians were tried on charges connected with homosexual activity (Chauncey, 1989; Haggerty, 2003; Murphy, 1988). The Newport investigation may have led the military to adopt its earliest unofficial rationale for excluding homosexuals, which primarily reflected an attempt to punish sexual activity between men rather than declarations of sexual orientation. Although infrequent, the record of sodomy cases between 1919 and 1932 suggests a belief by military leaders that homosexual behavior tended to destroy good morals and had a detrimental effect on the functioning of the unit (Haggerty).

The Newport scandal occurred at a time when society's understanding of sexuality was undergoing a profound change. By the end of the 19th century, medicine and psychiatry had begun to compete successfully with religion and the law for jurisdiction over sexuality. As a consequence, discourse about homosexuality expanded beyond the realms of sin and crime to include pathology. This historical shift was generally considered progressive at the time because a sick person was less blameful than a sinner or criminal. It was also around this time that the modern notions of "the homosexual" and "the heterosexual," that is, the idea that individuals could be defined in terms of their sexual attractions and behaviors, began to emerge in medical discourse.

From the outset, homosexuality was defined in opposition to normalcy. Indeed, Karl Maria Benkert, the Hungarian writer widely credited with coining the term *homosexual* in 1869, originally contrasted it to *normalsexual*. *Heterosexual* did not emerge until later as the preferred term for describing sexual attraction to and behavior with the other sex (Dynes, 1985). Even within medicine and psychiatry, however, homosexuality was not universally viewed as a pathology in the early 20th century. Richard von Krafft-Ebing (1900) described it as a degenerative sickness in his *Psychopathia Sexualis*, but Havelock Ellis (1901) urged that homosexuality be considered a normal variant of human behavior, like left-handedness. Sigmund Freud

(1905/1953) believed that homosexuality represented a less than optimal outcome for psychosexual development, but nevertheless asserted in a now famous 1935 letter that "it is nothing to be ashamed of, no vice, no degradation, it cannot be classified as an illness" (Freud, 1951, p. 786).

During the 1940s, however, American psychoanalysis—the dominant theoretical framework in psychiatry—broke with Freud. Sandor Rado (1940, 1949) rejected Freud's theory of innate bisexuality, arguing instead that humans are naturally heterosexual. When normal heterosexual outlet proves too threatening, he argued, homosexuality represents a "reparative" attempt to achieve sexual pleasure. Thus, Rado proposed that homosexuality is a phobic response to members of the other sex. His position, and other theoretical accounts that pathologized homosexuality, soon became dominant in American psychoanalysis (for a brief history, see Bayer, 1987).

They also became wedded to official U.S. military policies concerning homosexuality. Previously, homosexual behavior was classified as a criminal offense and subject to sanction but homosexual individuals were not officially barred from military service (Haggerty, 2003; Osburn, 1995). As it prepared for World War II, however, the military sought to exclude homosexual persons from its ranks, based on a medical rationale. Psychiatry's view of homosexuality as an indicator of psychopathology was introduced into the military and psychiatric screening became part of the induction process. In 1942, for example, revised Army mobilization regulations included for the first time a paragraph defining both the homosexual and the "normal" person and clarifying procedures for rejecting gay draftees (Bérubé, 1990; Meyer, 1996).

Despite official policy, the ranks of the armed forces included many gay men and lesbians during World War II. Some of them became aware of their homosexuality only after they joined the service. Others were gay or lesbian but, motivated by a desire to assist the war effort, successfully circumvented the screening process and enlisted. Still others were detected at induction but were nonetheless accepted for service in the early years of the war when the need for personnel was greatest. As expansion of the war required that all available personnel be utilized, screening procedures were further loosened (Bérubé, 1990; D'Emilio, 1983). During the war, some military physicians and social scientists noted that many homosexual soldiers functioned as effectively as their heterosexual counterparts (Loeser, 1945; Menninger, 1948). Representing a minority view that conflicted with official policy, however, their reports were not taken seriously by military officials and were largely ignored for decades (e.g., Bérubé).

When the need for recruits diminished in the war's waning years, antihomosexual policies were enforced with increasing vigilance and many gay and lesbian service members were discharged involuntarily in a series of witch hunts (Bérubé, 1990). Ironically, the mass courts martial and discharges helped to stimulate the development of lesbian and gay communities and the modern movement for gay rights. Because they were socially ostracized, often unable to secure employment, and ineligible for benefits under the GI Bill of Rights as a result of their undesirable discharge as a "sexual psychopath," men and women ejected from the military for homosexuality often chose not to return to their hometowns. Instead they stayed in the major port cities and centers of war industry—including San Francisco, Los Angeles, and New York—where many first encountered other gay people during the war and where many landed after separating from the military. Many homosexuals who had avoided detection or prosecution in the military made similar decisions to locate in large port cities upon discharge. Thus, large and fairly visible gay communities (complete with social and commercial institutions, such as bars) rapidly emerged in many American cities at the end of the war (D'Emilio, 1983).

In 1948 and 1953, Alfred Kinsey and his colleagues at Indiana University published their famous reports on sexual behavior in the human male (Kinsey, Pomeroy, & Martin, 1948) and the human female (Kinsey, Pomeroy, Martin, & Gebhard, 1953). Based on approximately 18,000 interviews with people from all around the United States, Kinsey's findings that homosexual experiences were fairly common shocked a country that viewed homosexuality as a rare form of deviance whose practitioners were visibly different from "normal" people. It was also around this time that Ford and Beach (1951) published their book length comparative study documenting the existence of homosexual behavior in many nonhuman species and its acceptance in a large number of human cultures. The scholarship of the Kinsey group and Ford and Beach (1951) challenged widespread assumptions that homosexuality was practiced only by a small number of social misfits. Nevertheless, homosexuality was included in the first *Diagnostic and Statistical Manual* (DSM) of the American Psychiatric Association in 1952 (American Psychiatric Association, 1952).

After World War II, the U.S. military continued to prohibit same-sex sexual behavior in its ranks but increasingly viewed a homosexual orientation per se as undermining the military. Throughout the 1950s and 1960s, acknowledging a homosexual orientation barred an individual from military service (Williams & Weinberg, 1971). In the 1970s, however, a new social movement emerged in the United States that pressed for civil rights for gay men and lesbians (Adam, 1995). That movement inspired many sectors of society to reevaluate longstanding assumptions about homosexuality. In 1973, informed by the weight of research evidence and changing societal norms, the American Psychiatric Association's Board of Directors voted to remove homosexuality as a diagnosis from the Diagnostic and Statistical Manual of Mental Disorders (Bayer, 1987; Minton, 2002). The American Psychological Association (APA) endorsed the psychiatrists' actions and urged its members to work to eradicate the stigma historically associated with a homosexual orientation (Conger, 1975).

The military, however, did not eliminate its policy. Legal challenges to the military in the 1970s, mounted by Leonard Matlovich and others (Hippler, 1989), were largely unsuccessful. Nevertheless, they highlighted the wide latitude of discretion afforded to commanders in implementing existing policy and the consequent variation in the rigor with which it was enforced. They also resulted in court orders that the military justify its exclusion of homosexuals more clearly (Osburn, 1995). In response, the Department of Defense (DoD) formulated a new policy in 1981 which declared unequivocally that homosexuality is incompatible with military service (DoD Directive 1332.14, 1982). Under this policy, nearly 17,000 men and women were discharged because of homosexuality in the ensuing decade (General Accounting Office, 1992a). The Navy was disproportionately represented, accounting for 51 percent of the discharges even though it comprised only 27 percent of the active force during this period. Statistical breakdowns by gender and race revealed that, for all services, white women were discharged at a rate disproportionate to their representation: white females represented 6.4 percent of personnel overall but 20.2 percent of those discharged for homosexuality (General Accounting Office, 1992b).

By the end of the 1980s, reversing the military's policy was becoming a national priority for advocates of gay and lesbian civil rights. An increasing number of lesbian and gay male members of the armed services came out publicly and vigorously challenged their discharges through the legal system. Many national organizations officially condemned the DoD's policy and many colleges and universities banned military recruiters and Reserve Officers Training Corps (ROTC) programs from their campuses. In 1992, legislation to overturn the ban was introduced in the U.S. Congress.

With the 1992 election of President Bill Clinton, whose campaign platform had included a promise to "issue executive orders to repeal the ban on gay men and lesbians from military or foreign service" (Clinton & Gore, 1992, p. 64), the military policy seemed to be on the verge of elimination. Shortly after his inauguration, President Clinton asked the Secretary of Defense to prepare a draft policy to end discrimination on the basis of sexual orientation, and he proposed to use the interim period to resolve the practical problems related to implementing a new policy.

Clinton's initiative, however, was greeted with intense opposition from the Joint Chiefs of Staff, members of Congress, the political opposition, and a considerable segment of the U.S. public. After lengthy public debate and congressional hearings, the President and Senator Sam Nunn (D-GA), chairperson of the Senate Armed Services Committee, reached a compromise, which they labeled "Don't Ask, Don't Tell, Don't Pursue" (hereafter referred to as "Don't Ask, Don't Tell," or DADT). Under its terms, military personnel would no longer be asked about their sexual orientation and would not be discharged simply for being gay. Demonstrating a propensity to engage in sexual conduct with a member of the same sex, however, would constitute grounds for discharge. In the fall of 1993, Congress voted to codify most aspects of the ban. Meanwhile, the civilian lower courts issued contradictory opinions about the policy, some upholding its constitutionality and others ordering the reinstatement of openly gay military personnel who were involuntarily discharged (Jacobson, 1996). Higher courts, however, consistently upheld the policy, and the U.S. Supreme Court has never reviewed its constitutionality.

DADT has remained in effect since 1993. Discharges generally increased during the 1990s, and harassment of gay and lesbian personnel appeared to intensify in some locales. With the beginning of the new century, the White House and Congress were controlled by Republicans who were on record opposing service by openly gay personnel. Prospects for eliminating the ban appeared slim. In 2002 and 2003, however, calls for changing the policy gained new momentum. Following the September 11, 2001, attacks on the World Trade Center and the Pentagon, the war on terrorism and U.S. military involvement in Afghanistan and Iraq created a need for more personnel. In that context, many objected when nine military linguists— including six who were fluent in Arabic—were discharged in 2002 after their homosexuality became known (Heredia, 2002). In 2003, three high-ranking retired military officers publicly disclosed their homosexuality and challenged the DADT policy's legitimacy (Files, 2003). Throughout this time, public opinion appeared to favor allowing service by openly gay personnel. A December, 2003, Gallup poll registered 79 percent of American adults (including 68 percent of self-described conservatives) in favor of allowing gay men and lesbians to serve openly (Carlson, 2003).

Whereas psychiatry's early assumption that homosexuality is a mental illness was incorporated into military policy before World War II, the mental health profession's repudiation in the 1970s of its earlier views did not have the same impact. Psychiatrists and psychologists are no longer employed to screen out gay men and lesbians at the time of their initial enlistment. Nevertheless, military mental health providers experience pressures from superior officers to report information about service members' homosexual feelings or behaviors disclosed to them during therapy. Indeed, legal limits to confidentiality often create conflicts for mental health professionals who work in military settings (Barnett & Jeffrey, 1996).

A complete history of the U.S. military's reactions to homosexuality is too long and complex to detail in the present chapter (for more extensive accounts, see Bérubé, 1990; Burg, 2002; Haggerty, 2003; Lehring, 2003; Murphy, 1988). From the brief historical summary presented here, three general conclusions are relevant for understanding current policies. First, in large part because its existence predates modern notions of sexual orientation, the U.S. military historically has attempted to craft policies that deal with both homosexual *behavior* and personnel who have a homosexual *identity.* Second, perhaps reflecting tensions between these two aspects of sexuality, military policy has been repeatedly modified over the past century. This has included effectively suspending enforcement of prohibitions on gay personnel when troops were needed for combat. Third, medicine, psychiatry, and psychology played an important role in shaping the military's reactions to homosexuality in the first half of the 20th century, but current military policy does not reflect contemporary psychological and psychiatric thinking.

Current Rationales for Exclusion

Over the past 50 years, military and political officials have articulated many different rationales for excluding gay and lesbian service members. At various times, they have argued that gay men and lesbians are mentally and physically unfit for military service, pose security risks, engage in sexual misconduct more often than their heterosexual counterparts, threaten unit cohesion, and violate the privacy of heterosexual service members (Osburn, 1995).

Some of these rationales are no longer credible to most military officials and scholars. Since the 1980s, a consensus has emerged among policy makers that homosexual men and women are fully capable of serving in the military and that many have done so despite policies that officially excluded them. During House Budget Committee hearings in 1992, for example, General Colin Powell, then-chairman of the Joint Chiefs of Staff, stated that the reason for keeping lesbians and gay men out of the military "is not an argument of performance on the part of homosexuals who might be in uniform, and it is not saying they are not good enough" (House Budget Committee Hearing, 1992, p. 112). He further characterized individuals "who favor a homosexual lifestyle" as "proud, brave, loyal, good Americans." In 1991 testimony before the same House committee, then-Secretary of Defense Dick Cheney referred to the policy of the time concerning gay people and security clearances as "an old chestnut" (GAO, 1992a; House Budget Committee Hearing, 1991).

What remains contested is whether the presence of acknowledged gay men and lesbians in the military would adversely affect heterosexual service members because of the latter's discomfort with homosexuality and gay people (MacCoun, 1996). Thus, the unit cohesion and privacy rationales now dominate the discussion of whether gay men and lesbians could serve openly in the U.S. military without compromising military effectiveness.

Unit Cohesion

The unit cohesion rationale is the official justification for the current DADT law and policies that regulate gay and lesbian service members, and it is premised on the idea that the military must exclude known gay and lesbian service members if it is to maintain morale, good order, and discipline—qualities associated with unit cohesion (U.S. Code 654, 1993). According to this perspective, heterosexual service members dislike gay men and lesbians to such an extent that they would be unable to work with them and trust them with their lives, thereby destroying the bonds necessary for units to function effectively (Miller & Williams, 2001). This rationale emerged in the policies articulated by the military in 1975 and 1981 in response to court decisions (Osburn, 1995).

The research literature on cohesion is vast, and the construct has been defined, described, and measured in numerous ways, often reflecting prevailing societal conditions and the values and interests of the scholars conducting the research (Siebold, 2000, Volume 1 of this set). Early academic research on cohesion tended to define it as a property of the group that resulted from positive social relationships among group members (e.g., Lott & Lott, 1965). The military has often related cohesion to combat, emphasizing the loyalty that service members feel toward each other, the group, and their leaders as they accomplish dangerous and life-threatening missions (e.g., Henderson, 1985). Wong, Kolditz, Millen, and Potter (2003), for example, argued that U.S. soldiers in Operation Iraqi Freedom developed trusting relationships, or cohesion, by withstanding hardship and enduring austere conditions together, and that these emotional bonds played a primary role in motivating them to fight.

Cohesion is not a unitary construct and multiple dimensions of cohesion have been discussed in the research literature. Perhaps the most common distinction made by behavioral scientists is between *social cohesion* (the nature and quality of the emotional bonds of friendship, liking, caring, and closeness among group members) and *task cohesion* (members' shared commitment to achieving a goal that requires the collective efforts of the group). A group displays high social cohesion to the extent that its members like each other, prefer to spend their social time together, enjoy each other's company, and feel emotionally close to one another. A group with high task cohesion is composed of members who share a common goal and who are motivated to coordinate their efforts to achieve that goal as a team (MacCoun, 1996).

The debate about the correlation between group cohesion and performance continues (Kier, 1998; Guzzo & Dickson, 1996). For example, based on interviews with approximately 40 service members who reported on their own motivations for fighting during combat in Iraq, Wong et. al. (2003) argued that social cohesion is an important determinant of unit performance. While their approach may have yielded an accurate impression of respondents' perceptions, however, it is not methodologically adequate for determining whether combat effectiveness actually resulted from social cohesion or another source for which they failed to control, in particular task cohesion.

Indeed, most scholars agree that social cohesion cannot be seen as the primary cause for high levels of military performance (Segal & Kestnbaum, 2002). Rather, task cohesion seems to be more important (Kier, 1998; Lott & Lott, 1965; MacCoun, 1996; Mullen & Copper, 1994). Successfully accomplishing a challenging task as a group, combined with familiarity but not social similarity, increases small-unit cohesion (Bartone, Johnsen, Eid, Brun, & Laberg, 2002). Effective leadership at the unit level is also a key element for creating cohesion (Siebold & Lindsay, 2000). After reviewing military and civilian studies of cohesion and performance, MacCoun (1996) concluded that task cohesion — not social cohesion or group pride — drives group performance. He pointed out that when social cohesion is too high, deleterious consequences can result, including excessive socializing, groupthink (the failure of a highly cohesive group to engage in effective decision-making processes; Janis, 1972), insubordination, and mutiny (Kier, 1998; MacCoun). MacCoun concluded that the impact—if any—of a new sexual orientation policy would be on social cohesion. Because coworkers can perform effectively as a team without necessarily liking each other, he argued, such a reduction in cohesion would be unlikely to reduce the military's ability to complete its mission successfully.

Thus, notwithstanding a few studies such as that by Wong et. al. (2003), the literature raises serious questions about the validity of the unit cohesion rationale (Kier, 1998). Because unit cohesion is more influenced by the successful completion of tasks and sharing of common goals than by social similarity, the presence of known gay or lesbian service members should have little negative impact so long as they share the same goals as their colleagues (Kier; MacCoun, 1996).

Another problem with the unit cohesion rationale is that it fails to acknowledge that most gay and lesbian service members exercise considerable discretion in revealing their homosexuality to others and are likely to continue doing so even if DADT is eliminated (Herek, 1996; MacCoun, 1996). Research on foreign militaries suggests that when bans on homosexual service members are lifted, relatively few gay and lesbian personnel disclose their sexual orientation. Although the Canadian military estimated that 3.5 percent of its personnel were gay or lesbian, for example, the Department of National Defence received only 17 claims for medical, dental, and relocation benefits for same-sex partners in 1998, six years after Canada lifted its ban. This suggests that service members were reluctant to identify themselves by requesting benefits. Similarly, only 33 soldiers identified themselves openly as gay or lesbian to a research team three years after Australia lifted its ban, although it is reasonable to assume that the actual number of gay service members was considerably larger (Belkin, 2003). If most gay and lesbian service members do not reveal their sexual orientation, it seems unlikely that their homosexuality would pose a serious threat to the effective operation of their unit (Belkin & Bateman, 2003; Kier, 1998; MacCoun, 1996).

Finally, even when a unit includes openly gay and lesbian personnel, experience does not indicate that cohesion suffers as a consequence. Bérubé (1990) provided extensive evidence that many lesbians and gay men served more or less openly in the U.S. military during World War II. Their sexual orientation was known to many of their heterosexual comrades, and they served effectively in combat with the respect and admiration of those comrades. More recently, the literature includes case studies of individuals such as Margarethe Cammermeyer and Perry Watkins who served openly without undermining their units' cohesion (Osburn, 1995). More generally, in countries that have lifted gay bans, there have been no reports that the small number of gay and lesbian personnel who came out compromised military performance, readiness, or unit cohesion in any way. The fact that 24 countries have lifted their bans on homosexual service members without undermining cohesion suggests that the U.S. military's rationale may not reflect military necessity (Belkin, 2001, 2003; Belkin & Bateman, 2003; Belkin & Levitt, 2001; Belkin & McNichol, 2001). Indeed, the U.S. military itself has refrained from enforcing the ban when personnel were needed for combat operations, the time when cohesion matters most to the military mission. As noted above, many homosexual recruits were accepted and retained for service during World War II when all available personnel were needed (Bérubé, 1990). And during the first Gulf War, the ban was effectively suspended via stop-loss order without any apparent impact on cohesion or readiness.

Privacy

Even while the unit cohesion rationale continues to be debated, a privacy rationale has been articulated with increasing frequency in discussions of the DADT policy (Belkin & Embser-Herbert, 2002; Frank, 2000). This rationale states that the presence of gay men and lesbians violates the privacy or modesty rights of heterosexual service members who feel they should not be forced to shower or live in close quarters with homosexuals of their same sex (Bianco, 1996; Moskos, 1994; Ray, 1993; Wells-Petry, 1993). The question of heterosexual and homosexual men showering together has been one of the most emotionally charged issues in the debate over gay people in the military

(Belkin & Bateman, 2003; Kaplan, 2003; Kendall, 1993). Whereas some scholars maintain that the current policy on gay men and lesbians in the military protects the privacy of heterosexual service members (Wells-Petry, 1993), a growing body of research challenges this assumption, suggesting that lifting the ban would have no negative impact on service members' privacy. Indeed, some have argued that by sparing heterosexual service members from interrogations about the suspected homosexuality of other personnel and by removing pressures to prove their heterosexuality (which is accomplished typically by exaggerating their conformity to stereotypical gender norms), eliminating the ban would actually enhance the privacy of all members of the military (e.g., Belkin & Embser-Herbert,; Herbert, 1998).

As Belkin and Embser-Herbert (2002) noted, the privacy rationale depends on two central premises. First, in spite of the numerous other personal sacrifices that military service requires, service members should be allowed to maintain some control over the exposure of their bodies in intimate settings. Just as the military segregates men from women for intimate activities such as showering and using toilet facilities, proponents of the privacy rationale argue, homosexuals and heterosexuals should likewise perform such tasks apart from each other. Because such segregation ultimately is not feasible, homosexuals should be excluded (Belkin & Bateman, 2003; Shawver, 1995; Moskos 1994). A second, implicit premise of the privacy rationale is that a privacy injury takes place whenever a heterosexual becomes aware that a homosexual person is seeing his or her naked or partially clothed body (Wells-Petry, 1993). Underlying this premise may be the notion that gay men and lesbians are disproportionately likely to be sexual predators who use seduction or coercion to force sex on unwilling heterosexual service members (Belkin & Bateman, 2003; Belkin & Embser-Herbert, 2002).

As Kaplan (2003) and Shawver (1995) suggested, the privacy rationale is based partly on the assumption that heterosexuals in the military do not currently shower or share latrines with homosexuals, that is, current policy prevents heterosexuals from encountering homosexuals in intimate environments. However, many heterosexuals in the military already are aware of gay and lesbian peers (Evans, 2002; Osburn, 1995). Out of 368 officers and enlisted personnel in the U.S. Navy and Marine Corps surveyed by Bicknell (2000), for example, 20 percent personally knew a homosexual service member and another 22 percent were unsure if they did. Similarly, out of 394 female veterans and active-duty service members surveyed by Herbert (1998), 79 percent of the women who identified as heterosexual said they knew women in the military who were lesbian or bisexual. Thus, heterosexual service members currently serve with colleagues they know to be homosexual, and some scholars have argued that Don't Ask, Don't Tell does little to preserve heterosexual privacy rights in this regard (Belkin & Bateman, 2003; Belkin & Embser-Herbert, 2002).

If heterosexual and homosexual service members already serve together, why haven't privacy problems erupted on a mass scale? One likely reason is that in most cases social norms dictate behavioral strategies whereby service members negotiate potential violations of privacy. These interaction patterns, which include mutual gaze aversion and similar behaviors, were termed *civil inattention* by Goffman (1963) and the *etiquette of disregard* by Shawver (1995). They operate routinely in civilian life with the consequence that homosexuals and heterosexuals routinely share settings such as public restrooms and locker rooms with few problems (Shawver). In most military settings, civil inattention and the etiquette of disregard prevent the occurrence of situations in which service members (heterosexual and homosexual alike) feel their privacy has been violated. They allow heterosexuals to maintain the assumption that no homosexuals are present in showers and latrines, whether or not this is truly the case.

A second reason that relatively few violations of privacy are perceived is that people adapt their personal standards of bodily modesty to new circumstances when necessary (Shawver, 1987). Such adaptation has been observed in a variety of settings, including college dormitories (Vivona & Gomillion, 1972), medical environments (Millstein, Adler, & Irwin, 1984), and prisons (Shawver, 1987; Shawver & Kurdys, 1987). Female U.S. military personnel in the 1991 Persian Gulf War reported that modesty needs often assumed less importance than other needs, such as hygiene, and they adjusted to a general lack of privacy for dressing, bathing, and using the latrine (Schneider & Schneider, 1992).

Finally, concerns about personal modesty are rapidly being addressed by new environmental designs in military facilities. Belkin and Embser-Herbert (2002) argued that because the new 1+1 barracks design standard will soon provide most service members with their own bedroom and a bathroom shared with just one other person, the gang latrine is a relic of the past for most military personnel most of the time. Even in overseas combat deployments and on submarines, many if not most service members shower in single-stall settings. These architectural changes, Belkin and Embser-Herbert argued, make the privacy rationale no longer valid.

Prospects for Change

Even if statutory and political barriers to allowing openly gay personnel to serve were to vanish overnight, the military would still face the prospect of implementing a new policy in a domain that has evoked intense emotional arguments on both sides. In this section of the chapter, we examine some practical issues relevant to replacing the DADT policy with one that does not discriminate against personnel on the basis of their sexual orientation.

As noted above, even most supporters of exclusionary policies acknowledge that lesbian and gay personnel are no less capable than heterosexuals of successfully performing the duties required by military service. To the extent that problems are associated with implementing a nondiscriminatory policy, therefore, they can be expected to stem largely from the attitudes, reactions, and conduct of heterosexual personnel. In the following paragraphs, we discuss two foci for change: the organizational culture in which heterosexual personnel work; and their behavior, attitudes, and beliefs. (For more detailed consideration of the points raised here, see Belkin, in press; Herek, 1993; Kauth & Landis, 1996; MacCoun, 1996; Sarbin, 1996; Zellman, 1996).

Kelman's (1961) model of behavior change provides a useful vocabulary for this discussion. It distinguishes change that occurs as a result of *compliance* (changing one's behavior as a result of external coercion) from change based on *identification* (adoption of the target behavior because the individual regards it as consistent with her or his identity or self-concept) and *internalization* (acceptance of the target behavior as congruent with one's own value system). Whereas initial reductions in discriminatory behavior in response to a new policy will probably reflect compliance, such changes will be more stable and long-lasting to the extent that heterosexual personnel come to regard nondiscrimination against gay personnel as consistent with their professional identities as members of the armed forces (i.e., identification) and with their personal values of fair and equal treatment for all service members (internalization).

Organizational Change

Any attempt to integrate openly gay and lesbian personnel into U.S. military life necessarily involves institutional change. Fortunately, the military has extensive experience with making structural changes to integrate new categories of personnel into its ranks, including women and members of racial, ethnic, and religious minorities (Evans, 2003; Kauth & Landis, 1996; Thomas & Thomas, 1996). In addition to revisiting the lessons learned from those experiences, the military can make use of social science knowledge about organizational change and policy implementation. This research literature suggests several important steps for effective policy implementation.[3]

First, the effectiveness of the new policy will depend on whether the military applies a single standard of conduct to all personnel. Based on the experiences of other military forces that have integrated gay men and lesbians, a workable standard would emphasize that each individual is to be judged on the basis of her or his performance relevant to military goals (i.e., that everyone should be judged on her or his own merits); that all personnel must respect each other's privacy (e.g., that intimate situations such as sleeping quarters and the latrine are not sexual); that interpersonal harassment—whether verbal, sexual, or physical—will not be tolerated, regardless of the genders of people involved; and that no service member will be permitted to engage in conduct that undermines unit cohesion.

Second, whether or not organizational members comply with a mandated policy is affected by two factors: their own calculations concerning the likelihood that it will be strictly enforced and compliance failures detected, and the severity of sanctions for noncompliance (Zellman, 1996). Compliance is more likely to the extent that enforcement is perceived to be strict and that noncompliance carries high costs. Consequently, the most effective policies are formulated so that the implementation plan includes *pressure* (i.e., clear enforcement mechanisms and high sanctions for noncompliance) and *support* for effective implementation (i.e., adequate resources, allowances for input from lower levels of the organization into the implementation process, and rewards for effective implementation) so that individuals perceive that their own self-interest lies in supporting the new policy.

Third, leaders play a critical role in changing the perceptions of the junior ranking personnel who actually implement a policy so that the latter come to view it as consistent with their own self-interest and with the organizational culture (identification and internalization, in Kelman's terminology). Thus, a new policy's effectiveness will depend on statements of clear support from the highest levels of leadership. Integration will be successful if upper-level commanders send strong, consistent signals of their support for the new policy and their commitment to ensuring behavioral compliance with it (MacCoun, 1996; Zellman, 1996).

Fourth, the policy's success will depend on whether lower-level leaders are convinced that active monitoring and support for a new policy will be noticed and rewarded, and that breaches of policy by subordinates will be considered instances of leadership failure. Although some militaries that successfully lifted their gay bans do not provide any training on their new policies, it seems likely that a minimal amount of training would help leaders address and solve challenges related to implementation. Zellman (1996) argued that leadership training should be designed to create *fixers*—people who care about successful implementation, have the skills necessary to anticipate and identify implementation problems, and can make adjustments to improve the implementation process. To be effective fixers, leaders must be allowed enough discretion so they can act to correct implementation problems. At the same time, this discretion must be bounded by behavioral monitoring and strict enforcement of a code of professional conduct. Leaders must be provided with clear procedures for reporting problems, and they must be convinced that accurate information about implementation problems is valued (i.e., that compliance difficulties do not indicate a failure of leadership).

Fifth, as noted by Zellman (1996), policies are more easily implemented to the extent that they are simple; reflect a cause-and-effect relationship that organizational members agree is valid; and are narrow in scope, that is, they involve small changes and few people. In this light, indications that officers and enlisted personnel do not understand the DADT policy is problematic. Research with Naval officers, for example, indicated that many of them did not clearly understand then-current policy on sexual orientation and this misunderstanding may have affected their enforcement of it (Sarbin, 1996).

Finally, policies imposed from outside an organization (or from outside the local site of the organization, e.g., a post or base) often meet with resistance because they are perceived as incompatible with local organizational culture. Such policies can challenge the value placed on learning from local experience in the organization, threaten deeply held beliefs concerning local organizational autonomy, and even be perceived as endangering the organization's survival. Given the resistance to change inherent in large organizations—especially to a policy that is widely perceived as inconsistent with the organization's existing culture—a new policy will work best if personnel are persuaded that it will not be harmful to the organization or to themselves, and may even result in gains (Zellman, 1996).

Individual Change

Once the military as an organization is committed to changing its policy toward service by gay and lesbian personnel, it will be possible to consider the factors that affect individual change. Two types of change are relevant to the present discussion: (a) changes in heterosexuals' conduct toward gay men and lesbians, and (b) changes in their attitudes and beliefs about homosexuality, gay personnel, and relevant military policies.

Early military programs designed to eliminate racial conflicts were premised on the assumption that change could best be facilitated by changing whites' attitudes and beliefs about blacks and other minorities. Such programs included sensitivity training and educational sessions about, for example, black culture and history (Kauth & Landis, 1996; Thomas, 1988). Systematic evaluation of those programs, however, suggested that such attempted consciousness raising often met with resistance, resentment, and hostility from whites who were required to participate in it (Thomas, 1988). By the time a 1973 training manual was published, a clear distinction was being drawn between attitudes (i.e., prejudice) and behavior (i.e., discrimination), with policy implementation focusing on the latter (Department of the Army, 1973).

It is reasonable to conclude that a similar distinction between private beliefs and public conduct will facilitate implementation of a new sexual orientation policy. To make this distinction, however, the military will have to identify the specific types of behavior that officers and supervisors must learn in order to implement the policy. This will require distinguishing between behavior that simply expresses private beliefs and that which is discriminatory or harassing. It also will entail identification of the behavioral skills that heterosexuals need to learn in order to establish civil working relationships with gay personnel.

Whereas a new policy concerning homosexual personnel will ultimately focus on behavior, understanding the social psychological processes that shape heterosexuals' attitudes and beliefs will ultimately prove useful for implementing it. Attitudes influence behavior both directly (when individuals deliberate about their intentions to act and consciously use their attitudes to inform their conduct) and indirectly (when attitudes unconsciously shape how an individual perceives and defines a situation). Global attitudes often are not particularly useful for predicting a specific behavior because many other factors play a role in determining whether a behavior occurs, including characteristics of the immediate situation, social norms, the actor's ability to enact the behavior, and the actor's attitudes toward performing the behavior. However, those global attitudes are correlated with general patterns of behavior across a variety of settings, times, and forms (Ajzen, 1989; Ajzen & Fishbein, 1980; Fazio, 1990). Within this context, an understanding of heterosexuals' negative attitudes toward gay men and lesbians is important for understanding general patterns of behavior, even though such attitudes will not predict an individual heterosexual's specific behaviors in all situations.

Surveys of the civilian population indicate that hostility toward gay men and lesbians has declined in recent years (Herek, 2002; Yang, 1997). Comparable data from active duty personnel are generally lacking, making it difficult to identify attitude trends within the military. Some studies indicated strong opposition to lifting the ban among enlisted personnel in the early 1990s (Miller, 1994) and among military elites in 1999 (Miller & Williams, 2001). In another study, however, 64 percent of Naval officers disagreed with the statement that they "feel uncomfortable in the presence of homosexuals and have difficulty interacting normally with them" (Bicknell, 2000, p. 170). Bicknell (2000) also found that 71 percent of Naval officers and 74 percent of sailors agreed with the statement "Compared with my peers, I consider myself more tolerant on the issue of homosexuals in the military" (p. 173). Comparisons across these studies are difficult because they were conducted with convenience samples and used different methodologies and survey questions.

A more recent study with a national probability sample indicates that sentiments within the military are not uniformly antigay. In a 2004 telephone survey, 50 percent of junior enlisted personnel in a sample of 371 active military personnel (including members of the National Guard and Reserves) believed that gays and lesbians should be allowed to serve openly; for the total sample, the figure was 34 percent (Annenberg Public Policy Center, 2004). Taken together, these findings indicate that attitudes toward current policy vary within the armed forces and suggest that the personal attitudes of individual service members may constitute a less significant obstacle to change than has been widely assumed. Reflecting these patterns, (Ret.) General Wesley Clark stated on NBC's *Meet the Press* that the "temperature of the issue" has cooled over the past decade, and that service members "were much more irate about this issue in the early '90s than I found in the late '90s" (Fischer, 2003).

In addition to describing the prevalence of positive and negative attitudes, empirical research on heterosexuals' attitudes toward homosexuality in the civilian sector has consistently yielded correlations between those attitudes and other variables that are relevant to the present discussion. For example, heterosexual males generally express greater hostility toward homosexuality than heterosexual females, especially toward gay men (Herek, 2002; Kite & Whitley, 1998). Negative attitudes toward homosexuality and gay rights are also correlated with traditional attitudes toward gender roles, political conservatism, strong religiosity, and psychological authoritarianism (e.g., Herek, 2000; Kite & Whitley, 1998; Whitley, 1999; Yang, 1997). To the extent that these and related characteristics are widespread among military personnel (Stiehm, 1992; Thomas & Thomas, 1996; Zellman, 1996), the persistence of some degree of negative attitudes toward homosexuality among military personnel is not unexpected.

As noted above, initial cooperation with a new nondiscriminatory policy is likely to reflect mere compliance in many cases. Over time, however, it is reasonable to expect that personnel will conform to the policy not only because they fear the negative consequences of noncompliance but also because they feel that nondiscriminatory behavior is consistent with their identity as a member of the armed forces and because they have internalized the institutional values on which the policy is based.

In addition, it seems likely that a policy change will result in changes in the attitudes some heterosexual personnel hold toward gay and lesbian service members. What is the basis for this expectation?

First, eliciting behavioral change through the organizational mechanisms described above may in itself lead to some degree of attitude change. This is especially likely after heterosexual personnel interact in a positive manner with gay and lesbian peers in the absence of overt threats of punishment. Two well-known social psychological theories predict that attitude change will occur under these circumstances. Cognitive dissonance theory predicts that inconsistency between heterosexuals' positive behaviors toward gay people and their negative attitudes will produce an unpleasant psychological state and they may resolve this dissonance by changing their attitudes. Self-perception theory predicts that heterosexuals will infer from their own nonprejudiced behavior that they actually do not harbor significant private prejudices against gay people. In both cases, the likely outcome is attitude change (for a review, see Eagly & Chaiken, 1993).

Second, a nondiscriminatory policy will create opportunities for some heterosexual personnel to interact with openly gay men and women. Provided that they meet certain conditions, such interactions are likely to have considerable impact on heterosexuals' attitudes toward gay personnel. They are most likely to foster more positive attitudes if they occur over an extended time period in a supportive environment where common goals are emphasized, where prejudice is negatively sanctioned, and where heterosexual personnel come to regard gay men and lesbians as individuals rather than as mere members of a disliked social category (Allport, 1954; Brewer & Miller, 1984; Pettigrew & Tropp, 2000).

This prediction is based on a large body of social psychological research on the *contact hypothesis* which, as originally described by Allport (1954), asserts that many forms of prejudice are reduced by equal status contact between majority and minority groups in the pursuit of common goals. Consistent with the contact hypothesis, heterosexuals with openly gay friends or acquaintances have been found to be more likely than others to hold accepting attitudes toward gay people in general (Herek & Capitanio, 1995, 1996; Herek & Glunt, 1993; Schneider & Lewis, 1984). This pattern may result partly from a preference among gay people for disclosing their sexual orientation to others perceived as likely to be already supportive (Herek & Capitanio, 1996; Herek & Glunt, 1993; Wells & Kline, 1987) but knowing an openly gay person is predictive of supportive attitudes even in demographic groups where hostility is the norm, e.g., among the highly religious and those with low levels of formal education (Schneider & Lewis, 1984). Thus, negative attitudes toward gay men and lesbians are likely to be reduced to the extent that working relationships develop between heterosexual and gay personnel, especially when heterosexual and homosexual personnel must work toward common goals and when discriminatory behaviors and overt expressions of prejudice are negatively sanctioned.

These relationships are likely to change heterosexuals' attitudes to the extent that they cause the latter to individuate and personalize gay people, that is, to perceive homosexuals as flesh-and-blood individuals rather than as members of an undifferentiated mass (Brewer & Miller, 1984). Individuation and personalization are more likely to occur when heterosexuals have opportunities to speak with a gay person and directly discuss the latter's experiences. If such interactions are not perceived by the heterosexual person as extremely threatening, they are likely to refute myths and stereotypes, change perceptions of social norms, and challenge the psychological functions served by negative attitudes.

Attitudes are more likely to change if heterosexual personnel have this sort of experience with more than one gay person. Surveys of the civilian population indicate that heterosexuals who know two or more gay people tend to have considerably more favorable attitudes toward gay people as a group than do those who know only one gay individual (Herek & Capitanio, 1996). This pattern may occur because knowing several members of a stigmatized group is more likely to foster recognition of that group's variability than is knowing only one group member (Wilder, 1978). Knowing multiple members of a group may also reduce the likelihood that their behavior can be discounted as atypical (Rothbart & John, 1985). Nevertheless, the potential impact of contact should not be overstated. As noted above, even under a new policy many gay and lesbian personnel will refrain from publicly disclosing their sexual orientation, which will mean that relatively few heterosexual service members will interact with even one openly gay person in their own unit (MacCoun, 1996).

Directions for Future Research

In its past efforts at implementing new personnel policies designed to eliminate discrimination against stigmatized minority groups, the military has relied heavily on social and behavioral science research for guidance and evaluation (e.g., Thomas, 1988). The military should follow a similar pattern for monitoring and evaluating a new policy concerning sexual orientation. It should be recognized, however, that the current policy has never been subjected to systematic evaluation. In suggesting directions for future research within the military, therefore, we caution against making policy change contingent on the results of such research. Indeed, signaling that the tenure of a new policy banning antigay discrimination will be based on the results of evaluation research could have the unintended effect of creating incentives for behavior that would sabotage the new policy. Instead, research should have the goals of monitoring compliance with a new policy, identifying problems with implementation and, when necessary, formulating solutions for those problems.

One level of research should focus on social psychological variables relevant to successful policy implementation. At this level, two types of information will be particularly useful. First, policy implementation will be facilitated by a clear understanding of heterosexual personnel's knowledge, beliefs, and attitudes related to homosexuality, gay people, and the new policy. Toward this end, descriptive survey research should be conducted on a regular basis to assess a variety of relevant variables, including the prevalence of various stereotypes, personnel's interpersonal contact experiences with gay men and lesbians, perceived social norms, and beliefs about the consequences of noncompliance with a new policy. Questions assessing these constructs could be integrated into questionnaires already administered to military personnel for other purposes. These data will enable the military leadership to monitor the effects of a new policy and to develop specific methods for improving its implementation. A related area for ongoing social psychological research is assessment of how well a new policy is understood by the officers who are responsible for implementing it. As noted above, one study indicated that many Naval officers did not clearly understand the DADT policy and this misunderstanding may have affected their enforcement of it (Sarbin, 1996). Ongoing research with military officers would be useful in identifying misinterpretations and misperceptions of current policy, and could offer guidelines for correcting those errors.

A second level of research should focus on organizational variables relevant to policy implementation. Examples of variables for monitoring at this level include the number of openly gay people serving, measures of unit performance (monitored in a way that permits comparisons between units with and without openly gay personnel, and within-unit comparisons before and after having openly gay personnel), and incidents of antigay harassment and violence. Data from these two levels of analysis could be usefully integrated. For example, the role of interpersonal contact could be assessed by examining correlations between unit performance and the extent to which personnel in that unit know a gay or lesbian peer.

Finally, comparative research on the experiences of different countries in integrating lesbian and gay personnel into their ranks will continue to be useful. No two militaries or national cultures are exactly the same and, consequently, the process of integration varies from one country to another. For example, some militaries, such as the Canadian Forces, are volunteer organizations that are not central to national identity whereas others, such as the Israel Defense Forces, are conscript militaries that play a more prominent role in the nation's consciousness (Belkin & Levitt, 2001; Belkin & McNichol, 2001). Understanding how different military organizations have implemented new policies within their respective cultural contexts will prove useful for understanding the roles played by cultural and organizational variables in implementing a new policy.

This brief discussion of research directions is based on an assumption that addressing any problems associated with implementing a new policy will require a focus on heterosexual personnel. This approach is consistent with the military's past efforts to integrate previously stigmatized minority groups into its ranks. When the military undertook to promote racial equality in the 1970s, for example, it located the core of the problem in the majority culture, as evidenced by the following passage from an Army race relations training manual:

> The root of the race problem is to be found, therefore, not in the victimized minorities where it so often is sought, but in the white-managed and controlled institutions which discriminate against them. This point is critical because it tells you what to work on if you are trying to eliminate racial discrimination. If white people and institutions managed by white people are responsible for the continued practice of racial discrimination, then it is they who must change if it is ever to stop. (Department of the Army, 1973, p. 10)

A comparable focus on heterosexuals will be necessary for implementing a new policy concerning sexual orientation. If a new policy treats gay personnel as no less capable than heterosexuals of successfully performing the duties required by military service, the problems associated with implementing it will stem primarily from the attitudes, reactions, and conduct of heterosexual personnel.

Conclusion

The military has adapted successfully to dramatic new policies in the past 50 years, including the integration of racial, ethnic, and religious minorities (Evans, 2003) as well as women. Social and behavioral research has played an important role in helping the military to meet those challenges. If faced with the prospect of implementing a new policy concerning sexual orientation, the military is likely to be able to meet that challenge as well. As in the past, empirical research will offer valuable guidance for confronting the challenge of change.

Notes

1. The authors express their deep appreciation to Geoffrey Bateman, Mark Eitelberg, Melissa S. Embser Herbert, Armando Estrada, Janice H. Laurence, and the editors of the *Handbook of Military Psychology*.
2. A brief *amicus curiae* submitted by historians to the United States Supreme Court in the case of *Lawrence v. Texas* (2003) provides an excellent history of sodomy laws in the United States. It is available on the Web at http://supreme.lp.findlaw.com/supreme_court/briefs/02-102/02-102.mer.ami.hist.pdf
3. The following discussion draws heavily from Zellman (1996).

References

Adam, B. D. (1995). *The rise of a gay and lesbian movement* (Rev. ed.). New York: Twayne Publishers.

Ajzen, I. (1989). Attitude structure and behavior. In A. R. Pratkanis, S. J. Breckler, & A. G. Greenwald (Eds.), *Attitude structure and function* (pp. 241–274). Hillsdale, NJ: Lawrence Erlbaum.

Ajzen, I., & Fishbein, M. (1980). *Understanding attitudes and predicting social behavior*. Englewood Cliffs, NJ: Prentice-Hall.

Allport, G. W. (1954). *The nature of prejudice*. Garden City, NY: Doubleday.

American Psychiatric Association. (1952). *Mental disorders: Diagnostic and statistical manual*. Washington, DC: Author.

Annenberg Public Policy Center. (2004). *Service members, families say Pentagon sent too few troops to Iraq, stressed National Guard and Reserves, should allow photos of coffins at Dover, Annenberg data show*. Washington, DC: Author. Retrieved October 22, 2004, from http://www.annenbergpublicpolicycenter.org/naes/2004_03_2military-data_10-16_pr.pdf

Barnett, J. E., & Jeffrey, T. B. (1996). Issues of confidentiality: Therapists, chaplains and health care providers. In G. M. Herek, J. B. Jobe, & R. Carney (Eds.), *Out in force: Sexual orientation and the military* (pp. 247–265). Chicago: University of Chicago Press.

Bartone, P. T., Johnsen, B. H., Eid, J., Brun, W., & Laberg, J. C. (2002). Factors influencing small-unit cohesion in Norwegian navy officer cadets. *Military Psychology, 14*, 1–22.

Bayer, R. (1987). *Homosexuality and American psychiatry: The politics of diagnosis* (Rev. ed.). Princeton, NJ: Princeton University Press.

Belkin, A. (2001). The Pentagon's gay ban is not based on military necessity. *Journal of Homosexuality, 41*(1), 103–130.

Belkin, A. (2003). Don't Ask, Don't Tell: Is the gay ban based on military necessity? *Parameters, 33*, 108–119.

Belkin, A. (in press). Would the elimination of Don't Ask, Don't Tell increase anti-gay violence? *Naval Institute Proceedings.*

Belkin, A. & Bateman, G. (2003). *Don't Ask, Don't Tell: Debating the gay ban in the military.* Boulder: Lynne Rienner Publishers.

Belkin, A., & Embser-Herbert, M. S. (2002). A modest proposal: Privacy as a rationale for excluding gays and lesbians from the U.S. military. *International Security, 27*, 178–187.

Belkin, A., & Levitt, M. (2001). Homosexuality and the Israeli Defense Forces: Did lifting the gay ban undermine military performance? *Armed Forces & Society, 27*, 541–566.

Belkin, A., & McNichol, J. (2001). Homosexual personnel policy of the Canadian forces: Did lifting the gay ban undermine military performance? *International Journal, 56*, 73–88.

Bérubé, A. (1990). *Coming out under fire: The history of gay men and women in World War Two.* New York: The Free Press.

Bianco, D. A. (1996). Echoes of prejudice: The debates over race and sexuality in the Armed Forces. In C.A. Rimmerman (Ed.), *Gay rights, military wrongs: Political perspectives on lesbians and gays in the military* (pp. 47–70). New York: Garland.

Bicknell, J. W. (2000). *Study of naval officers' attitudes toward homosexuals in the military.* Monterey, CA: U.S. Naval Postgraduate School.

Brewer, M. B., & Miller, N. (1984). Beyond the contact hypothesis: Theoretical perspectives on desegregation. In N. Miller & M. B. Brewer (Eds.), *Groups in contact: The psychology of desegregation* (pp. 281–302). Orlando, FL: Academic Press.

Burg, B. R. (2002). *Gay warriors: A documentary history from the ancient world to the present.* New York: New York University Press.

Carlson, D. K. (2003, December 23). Public ok with gays, women in military. *Gallup Poll News Service.* Retrieved April 12, 2005, from http://www.gallup.com

Chauncey, G., Jr. (1989). Christian brotherhood or sexual perversion? Homosexual identities and the construction of sexual boundaries in the World War I era. In M. B. Duberman, M. Vicinus, & G. Chauncey, Jr. (Eds.), *Hidden from history: Reclaiming the gay and lesbian past* (pp. 294–317). New York: New American Library.

Clinton, B., & Gore, A. (1992). *Putting people first: How we can all change America.* New York: Times Books.

Conger, J. J. (1975). Proceedings of the American Psychological Association, Incorporated, for the year 1974: Minutes of the annual meeting of the Council of Representatives. *American Psychologist, 30*, 620, 632–633.

D'Emilio, J. (1983). *Sexual politics, sexual communities: The making of a homosexual minority in the United States 1940–1970.* Chicago: University of Chicago Press.

Department of Defense Directive 1332.14 (1982, January 28). Part 1, Section H.

Department of the Army (1973). *Improving race relations in the Army: Handbook for leaders [Pamphlet 600-16].* Washington, DC: Author.

Dynes, W. (1985). *Homolexis: A historical and cultural lexicon of homosexuality.* New York: Gay Academic Union.

Eagly, A. H., & Chaiken, S. (1993). *The psychology of attitudes.* Ft. Worth, TX: Harcourt Brace Jovanovich.

Ellis, H. (1901). *Sexual inversion.* Philadelphia, PA: F. A. Davis.

Evans, R. L. (2002). U.S. military policies concerning homosexuals: Development, implementation and outcomes. *Law and Sexuality, 11*, 113–191.

Evans, R. L. (2003). *A history of the service of ethnic minorities in the U.S. Armed Forces.* Santa Barbara, CA: Center for the Study of Sexual Minorities in the Military.

Fazio, R. H. (1990). Multiple processes by which attitudes guide behavior. In M.P. Zanna (Ed.), *Advances in experimental social psychology* (Vol. 23, pp. 75–109). New York: Academic Press.

Files, J. (2003, December 10). Gay ex-officers say 'Don't Ask' doesn't work. *New York Times,* p. A18.

Fischer, B. (Executive Producer). (2003, June 15). *Meet the Press* [Television broadcast]. New York: National Broadcasting Corporation.

Ford, C. S., & Beach, F. A. (1951). *Patterns of sexual behavior.* New York: Harper & Bros.

Frank, N. (2000). What's love got to do with it? The real story of military sociology and "Don't Ask, Don't Tell." *Lingua Franca, 10*(7), 71–81.

Freud, S. (1951). A letter from Freud. *American Journal of Psychiatry, 107*, 786–787.

Freud, S. (1953). Three essays on the theory of sexuality. In J. Strachey (Ed. and Trans.), *The standard edition of the complete psychological works of Sigmund Freud* (Vol. 7, pp. 123–243). London: Hogarth Press. (Original work published in 1905).

Gade, P. A., Segal, D. R., & Johnson, E. M. (1996). The experience of foreign militaries. In G. M. Herek, J. B. Jobe, & R. Carney (Eds.), *Out in force: Sexual orientation and the military* (pp. 106–130). Chicago: University of Chicago Press.

General Accounting Office. (1992a). *Defense force management: DOD's policy on homosexuality.* (Document GAO/NSIAD-92-98). Washington, DC: Author.

General Accounting Office. (1992b). *Defense force management: Statistics related to DOD's policy on homosexuality.* (Document GAO/NSIAD-92-98S). Washington, DC: Author.

Goffman, E. (1963). *Behavior in public places: Notes on the social organization of gatherings.* New York: Free Press.

Guzzo, R. A., & Dickson, M. W. (1996). Teams in organizations: Recent research on performance and effectiveness. *Annual Review of Psychology, 47*, 307–338.

Haggerty, T. (2003). History repeating itself: A historical overview of gay men and lesbians in the military before "Don't Ask, Don't Tell." In A. Belkin & G. Bateman (Eds.), *Don't Ask, Don't Tell: Debating the gay ban in the military* (pp. 9–42). Boulder, CO: Lynne Rienner Publishers.

Henderson, W. D. (1985). *Cohesion: The human element.* Washington, D.C.: National Defense University Press.

Herbert, M. S. (1998). *Camouflage isn't only for combat: Gender, sexuality, and women in the military.* New York: New York University Press.

Heredia, C. (2002, November 15). Army discharges 6 gay foreign language students; Monterey institute follows Pentagon policy despite shortage of speakers of Arabic. *San Francisco Chronicle,* p. A2.

Herek, G. M. (1993). Sexual orientation and military service: A social science perspective. *American Psychologist, 48*, 538–549.

Herek, G. M. (1996). Why tell if you're not asked? Self-disclosure, intergroup contact, and heterosexuals' attitudes toward lesbians and gay men. In G. M. Herek, J. Jobe, & R. Carney (Eds.), *Out in force: Sexual orientation and the military* (pp. 197–225). Chicago: University of Chicago Press.

Herek, G. M. (2000). The psychology of sexual prejudice. *Current Directions in Psychological Science, 9*, 19–22.

Herek, G. M. (2002). Gender gaps in public opinion about lesbians and gay men. *Public Opinion Quarterly, 66*, 40–66.

Herek, G. M., & Capitanio, J. P. (1995). Black heterosexuals' attitudes toward lesbians and gay men in the United States. *Journal of Sex Research, 32*, 95–105.

Herek, G. M., & Capitanio, J. P. (1996). "Some of my best friends": Intergroup contact, concealable stigma, and heterosexuals' attitudes toward gay men and lesbians. *Personality and Social Psychology Bulletin, 22*, 412–424.

Herek, G. M., & Glunt, E. K. (1993). Interpersonal contact and heterosexuals' attitudes toward gay men: Results from a national survey. *Journal of Sex Research, 30*, 239–244.

Hippler, M. (1989). *Matlovich, the good soldier.* Boston: Alyson.

House Budget Committee Hearing. (1991, July 31). *Reuters transcript report,* Reuters News Service.

House Budget Committee Hearing. (1992, February 5). *Reuters transcript report,* Reuters News Service.

Jacobson, P. D. (1996). Sexual orientation and the military: Some legal considerations. In G. M. Herek, J. B. Jobe, & R. Carney (Eds.), *Out in force: Sexual orientation and the military* (pp. 39–61). Chicago: University of Chicago Press.

Janis, I. L. (1972). *Victims of groupthink: A psychological study of foreign-policy decisions and fiascoes.* Boston: Houghton Mifflin.

Kaplan, D. (2003). *Brothers and others in arms: The making of love and war in Israeli combat units.* New York: Harrington Park Press.

Katz, J. N. (1976). *Gay American history: Lesbians and gay men in the USA..* New York: Thomas Y. Crowell Company.

Kauth, M. R., & Landis, D. (1996). Applying lessons learned from minority integration in the military. In G. M. Herek, J. B. Jobe, & R. Carney (Eds.), *Out in force: Sexual orientation and the military* (pp. 86–105). Chicago: University of Chicago Press.

Kelman, H. C. (1961). Processes of opinion change. *Public Opinion Quarterly, 25*, 57–78.

Kendall, T. (1993). Shower/closet. *Assemblage, 20*, 80–81.

Kier, E. (1998). Homosexuals in the U.S. military: Open integration and combat effectiveness. *International Security, 23*(2), 5–39.

Kinsey, A. C., Pomeroy, W. B., & Martin, C. E. (1948). *Sexual behavior in the human male.* Philadelphia, PA: W. B. Saunders.

Kinsey, A. C., Pomeroy, W. B., Martin, C. E., & Gebhard, P. H. (1953). *Sexual behavior in the human female.* Philadelphia: W. B. Saunders.

Kite, M. E., & Whitley, B. E., Jr. (1998). Do heterosexual women and men differ in their attitudes toward homosexuality? A conceptual and methodological analysis. In G. M. Herek (Ed.), *Stigma and sexual orientation: Understanding prejudice against lesbians, gay men, and bisexuals* (pp. 39–61). Thousand Oaks, CA: Sage.

Krafft-Ebing, R. V. (1900). *Psychopathia sexualis, with especial reference to contrary sexual instinct: A medico-legal study.* Chicago: W. T. Keener.

Lawrence v. Texas, 539 US 558 (2003).

Lehring, G. L. (2003). *Officially gay: The political construction of sexuality by the U.S. military.* Philadelphia: Temple University Press.

Loeser, L. H. (1945). The sexual psychopath in the military service: A study of 270 cases. *American Journal of Psychiatry, 102,* 92–101.

Lott, A. J. & Lott, B. E. (1965). Group cohesiveness as interpersonal attraction: A review of relationships with antecedent and consequent variables. *Psychological Bulletin, 64,* 259–309.

MacCoun, R. J. (1996). Sexual orientation and military cohesion: A critical review of the evidence. In G. M. Herek, J. B. Jobe, & R. Carney (Eds.), *Out in force: Sexual orientation and the military* (pp. 157–176). Chicago: University of Chicago Press.

Menninger, W. C. (1948). *Psychiatry in a troubled world.* New York: Macmillan.

Meyer, L. D. (1996). *Creating GI Jane: Sexuality and power in the Women's Army Corps during World War II.* New York: Columbia University Press.

Miller, L. L. (1994). Fighting for a just cause: Soldiers' views on gays in the military. In W. J. Scott & S. C. Stanley (Eds.), *Gays and lesbians in the military: Issues, concerns, and contrasts* (pp. 69–85). New York: Aldine de Gruyter.

Miller, L. L., & Williams, J. A. (2001). Do military policies on gender and sexuality undermine combat effectiveness? In P. D. Feaver & R. H. Kohn (Eds.), *Soldiers and civilians: The civil-military gap and American national security* (pp. 361–402). Cambridge: MIT Press.

Millstein, S. G., Adler, N. E., & Irwin, C. E. (1984). Sources of anxiety about pelvic examinations among adolescent females. *Journal of Adolescent Health Care, 5,* 105–111.

Minton, H. L. (2002). *Departing from deviance: A history of homosexual rights and emancipatory science in America.* Chicago: University of Chicago Press.

Moskos, C. (1994). From citizens' army to social laboratory. In W. J. Scott & S. C. Stanley (Eds.), *Gays and lesbians in the military: Issues, concerns, and contrasts* (pp. 53–65). New York: Aldine de Gruyter.

Mullen, B., & Copper, C. (1994). The relation between group cohesiveness and performance: An integration. *Psychological Bulletin, 115,* 210–227.

Murphy, L. R. (1988). *Perverts by official order: The campaign against homosexuals by the United States Navy.* New York: Haworth.

Osburn, C. D. (1995). A policy in desperate search of a rationale: The military's policy on lesbians, gays, and bisexuals. *University of Missouri-Kansas City Law Review, 64,* 203–213.

Pettigrew, T. F., & Tropp, L. R. (2000). Does intergroup contact reduce prejudice: Recent meta-analytic findings. In S. Oskamp (Ed.), *Reducing prejudice and discrimination* (pp. 93–114). Mahwah, NJ: Lawrence Erlbaum.

Rado, S. (1940). A critical examination of the concept of bisexuality. *Psychosomatic Medicine, 2,* 459–467.

Rado, S. (1949). An adaptational view of sexual behavior. In P. H. Hoch & J. Zubin (Eds.), *Psychosexual development in health and disease* (pp. 159–189). New York: Grune & Statton.

Ray, R. D. (1993). Military necessity and homosexuality. In R. D. Ray (Ed.), *Gays: In or out? The U.S. military and homosexuals: A sourcebook* (pp. 1–136). New York: Brassey's.

Rothbart, M., & John, O. P. (1985). Social categorization and behavioral episodes: A cognitive analysis of the effects of intergroup contact. *Journal of Social Issues, 41*(3), 81–104.

Sarbin, T. R. (1996). The deconstruction of stereotypes: Homosexuals and military policy. In G. M. Herek, J. B. Jobe, & R. Carney (Eds.), *Out in force: Sexual orientation and the military* (pp. 177–196). Chicago: University of Chicago Press.

Schneider, D., & Schneider, C. J. (1992). *Sound off! American military women speak out.* New York: Paragon House.

Schneider, W., & Lewis, I. A. (1984). The straight story on homosexuality and gay rights. *Public Opinion, 16–20,* 59–60.

Segal, D. R., & Kestnbaum, M. (2002). Professional closure in the military labor market: A critique of pure cohesion. In D. M. Snider & G. L. Watkins (Eds.), *The future of the army profession* (pp. 441–458). Boston: McGraw-Hill.

Shawver, L. (1987). On the question of having women guards in male prisons. *Corrective and Social Psychiatry, 33*(1), 154–159.

Shawver, L. (1995). *And the flag was still there: Straight people, gay people and sexuality in the U.S. military.* New York: Harrington Park Press.

Shawver, L., & Kurdys, D. (1987). Shall we employ women guards in male prisons? *Journal of Psychiatry Law, 15,* 277–295.

Siebold, G. L. (2000). The evolution of the measurement of cohesion. *Military Psychology, 11,* 5–26.

Siebold, G. L., & Lindsay, T. J. (2000). The relation between demographic descriptors and soldier-perceived cohesion and motivation. *Military Psychology, 11,* 109–128.

Stiehm, J. H. (1992). Managing the military's homosexual exclusion policy: Text and subtext. *University of Miami Law Review, 46,* 685–710.

Thomas, J. A. (Ed.). (1988). *Race relations research in the U.S. Army in the 1970s: A collection of selected readings.* Alexandria, VA: U.S. Army Research Institute for the Behavioral and Social Sciences.

Thomas, P. J., & Thomas, M. D. (1996). Integration of women in the military: Parallels to the progress of homosexuals? In G. M. Herek, J. B. Jobe, & R. Carney (Eds.), *Out in force: Sexual orientation and the military* (pp. 65–85). Chicago: University of Chicago Press.

U.S. Code 654. (1993). Pub. L. 103 – 160 571, 107 Stat., 1547. Washington, D.C.: Government Printing Office.

Vivona, C. M., & Gomillion, M. (1972). Situational morality of bathroom nudity. *Journal of Sex Research, 8,* 128–135.

Wells, J. W., & Kline, W. B. (1987). Self-disclosure of homosexual orientation. *Journal of Social Psychology, 127,* 191–197.

Wells-Petry, M. (1993). *Exclusion: Homosexuals and the right to serve.* Washington, DC: Regnery Gateway.

Whitley, B. E., Jr. (1999). Right-wing authoritarianism, social dominance orientation, and prejudice. *Journal of Personality and Social Psychology, 77,* 126–134.

Wilder, D. A. (1978). Reduction of intergroup discrimination through individuation of the out-group. *Journal of Personality and Social Psychology, 36,* 1361–1374.

Williams, C. J., & Weinberg, M. S. (1971). *Homosexuals and the military: A study of less than honorable discharge.* New York: Harper and Row.

Wong, L., Kolditz, T. A., Millen, R. A., & Potter, T. M. (2003). *Why they fight: Combat motivation in the Iraq war.* Carlisle, PA: Strategic Studies Institute, U.S. Army War College. Retrieved September 1, 2004, from http://www.carlisle.army.mil/ssi/pdffiles/ 00172.pdf

Yang, A. S. (1997). Trends: Attitudes toward homosexuality. *Public Opinion Quarterly, 61,* 477–507.

Zellman, G. L. (1996). Implementing policy changes in large organizations: The case of gays and lesbians in the military. In G. M. Herek, J. B. Jobe, & R. Carney (Eds.), *Out in force: Sexual orientation and the military* (pp. 266–289). Chicago: University of Chicago Press.

PART IV

PERSPECTIVES ON THE MILITARY

CHAPTER 8

QUALITY OF LIFE AND SUBJECTIVE WELL-BEING AMONG MILITARY PERSONNEL: AN ORGANIZATIONAL RESPONSE TO THE CHALLENGES OF MILITARY LIFE

Michael J. Schwerin

Most folks are about as happy as they make up their minds to be.

–Abraham Lincoln

Quality of life (QOL) is an essential component of maintaining a high state of personnel and unit readiness in the U.S. Armed Forces. The U.S. Department of Defense (DoD) has the challenge of meeting the QOL needs of a large military force and its member families—over 1.4 million active duty service members, nearly 700,000 spouses, over 1.2 million children and minor dependents, as well as over 880,000 reserve component members and over 1 million family members of reservists (Office of the Under Secretary of Defense for Personnel & Readiness, 2004). Additionally, DoD and the services are attempting to keep pace with an ever-changing economy and meet the expectations of a new generation of employees while maintaining the military's focus on carrying out the U.S. national defense strategy.

Improving QOL for servicemembers has been a priority of the U.S. military leadership for years and is periodically reemphasized by service chiefs (e.g., the Chief of Naval Operations, Commandant of the U.S. Marine Corps, Chief of Staff of the U.S. Army, U.S. Air Force Chief of Staff) and the senior civilian leadership of the U.S. military, including the Commander in Chief. What varies in the message from these military leaders is a matter of emphasis and purpose—how will the services' approaches to QOL meet the needs of military personnel and their families and what do the services hope to gain from their investments in QOL?

While the strategies to facilitate QOL in the military vary, they all have one common objective—supporting the DoD's commitment to servicemembers and their families. In 2002, DoD established a "new social contract" that outlined the recipro-cal partnership between the DoD, service members, and their families. The nexus of this social contract is a covenant-like relationship among partners (Office of the Deputy Assistant Secretary of Defense, 2002), similar to a social exchange in which those people who commit to supporting their nation's defense (military, civilian, families, and retirees) can expect certain conditions to be met because of their serv-ice.[1] This commitment to supporting service members and their families was renewed in 2004 with a revised social contract in the First DoD Quadrennial QOL Review (Office of the Under Secretary of Defense for Personnel & Readiness, 2004). The revised social contract extends DoD's commitment to military personnel and their families by outlining a 20-year strategic plan for

> ensuring that the Department's performance goals for quality of life keep pace with the changing expectations of the American workforce and address the needs of the two-thirds of military families living off the installation as well as the Reserve Component. (Office of the Under Secretary of Defense for Personnel & Readiness, Appendix 3, p. i)

While the goal for DoD is to meet the QOL needs of military personnel and their families, "Ultimately, these are the factors that influence the Military Services' con-tinued readiness to fight and win the Nation's wars through recruiting, developing and retaining talented people" (Office of the Under Secretary of Defense for Person-nel & Readiness, Appendix 3, p. ii).

The objective of this chapter is to provide a brief overview of the relevant theories and perspectives that affect QOL initiatives and research in the military. First, I will begin with a discussion of those factors that comprise QOL and how these factors interact. I will present several definitions of QOL and distinguish QOL from other related concepts such as subjective well-being and psychological well-being. In the second section, I will describe several of the proposed mechanisms that de-scribe how QOL works—bottom-up models, top-down models, integrative models, and Multiple Discrepancy Theory (MDT). In the third section, I will describe some of the common objectives military organizations have in their focus on QOL (i.e., enhancing the lives and well-being of military personnel and their families and positively affecting military outcomes such as readiness and retention), and the research conducted in these areas. Finally, I'll conclude this chapter with a discus-sion of the implications of the various approaches the military takes in QOL, some of the limitations of the research conducted, and future directions for research in military QOL.

Definitions of QOL and Well-Being

QOL has been a topic of research for many years among military and civilian research organizations. Because QOL research has applications in a number of disci-plines (e.g., psychology, sociology, anthropology, medicine, and political science) it often seems as though there are as many definitions of QOL as there are researchers studying QOL.[2] QOL has been described by military organizations in a variety of ways. Drawing from recent QOL studies, QOL strategic planning documents, and Congressional testimony, each service's definition or approach to QOL can be compared (see Table 8.1). In addition to the U.S. military research on QOL, the Canadian National Defence has an active QOL research program supporting Canadian QOL initiatives. Beginning with the initiatives from the Standing Committee on National Defence and Veterans Affairs (1998), the Canadian National Defence first focused on addressing existing personnel and family support needs and then moved to more theory-based conceptualizations of QOL. Common to all of the definitions of QOL from military organizations is that QOL is a multidimensional concept that encompasses physical, psychological, and social well-being.

These definitions of QOL adopted by military organizations reflect a rich history of QOL research in nonmilitary settings. Gladis, Gosch, Dishuk, & Crits-Christoph (1999) described QOL as encompassing a wide array of constructs and measures that reflect some aspect of physical, social, or emotional functioning in order to quantify life satisfaction. The umbrella of QOL includes constructs such as life satisfaction, functioning, morbidity, social relationships, work performance, and adverse effects of (physical and psychological) treatments. Katschnig (1997) depicts QOL as "a loosely related body of work on psychological well-being, social and emotional functioning, health status, functional performance life satisfaction, social support and standard of living, whereby normative, objective, and subjective indicators of physical, social, and emotional functioning are all used" (p. 6). Evans and Cope (1989) portray QOL as a multidimensional construct where "certain actions or behaviors of an individual in response to particular environmental domains can be considered to represent a good quality of life" (p. 1). Like the definitions of QOL used by military organizations, conceptualizations and definitions of QOL in the civilian research literature focuses on the notion that QOL is multidimensional, it includes physical, social, and emotional well-being, and the assessment of QOL is based on the subjective experience of the individual.

One of the common notions among definitions of QOL is that well-being is a component of QOL. In the research literature there is a debate regarding which perspective of well-being is most meaningful. These perspectives are known as the *hedonic* and *eudaimonic* philosophies of well-being.

Hedonic Perspective of Well-Being

Kahneman et al. (1999) describe the hedonic view as those events that "make experiences and life pleasant and unpleasant" (p. ix). Well-being is a matter of how individuals perceive their life experiences and interactions rather than whether those life experiences are beneficial for their personal or professional growth.

Operationally, the study and subsequent measurement of the hedonic view of well-being is reflected by work in the area of subjective well-being. Diener, Suh, Lucas, and Smith (1999) define subjective well-being as "a broad category of phenomena that includes people's emotional responses, domain satisfactions, and global judgments of life satisfaction...we define [subjective well-being] as a general area of

Table 8.1
Conceptualizations of QOL in Military Organizations

Military Organization	QOL or Well-Being Position Statement
U.S. Air Force[1]	Core QOL priorities consist of adequate manpower, improved workplace environments, fair and competitive compensation and benefits, balanced amounts of time away from home or TEMPO, quality health care, safe and affordable housing, enriched community and family programs, enhanced education opportunities, manpower, and enhanced education opportunities.
U.S. Army[2]	Well-being is the personal—physical, material, mental, and spiritual—state of Soldiers [Active, Reserve, Guard, Retirees, Veterans], civilians, and their families that contributes to their preparedness to perform and support The Army's mission. From The Army's perspective, Well-Being is a "condition" resulting from a system of individual programs.
U.S. Navy[3]	A good QOL is a high level of physical and psychological well being, including a capacity for adaptation to life's changes and the social and economic resources necessary to sustain such a level.
U.S. Marine Corps[4]	The extent to which a person's physical and psychological needs are met and how this compares to expectations.
Canadian National Defence[5]	Quality of Life in the Canadian Forces (CF) is the degree to which the well-being, work environment and living conditions of our people and their families are consistent with evolving standards, while recognizing the unique demands of military service in accomplishing the mission of the CF.

1 Peterson, 2001, p. 17.
2 Keane, 2001, August 28, p. 4.
3 Naval Research Advisory Committee, 2001, p. 26.
4 Ditton, Bolmarcich, Moore, Webb, & Quinlan, 2003, pp. 1–2.
5 Directorate Quality of Life, 2005.

scientific interest rather than a single specific construct." (p. 277) Diener, Lucas, and Oishi (2002) further elaborate on subjective well-being by describing it as an amalgam of three distinct but related concepts: life satisfaction, positive affect, and the absence of negative affect.

There are a number of measures of subjective well-being including the *Subjective Happiness Scale* (Lyumbomirsky & Lepper, 1999), the *Well-Being Scale* (Tellegen, 1982), the *Life Characteristics Scale* (Campbell, Converse, & Rodgers, 1976), the *Life Domains Scale* (sometimes referred to as the *Life 3 Scale*; Andrews & Withey, 1976), and the *Satisfaction with Life Domains Scale* (Baker & Intagliata, 1982). Two of the most frequently used measures of subjective well-being (Lent, 2004) include Watson's work with the *Positive and Negative Affect Scale* (*PANAS*; Watson, Clark, & Tellegen, 1988) and the *Satisfaction With Life Scale* (*SWLS*; Diener, Emmons, Larsen, & Griffin, 1985).

The primary difference between the PANAS and the SWLS is how positive affect, negative affect, and overall well-being are measured. Watson et al. (1988) maintain the distinction between positive affect and negative affect, measuring these components of subjective well-being separately using independent subscales. In contrast, Diener and Emmons (1984) initially developed a measure that has independent positive affect and negative affect subscales but subsequent research moved toward a single measure of subjective well-being that encompassed positive affect, negative affect, and life satisfaction.

Eudaimonic Perspective of Well-Being

The eudaimonic view of well-being focuses more on the inner thoughts and intrinsic motivation and feelings of growth than a person's subjective feelings. For example, a person can have negative feelings about a work assignment yet personally and professionally grow from that experience. The emphasis in the eudaimonic view is on the challenges one experiences in life and how those challenges lead to a more productive life experience rather than simply feeling better.

The eudaimonic perspective is operationally defined by measures of psychological well-being. Research led by Ryff (1989, 1995; Ryff & Keyes, 1995; Ryff & Singer, 1998, 2000) describe psychological well-being "as the by-product of a life that is well-lived" (Ryff & Singer, 1998, p. 5). Psychological well-being was developed using a *construct-oriented* approach to measurement (Wiggins, 1973) with statements written from various theories of positive functioning. In all, these theories posit six dimensions: autonomy, personal growth, self-acceptance, purpose in life, environmental mastery, and positive relations with others. The psychological well-being measure has been shown to possess strong internal consistency reliability (alpha of between 0.86 and 0.93 for all six dimensions and six-week test-retest stability coefficient of between 0.81 and 0.85 for all six dimensions; Ryff, 1989). It has been routinely used as a global measure of subjective well-being in a wide range of settings and populations.

Analyses support the multidimensional structure, reliability, and validity of both psychological well-being and subjective well-being. Yet differences in the theoretical underpinning of the constructs remain: can well-being be characterized by living well (subjective well-being) or well living (psychological well-being)? Another difference is the measurement approach. While psychological well-being uses a classic personality test construction method where constructs are formed and there is a greater reliance on convergent and discriminant validity, measures of subjective well-being begin with a test construction approach but accommodate the notion of face validity. This distinction can lead to seemingly conflicting results between psychological well-being and subjective well-being scores (e.g., individuals score high on psychological well-being yet do not feel a sense of well-being as measured by subjective well-being scales). Yet another difference is the role individuals have in defining their own well-being. Psychological well-being scales use a constructionist approach where scores indicate well-being while subjective well-being scales rely on the individual to simply estimate overall well-being.

Ryan and Deci (2001) describe the difference between the hedonic and eudaimonic perspectives on well-being by saying that "well-being is probably best conceived as a multidimensional phenomenon that includes aspects of both the hedonic and eudaimonic conceptions of well-being" (p. 148). What is meaningful to those interested in measuring QOL and well-being among military personnel is an awareness that these philosophical distinctions are relevant in the measures, results, and conclusions that come from studies of QOL in the military as well as in the policies designed to enhance QOL for military personnel and families. While most studies of QOL and well-being focus on subjective well-being, the validity and usefulness of using one well-being measure over another (e.g., psychological well-being versus subjective well-being) among military personnel is an empirical question that has yet to be studied.

Proposed Models of the Action of QOL

Those conducting research in disciplines traditionally oriented to well-being and QOL examine causality predominantly with bottom-up, top-down, and integrative models. Understanding these models of action is important in determining whether personality, dispositional, or genetic factors affect perceptions of other facets of people's lives (top-down), whether situations, events, and the environment affects their perceptions of life as a whole (bottom-up), or whether there is an interplay of perceived experiences, one affecting the other (interactive or bi-directional).[3] With an idea of what factors affect global perceptions of QOL, military organizations can better identify philosophical approaches that drive policy. For example, should the military attempt to facilitate more positive perceptions of military life as a whole, implement initiatives to improve more positive perceptions of life domains, some combination of both, or some other approach?

Traditionally, studies of life domains and global ratings of life satisfaction use two primary models of action—bottom-up and top-down models (Diener, 1984).

Bottom-up models of action propose that individuals examine positive and negative areas of their lives (or life domains) or daily life events and then come to a summative, overarching perception about their overall perceived well-being (Brenner & Bartell, 1983; Bryant & Marquez, 1986; Campbell, Converse, & Rodgers, 1976; DeLongis, Folkman, & Lazarus, 1988; Haring, Okun, & Stock, 1984; Michalos & Zumbo, 1999; Okun, Olding, & Cohn, 1990; Stone, 1987; Weingarten & Bryant, 1987; Wood, Rhodes, & Whelan, 1989). For example, when individuals are asked how their life is overall, they consider their satisfaction with their job, family, friends, and financial status and base their global perceptions on how satisfied they are with each of these life domains—"I dislike military deployments, the pay is not worth being away from my family, I am not given the tools to do my job well…life is going pretty poorly now." The focus here is on external influences and how positive or negative those aspects of life are.

Top-down models of action propose that trait (i.e., personality) or dispositional factors affect global life perceptions and affect perceptions of subsequent life events (Costa & McCrae, 1984; Diener & Larsen, 1984; Headey & Wearing, 1989, 1991; Hotard, McFatter, McWhirter, & Stegall, 1989; Zika & Chamberlain, 1987). For example, if individuals are asked how their life is overall, they may respond that things are going well even though various aspects of their lives are not as positive as they would like—"I'm pretty satisfied with my life now even though I dislike military deployments, the pay is not worth being away from my family, and I need better equipment to do my job well—but things could be worse." Costa, McCrae, and Norris (1981) describe the top-down processing in the following way, "despite circumstances, some individuals seem to be happy people, some unhappy people" (p. 79).

More recently, studies comparing the power of different models to predict QOL examined top-down models, bottom-up models, and a combination of the two (termed integrative models). Generally, these studies find support for integrative models (Brief, Butcher, George, & Link, 1993; David, Green, Martin, & Suls, 1997; Feist, Bodner, Jacobs, Miles, & Tan, 1995; Hart, 1999; Heller, Watson, & Ilies, 2004). For example, in a meta-analytic study of personality, domain satisfactions, and life satisfaction, Heller, Watson, and Ilies tested all three models and found support for both top-down and integrative models. In a study of global personality dimensions and objective life circumstances, Brief, Butcher, George, and Link (1993) found that both domain-specific indicators (i.e., health indicators) and trait factors (i.e., negative affect) affect subjective well-being. Hart (1999) examined domain-specific indicators (work and non-work domain satisfaction) as well as trait factors (i.e., neuroticism and extraversion) in predicting subjective well-being among a sample of police officers. Findings supported the importance of state factors (i.e., non-work and work factors) and some trait factors in predicting subjective well-being as measured by life satisfaction.

Another model of action for QOL is the *Multiple Discrepancies Theory* or MDT framework (Michalos, 1985). MDT states that life satisfaction is a function of discrepancies between what relevant others have, previous experiences (what one had in the past), what one expects to have, what one feels they deserve, and what one believes they want and need. Unique to this model of action in QOL is the role of expectations and perceived inequities between what an individual believes they deserve and what they have acquired. MDT aspects are frequently incorporated in QOL research for a more complete assessment of motivational factors that affect perceptions of satisfaction (Cohen, 2000; Lance, Mallard, & Michalos, 1995; Schulz, 1995). While useful, MDT comparisons are sometimes difficult for military personnel since their pay, benefits, work stressors, and non-work stressors do not make for easy comparisons to the situations of friends and family working in the civilian employment sector.

QOL Research Objectives for Military Organizations

DoD and each of the services have the significant challenges of addressing the QOL needs of service members and families. Typically, DoD provides guidance as the services develop initiatives and support programs to reach out and serve military personnel and families. These QOL programs come at a significant cost. In fiscal year 2003, the budget for community support program funding was $3.8 billion (Office of the Deputy Assistant Secretary of Defense, 2002) and in order to meet the objectives in the QOL Quadrennial Defense Review (Office of the Under Secretary of Defense for Personnel & Readiness, 2004), the costs will be a great deal more.

In addition to the challenge of developing the QOL programs, the services are faced with acquiring the resources and funding to carry out the mission of these QOL programs. QOL program managers and resource sponsors compete with other defense priorities such as military hardware, defense systems, installations, and infrastructure. In order to compete for program funding, QOL program managers need to demonstrate (1) that the programs are effective in addressing the needs of military personnel and their families, and (2) that there is some return on investment that relates to outcomes of interest for the military—typically, recruiting, readiness, and retention.

Each of the services have similar objectives in studying life needs, demonstrating QOL program efficacy, and examining the relationship between QOL and outcomes such as readiness and retention. Although the services have common research objectives, there is no DoD-wide coordinated research initiative conceptualizing and measuring QOL, developing standard practices of program evaluation, and resourcing research to this end. One effect of the autonomy in conceptualizing QOL programs and research practices is that each of the services developed their own approaches to quantify QOL needs and the satisfaction with and impact of their QOL programs.

DoD (with research conducted by the Defense Manpower Data Center and the Military Family Research Institute) and each branch of the armed services conducted QOL research to evaluate progress in addressing their QOL objectives. The 2004 QOL Quadrennial Defense Review describes the QOL research conducted by the U.S. military (Office of the Under Secretary of Defense for Personnel & Readiness,

2004). Here, authors describe essentially four types of QOL-related studies conducted by the U.S. military—need assessments, program evaluations, customer satisfaction surveys, and life domains (QOL and subjective well-being) studies.

While each of the services claim to conduct comprehensive assessments of QOL, a closer examination of these studies reveals that some QOL studies are more accurately described as studies of QOL program satisfaction. For example, several services purport to measure QOL but results presented in the QOL Quadrennial Defense Review actually describe satisfaction with QOL programs rather than satisfaction with life domains apart from the program[4] (see Table 8.2). The remainder of this chapter will describe the leading approaches in the U.S. military in QOL program implementation and research examining the relationship between life needs and readiness and retention intent.

U.S. Air Force Community Needs Assessment Survey, Community Capacity Model, and Chief of Staff QOL Survey

Much of what the Air Force does in terms of QOL is guided by the Air Force Community Needs Assessment Survey and the Community Capacity Model. The Air Force Community Capacity Model was developed from civilian research designed to facilitate community-centered linkages among people, neighborhoods, and service agencies. First explored for use with the Air Force, Bowen, Martin, and Mancini (1999) and senior leaders in the Air Force conducted an assessment of community in nine Air Force base areas. Results and recommendations from this work led to the development of community building initiatives to build formal and informal networks to provide social support and a greater sense of well-being among Air Force personnel and their families.

The Air Force Needs Assessment Survey, first conducted in 1993 but significantly aligned with the Air Force Community Capacity Model in 2003, is administered every two years to a random sample of over 180,000 active duty and reserve Air Force personnel and their spouses. Measures on the need assessment survey include indicators of QOL program use and satisfaction as well as items that reflect subjective well-being (e.g., physical and emotional well-being). Survey results are distributed via an interactive analysis and reporting web portal where base-level working groups can access data, conduct queries of the data, and generate reports comparing their installation with other installations of a similar size. This needs assessment survey is a key source of information that is an example of how survey results inform community initiatives and action planning through a structured communication, implementation, and feedback network.

The infrastructure and engine of QOL in the Air Force rests in the QOL working groups—the Community Action Information Boards and the Integrated Delivery Systems. These Air Force, Major Command, and installation-level Community Action Information Boards facilitate community-centered linkages among Air Force personnel and their families, formal Air Force agencies (e.g., Major Commands, installation-level leaders, and family support centers), and informal Air Force groups

Table 8.2
Research Approach for Studying QOL in Military Organizations

Military Organization	QOL Research Approach															
	Needs Assessment				Program Evaluation				Program Satisfaction				Life Domains/QOL			
	AD	AS	RC	RS	AD	AS	RC	RS	AD	AS	RC	RS	AD	AS	RC	RS
Defense Manpower Data Center (DoD-wide)	✓	✓	✓	✓					✓	✓	✓	✓	✓		✓	
U.S. Air Force	✓								✓				✓			
U.S. Army	✓	✓							✓							
U.S. Navy	✓	✓			✓				✓	✓	✓		✓	✓		
U.S. Marine Corps	✓	✓			✓				✓	✓			✓			
Canadian National Defence	✓								✓				✓			

Note: AD = Survey of Active Duty Personnel; AS = Survey of Active Duty Spouses; RC = Survey of Reserve Component Personnel; RS = Survey of Reserve Component Spouses.

(e.g., neighborhood support groups, First Sergeants Council, etc.). A subcommittee of the Community Action Information Boards is the Integrated Delivery System—created at each level described above to examine needs assessment data, other sources of QOL, and personnel data, and to prioritize and to address Air Force community concerns (whether at the installation, Major Command, or Air Force level). Here, Air Force personnel, families, and leaders share the responsibility and benefits of community-building. For example, if data from community needs assessment identify a need for additional child-care outside of typical hours for the base child development center, members of the Integrated Delivery System might help in recruiting more providers for off-hour childcare needs.

Illustrated by Figure 8.1, community capacity is built by formal military organizations, formal community agencies, and informal community connections. As these three sources of support integrate, the members of those communities experience increased "shared responsibility and…collective competence" (p. 6) that "allows members and families to remain resilient in meeting mission requirements" and

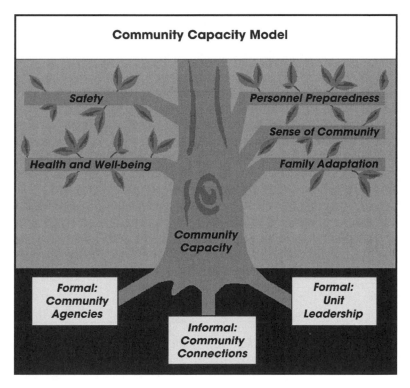

Figure 8.1
The U.S. Air Force Community Capacity Model

Source: Bowen, Orthner, Martin, & Mancini, 2001.

manage "their personal, family, and work responsibilities" (p. 10; Bowen, Martin, & Mancini, 1999).

Administered every two and a half years, the Air Force Chief of Staff QOL Survey (2002) is a measure of work life, non-work life, and program satisfaction. Work life areas of interest include manpower, personnel tempo (PERSTEMPO) and operational tempo (OPTEMPO), workplace environment, and aspects of the workplace setting (i.e., physical attributes of the work environment). Non-work life factors examined include general well-being, compensation and benefits, health care, housing, community and family programs, and education opportunities. Surveys are sent to a stratified random sample of active duty and civilian Air Force personnel via email-only surveys.

The objective of this survey is to track changes in work life, non-work life, QOL program satisfaction, and retention plans across time. Descriptive results and drill-down analyses examine results by categories including: officer and enlisted, officer grade (i.e., company grade or field grade), term of enlistment (i.e, first term, second term, or career), and job type (i.e., pilot, non-pilot, enlisted). Data from this study augments data from the Air Force Community Needs Assessment survey, serving as an indicator of quality of work life that is not captured on the Needs Assessment survey.

Retention analyses consist of descriptive analyses by group of retention intent. Further in-depth analyses explore the relationship between retention intent and aspects of Air Force life like QOL issues and TEMPO. While the Air Force QOL survey appears to be a good source of data for exploratory analyses on the relationship between work life, non-work life, QOL, and retention, there is no published research examining the relationship among these variables. The QOL/retention link is further clouded by data limitations on the Air Force QOL Survey. One item that examines QOL issues that affect retention lists only eight QOL factors for respondents to rank order: manpower, workplace environment, compensation/benefits, TEMPO, health care, housing, community and family support programs, and educational opportunities. Unfortunately this list of QOL issues is far from exhaustive and does not include many non-work or family factors.

U.S. Army and the Well-Being Campaign Plan

In 2001, the Army acknowledged a lack of strategic focus in the myriad of soldier and family support programs and sought to establish a framework that could guide QOL and well-being initiatives. The goal is to align QOL and well-being programs and support soldiers in order to enhance soldier readiness and retention. The scope of the Army Well-Being Campaign Plan (Keane, 2001, August 28) extends beyond QOL and incorporates aspects of psychological well-being, with one objective being to provide "opportunities for Soldiers, civilians, and their families to enhance their personal self-reliance and resilience as they pursue their unique individual aspirations" (p. 4). A model of the Army Well-Being Plan illustrates the concept that the Army well-being consists of both subjective well-being and

Figure 8.2
Army Well-Being Model

Source: Keane, 2001, January 5.

psychological well-being with individual well-being and mission preparedness as primary objectives (see Figure 8.2).

Research supporting the Army Well-Being Campaign Plan consists of metrics used to track progress toward several lines of well-being initiatives—command programs, pay and allowances, health care, housing, and workplace environment, education, family programs, and morale, welfare, and recreation. The Army Well-Being Campaign Plan framework is an aggressive plan to ensure that QOL program resource sponsors effectively fund, and command leaders effectively implement and support, well-being programs at the local level.

The Army focuses on studies of program satisfaction and satisfaction with well-being programs and perceived satisfaction with overall quality of Army life. The Sample Survey of Military Personnel tracks 58 items indicating soldier satisfaction with well-being programs and reasons for considering leaving military service. The Sample Survey of

Military Personnel is augmented with the Survey of Army Families, a survey that measures spouse satisfaction with Army well-being programs and overall quality of Army life. Research evaluating the effectiveness of well-being programs serves as a metric that identifies programs or components of programs that are either (1) not effective, (2) not meeting program standards, or (3) are operating above standards and thus providing services that are beyond what personnel want or need).

In a study of the relationship between Army and personal factors and readiness, Burnam, Meredith, Sherbourne, Valdez, & Vernez (1992) conducted a survey of soldiers and spouses (for those who were married) to test a conceptual framework derived from Vernez and Zellman (1987). This model conceptualized a model of action that could be interpreted as a bottom-up model of QOL where factors external to the Army (i.e., non-work factors such as individual characteristics, family structure, and spouse characteristics), factors internal to the Army (e.g., indicators of PERSTEMPO and working hours), and the relationship of soldier perceptions of these factors and well-being (measured by emotional well-being, depression, and marital satisfaction) all affect soldier well-being. Next, the Burnam et al. conceptual model hypothesized a relationship between well-being and Army outcomes—readiness and use of QOL programs (see Figure 8.3).

Analyses were conducted to examine various stages of the Vernez and Zellman (1987) conceptual model: family and Army environment/practice variables related to well-being, well-being variables related to readiness, and family and Army environment/practice variables related to QOL program use. Results indicated that there were significant relationships between well-being and readiness. These findings support (1) an interrelated (but not fully integrated) model of work and non-work factors affecting QOL, (2) the relationship between QOL and readiness, and (3) preliminary exploration of a bottom-up model of QOL.

Other research studies that precede the Army Well-being Campaign Plan examined soldier retention, aspects of work and non-work domains, and organizational influences on retention such as the effects of job satisfaction (Woefel & Savell, 1978), organizational commitment (Gade, Tiggle, & Schumm, 2003), deployment (Rosen & Durand, 1995; Schumm & Bell, 2000; Segal, Rohall, Jones, & Manos, 1999) and PERSTEMPO (Alderks, 1998; Bell, Schumm, & Martin, 2001; Sticha et al., 1999). While aspects of work and non-work domains were included in each of these studies, non-work domains were operationalized in a variety of ways (i.e., work–family conflict, marital/family conflict, family adjustment, and family well-being). For example, Sticha et al. used data from the Sample Survey of Military Personnel and conceptualized QOL as consisting of family factors (i.e., satisfaction with time away from family, satisfaction with services and family programs, spouse support of Army career), financial factors (i.e., satisfaction with pay, confidence that the Army will protect benefits/retirement), and general satisfaction (i.e., satisfaction with overall quality of life, unit/self morale, satisfaction with leadership, and satisfaction with work tasking). Segal et al. operationalized family factors as family adjustment to the deployment and concern for family well-being (e.g., concern for family's psychological and physical well-being).

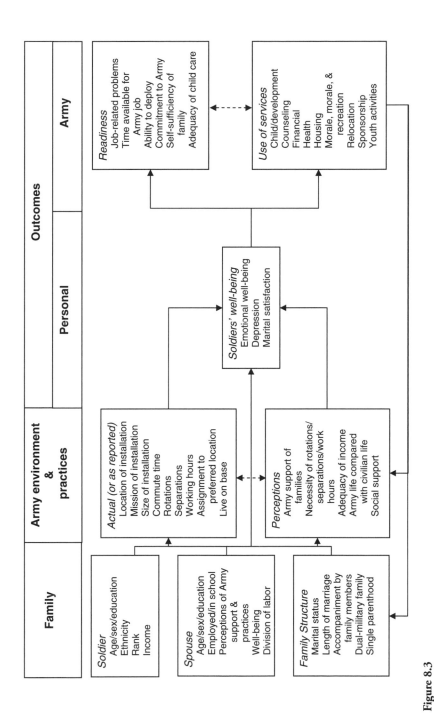

Figure 8.3
Conceptual Framework for Analysis of Soldiers' Army Outcomes

While the objective of each study cited in the examples above is not to measure QOL, the variability in how QOL/family well-being factors were operationalized is quite different and potentially problematic. Differences in the psychological processes implicit in the family well-being construct (i.e., work/family conflict, satisfaction with needs being met, concern for family well-being, and family adjustment) limit our ability to generalize results across studies within the Army and among the services. Differences in how non-work factors are operationalized and measured is a recurring issue in many military personnel surveys and warrants further research.

U.S. Marine Corps QOL Survey

Since the early 1990s, the Marine Corps QOL research program had two areas of focus—QOL needs/life domains and QOL programs. QOL program studies included customer satisfaction surveys, need assessments, and program evaluations. In their approach to evaluating USMC QOL programs, researchers used a cluster evaluation approach where one asks program users about program-specific outcomes and higher-order outcomes that cross a series of programs. The USMC QOL program evaluation study asked users of nearly 20 QOL programs to rate program satisfaction (e.g., how satisfied were you with the hours, customer service, services provided, etc.) as well as program impact on several higher-order outcomes—program "reasons for being" such as contribution to satisfaction with life in the USMC (Kerce, 1998; Kerce, Sheposh, & Knapp, 1999). Results provided data that indicated that program users were very satisfied with QOL programs and that programs were meeting their objectives in terms of addressing QOL needs.

Kerce (1995) was the first to study QOL and subjective well-being with the goal of developing a life domain model of QOL among U.S. Marine Corps personnel. The USMC QOL life domain studies focused on rating satisfaction with areas of one's life and examining the relationship between those life needs and organizational outcomes, such as personnel readiness, retention, and job performance (Kerce, 1995). It was thought that by identifying life domains with low perceived satisfaction that policy could be affected to increase service member satisfaction in those life need areas. The measurement method used a domain-based approach (Andrews & Withey, 1976; Campbell et al., 1976; Cantril, 1965; Flanigan, 1978) to evaluate QOL among active duty service members. In Kerce's study of Marine Corps QOL, 11 life domains were identified through interviews with Marine Corps personnel and a review of the civilian literature. Life domain satisfaction was captured by items measuring overall domain satisfaction (e.g., overall satisfaction with housing) and satisfaction with aspects of each domain (e.g., satisfaction with aspects of one's housing—attractiveness, amount of space, location, cost, etc.). Kerce (1995) recognized the need to collect objective and subjective QOL data (Buddin, 1998; Cheng, 1988; Diener & Diener, 1995; Rootman, 1996; Sirgy et al., 1995) in order to cover a broad range of influences on organizational outcomes. While Kerce (1995) tested various models using objective and subjective indicators of QOL, analyses indicated that models using only subjective indicators of QOL facilitated adequate model fit.

The Kerce (1995) model proved to be a significant contribution to the military QOL literature—this was the first model that sought to link life needs to organizational outcomes. Kerce's conceptual model proposes a bottom-up model of action where life domains were related to overall QOL, which in turn was related to several organizational outcomes. Other components viewed as theoretically relevant to QOL in the military were included in this conceptual model such as trait factors (optimism), components from a MDT perspective (i.e., comparisons between civilian life and military life), and person–job fit. These additional factors (i.e., trait factors, MDT items, and person–job fit) are typical of a top-down approach but the emphasis of Kerce's conceptual model is bottom-up (see Figure 8.4). Structural Equation Modeling (SEM) analyses were planned to identify life domains with significant relationships to global QOL and provide decision support to Marine Corps policy makers regarding life needs that were key drivers of QOL and military outcomes such as readiness, job performance, and retention intent.

Because life domains vary in their relevance for different groups of marines as a function of marital and family status (e.g., marines without children could not rate their satisfaction with their relationship with their children), SEM analyses were conducted separately for married marines with children, married marines without children, and single marines without children. Analyses provided support for Kerce's conceptual model with life domains related to global QOL that was subsequently related to military outcomes. Figure 8.5 illustrates results for enlisted marines without children. Here life domains of Self (personal development), Job (job satisfaction), and Residence were related to Global QOL and QOL was subsequently related to readiness and retention intent. A third organizational outcome, Workplace Performance, was affected by satisfaction in domains of Self and Friends and Friendship.

Results from this model could be used by Marine Corps decision-makers to identify life domains that were key drivers of QOL and organizational outcomes. For example, if the life domain for *residence* was identified as having the lowest rated satisfaction among marines and a significant effect on global QOL (and global QOL having a significant relationship with readiness and retention), Marine Corps leadership could prioritize resources in hopes of targeting improvements to life needs that would have the greatest return (in terms of QOL, readiness, and retention) on investment. In this example, improvements with enlisted barracks would positively affect satisfaction ratings of the residence domain, global ratings of QOL, and consequently affect Marine readiness and retention.

White, Baker, and Wolosin (1999) conducted a follow-up study of QOL among USMC personnel using the Kerce (1995) bottom-up model of QOL. Results were similar to those found by Kerce (1995) supporting the notion that life domains had little direct effect on organizational outcomes and that the mediating variable of global QOL was important in predicting career intentions.

Ditton, Bolmarcich, Moore, Webb, & Quinlan (2003) conducted the third QOL study for the USMC, administering QOL measures nearly identical to those used by Kerce (1995) and White et al. (1999) to four groups of people in the Marine Corps community—active duty marines, spouses of active duty marines, independent duty

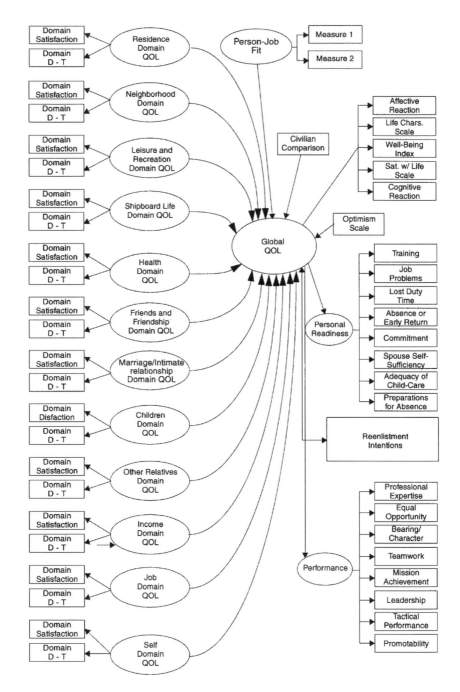

Figure 8.4
The U.S. Marine Corps Conceptual Model of QOL

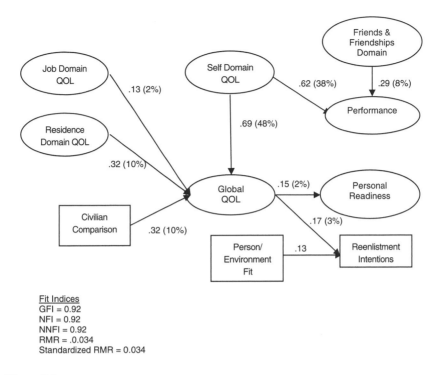

Fit Indices
GFI = 0.92
NFI = 0.92
NNFI = 0.92
RMR = .0.034
Standardized RMR = 0.034

Figure 8.5
The U.S. Marine Corps QOL Model for Single Marines without Children (percent variance accounted for among constructs indicated in parentheses)

Source: Kerce, 1995.

marines (those personnel on active duty stationed in areas without access to military personnel and family support programs), and production recruiters (personnel in high stress assignments who are oftentimes stationed in areas without access to military personnel and family support programs). Measures were similar to those used in previous USMC QOL studies with the additional MDT items (Michalos, 1985; 1991) used to test a broader range of influences on QOL, readiness, and retention. Again, using SEM, data were applied to the Kerce (1995) model where global QOL was affected by satisfaction with various life domains and global QOL was thought to significantly affect readiness and retention intent. Results were similar to those of Kerce (1995) and White et al. (1999) with models supporting a bottom-up model of QOL.

Findings from these three studies of QOL indicated that (1) life domain satisfaction varied as a function of marital and family status, (2) life domains of job and self consistently appeared as key drivers of QOL, and (3) there was a significant relationship between QOL and readiness and retention. Each year this study has been conducted, results from these studies have been instrumental in prioritizing QOL resource allocation and informing command leadership of the QOL issues that are important for marines and their families. While we know how satisfied marines are with life domains and that there is a relationship to readiness and retention intent we have yet to determine the reasons for their satisfaction (or lack of satisfaction). Often, the "why" questions are answered by focus group interviews to gather the qualitative reasons for the quantitative rating. This additional step in the research process could help the USMC move to a level of specificity that makes this information much more meaningful and actionable.

U.S. Navy QOL Survey

Much like the Marine Corps, the Navy divided their QOL research agenda into several distinct components—customer satisfaction, needs assessment, and QOL life domains surveys. Among the first to study QOL and subjective well-being among Navy personnel were Booth-Kewley and Thomas (1993) and Wilcove (1994). Both research teams used a domain-based approach to evaluate QOL among active duty service members, but the Navy opted not to fund further QOL research using a life domains approach. From 1994 to 1999, the U.S. Navy focused on evaluating satisfaction with specific QOL programs and needs assessments of leisure needs rather than individual life needs.

Inspired by a 1996 Navy Inspector General report critical of the Navy's lack of a systematic, recurring approach for evaluating shipboard habitability/QOL (Navy Inspector General, 05 May 1996), Navy leaders decided to return to using a domain-based approach to evaluate QOL (now including shipboard QOL) and added a program evaluation component to measure use, satisfaction, and impact (on readiness and retention) of QOL programs. Navy researchers used Kerce (1995) as a model for the Navy QOL Survey and the Kerce (1998) program evaluation methodology as a model for the program-specific evaluation of Navy QOL programs. The objective of the Navy QOL program/cluster evaluation[5] was to examine program users' perceived satisfaction of the program and impact both in terms of helping with the concern that led patrons to use the QOL program and the program meeting broader QOL program objectives (Schwerin, Michael, Glaser, & Farrar, 2002). Results indicate that there is a significant relationship between program satisfaction, programs meeting broader/global QOL objectives, and military outcomes such as perceived readiness and retention intent (Kelley, Schwerin, Farrar, & Lane, 2005a; Kelley et al., 2005b; Schwerin et al., 2002).

In 1999, the Navy administered the Navy QOL Survey (Wilcove & Schwerin, 2002) using QOL measures nearly identical to those used by Kerce (1995). Using data from that life domains survey, Wilcove, Schwerin, & Wolosin (2003) attempted to apply the Kerce (1995) model to Navy personnel but several variables included in Kerce's model were not significantly correlated with QOL (i.e., person–job fit and civilian comparisons—a finding also cited in Ditton et al. 2003) and the overall model did not possess adequate goodness of fit.

Their inability to adapt the U.S. Marine Corps life domain model to the Navy led researchers to the consideration of other models of QOL. Citing the work/non-work dichotomy previously validated by Hart (1999), Wilcove et al. (2003) conducted exploratory analyses of the variables used to measure the major areas of life experience (i.e., life domains) assessed by the 1999 Navy QOL Survey. Exploratory factor analyses confirmed the existence of two overarching factors into which life domains could be partitioned: work and non-work.

Following the Hart (1999) QOL theoretical framework, Wilcove et al. (2003) conducted exploratory SEM analyses and confirmed the Hart (1999) model indicating a direct link between non-work (personal) domains and retention intent. In the Wilcove et al. (2003) model, life domains were related to work and non-work factors. Non-work (or personal) factors had a significant, direct relationship to retention intent while work factors had a significant indirect effect (mediated by organizational commitment) with retention intent (see Figure 8.6). Hindelang, Schwerin, & Farmer (2004) tested the Wilcove et al. (2003) model using USMC data from the White et al. (1999) U.S. Marine Corps QOL survey with results indicating that the Wilcove et al. (2003) QOL model also fit USMC QOL data.

Results from Wilcove et al. (2003) and Hindelang et al. (2004) produced several meaningful findings. First, results support U.S. Marine Corp QOL modeling studies (Ditton et al., 2003; Kerce, 1995; White et al., 1999) and civilian studies (Hart, 1999) that broadly conceptualized work and non-work factors as having a significant effect on retention intent. Second, while models of action were not tested, results appear to support findings from USMC QOL modeling studies that QOL operates in a bottom-up fashion. Third, Navy QOL modeling studies incorporate, for the first time, a domain for shipboard life, which was significantly related to both work and non-work factors. This indicates that shipboard life (a parallel for USMC, Army, and Air Force might be "life in the field" or "life while deployed") is a life domain that needs to be included in future assessments of QOL and ought to be considered as having a significant effect on retention intent. Finally, these studies (e.g., Hindelang et al.; Wilcove et al., 2003) identified a model of QOL and retention intent that generalizes across services (Navy and Marine Corps).

Future Directions

All of these studies, models, and research approaches yield some exciting results and opportunities in QOL and personnel research among military personnel. As we have seen through the different conceptualizations of QOL used by military organizations, organizational approaches to QOL vary by service. The Air Force integrates QOL studies with needs assessment and an infrastructure to make QOL data a source of empowerment and goals for members of the Air Force community. Similarly, the Army uses QOL data as a metric for tracking progress on the Army Well-Being Plan. The Navy and Marine Corps use QOL data as an indicator of work and non-work life satisfaction and examine the relationship between these life needs and retention. Unlike the Navy, the Marine Corps

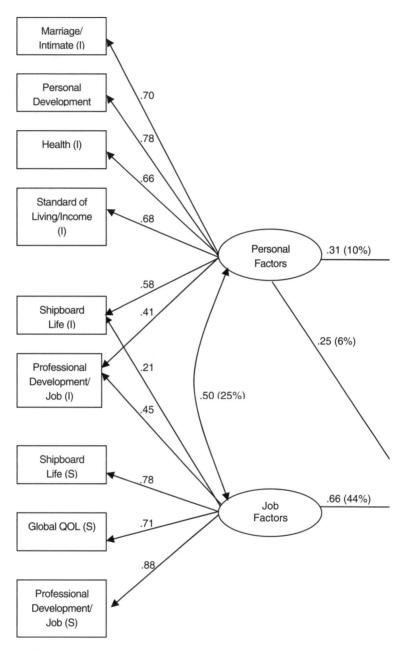

Figure 8.6
USN QOL Model for Unmarried First-Term Enlisted Sailors without Children (percent variance accounted for among constructs indicated in parentheses)

Source: Wilcove, Schwerin, & Wolosin, 2003.

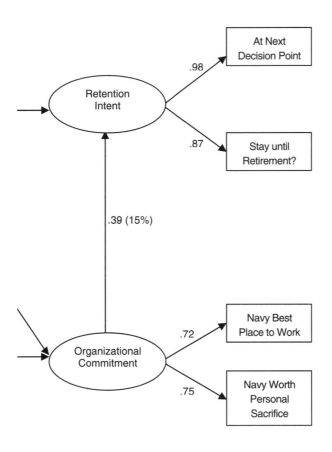

Fit Indices
AGFI = 0.94
CFI = 0.99
NFI = 0.97
RMR = 0.05
RMSEA = 0.04

At Next
Decision Point

.98

Retention
Intent

.87

Stay until
Retirement?

.39 (15%)

Navy Best
Place to Work

.72

Organizational
Commitment

.75

Navy Worth
Personal
Sacrifice

uses QOL data for prioritizing resource allocation and as a source of insight for leadership training.

Although approaches to measuring and analyzing QOL data vary among services, there are a number of methodological considerations for future QOL research. More work is needed in defining QOL, developing reliable and valid measures of QOL that reflect work life and non-work life, and analyzing the relationship between QOL and military outcomes of interest.

Definitions of QOL cited earlier in this chapter note that QOL consists of physical, social, emotional, and psychological well-being. Additionally, well-being can vary in how it is conceptualized—subjective well-being (hedonic) or psychological well-being (eudaimonic). These differences should be a starting point in how QOL measures are designed and test/survey items written. For example, current measures of QOL used by DoD and the services are all based on a subjective well-being (or hedonic) definition but may elicit ratings that are based on different aspects of QOL (see Table 8.3). QOL items used by the Army and Air Force ask respondents to rate their satisfaction with the "Army as a way of life" or "your quality of life in the Air Force." Including a reference to the Army or Air Force in the QOL item may restrict the frame of experiences the respondents consider. They may only consider QOL as it relates to their military job and not their life taken as a whole. The Navy and Marine Corps use measures that are more global and refer to their life as a whole—"your life overall." Here respondents may interpret these items as asking about satisfaction with all aspects of their life, work and non-work, a truly broad QOL definition.

Aligning military QOL research with the civilian research in QOL and in-depth testing of QOL measures prior to administration can help us identify sources of measurement error and respondent error in the data. The difference in item wording raises an empirical question that could be tested—what aspects of QOL do respondents consider in their rating of QOL? Cognitive testing (Tourangeau, 1984; Willis, 2004) is just one step in survey item pre-testing that helps researchers identify several potential sources of error including (1) question comprehension, (2) retrieval of relevant information from memory, (3) decision processes, and (4) response processes (Tourangeau, 1984).

In addition to measurement issues related to assessing global QOL, other measurement issues exist in measuring work life and non-work life. With a wealth of civilian and military research in work-life measurement, scales for job satisfaction, organizational commitment, fairness and equity of performance appraisal, actual operations tempo, and aspects related to perceptions of operations tempo provide good coverage for measuring work life.

One area for improving measurement of work life is assessment of life while deployed or in the field. Because the Navy QOL Survey originated from concerns with shipboard habitability, in-depth measures of shipboard QOL were included in Navy QOL surveys. These shipboard QOL items include overall satisfaction with shipboard life, the physical environment (i.e., lighting, temperature, motion, and vibration), facilities (i.e., berthing, personal storage space, mattresses, and

Table 8.3
Measures of Global QOL Used by U.S. Military QOL Surveys

Branch of U.S. Military & Survey Title	Global QOL Measure
DoD—Status of Forces Survey of Active Duty Members (March, 2003)	Overall, how satisfied are you with your military way of life?
Air Force—Air Force Chief of Staff QOL Survey (2002)	Overall, how satisfied are you with your quality of life in the Air Force?
Army—Sample Survey of Military Personnel (SSMP)	Overall, how satisfied are you with the Army as a way of life?
Navy—Navy QOL Survey (2002)	How satisfied are you with your life overall? How satisfied are you with the military way of life? How do you feel about your life at the present time?
Marine Corps—USMC QOL Survey (2002)	Which point on the scale below best describes how you feel about your life as a whole at this time? [1 – 7 scale from "terrible" to "delighted"] (Andrews & Withey, 1976) Now, once again, about your life as a whole, considering all aspects of life that have been covered in this survey, please indicate how much you agree or disagree with each statement (SWL; Diener et al., 1985): In most ways, my life is close to ideal The conditions of my life are excellent I am satisfied with my life So far, I have gotten the most important things I want in life If I could live my life over, I would change almost nothing

shower/head fixtures), shipboard services (i.e., food, recreation activities, Internet access, and postal services), and social needs (i.e., contact with family/friends ashore, feeling a part of the work team/division, ability to socialize with friends on the ship). Analyses of Navy QOL data indicate that satisfaction with shipboard QOL has a significant effect on QOL and retention. It would seem that similar measures of satisfaction with QOL in field settings while deployed should be included on QOL measures used by other branches of the military.

Measures of non-work life vary significantly among the services. Some QOL measures focus on the use and satisfaction with QOL programs that address non-work life and family concerns (i.e., childcare, family support programs, and residence), work–family conflict (i.e., the extent that work interferes with family life), or family–work conflict (i.e., the extent that family life interferes with work) (Netemeyer et al., 1996). Other QOL measures examine satisfaction with non-work life and satisfaction with family relationships apart from use and satisfaction with QOL programs. Program use and satisfaction are measured on other customer satisfaction or needs assessment surveys.

This raises another empirical question that has yet to be fully studied—what is the relationship between work and non-work factors and do these relationships indicate work/family conflict in the military? In terms of QOL studies cited earlier in this chapter, the research question at hand is whether work and non-work factors are correlated (supporting a spillover model) or whether they are uncorrelated (supporting a segmentation model). Previous studies using military personnel data from New Zealand Army personnel (Capon, Chernyshenko, & Stark, 2004) and Canadian Forces personnel (Dobreva-Martinova, Villeneuve, Sharp, Otis, & Coulombe, 2004) failed to demonstrate a relationship between either work–family conflict or work-life balance and retention intent. Such findings suggest a segmentation model: work may predict retention intent but the interface between work and non-work life does not. Several other research studies (Hart, 1999; Headey, Glowacki, Holmstron, & Wearing, 1985; Williams & Alliger, 1994) support a spillover model where work and non-work domains have a significant role in predicting QOL or retention. More research could be conducted to determine (1) which measure is more relevant to capturing non-work life needs—work–family conflict or non-work life domain satisfaction, (2) how do work–family conflict and non-work life domain satisfaction interact —are these measures independent or is there significant overlap between the two (and where is that overlap), and (3) what implications do these findings have for the nature of the life needs model—is work life and non-work life correlated (supporting a spillover model) or uncorrelated (segmentation model).

Other measurement issues exist in assessing the state component of QOL and subjective well-being. Kahneman (1999) argues that experience sampling ought to be used in subjective well-being research and Beal and Weiss (2003) further describe ecological momentary assessment in organizational settings. For example, rather than asking respondents to provide an overall estimation of QOL or well-being, one could develop methods to use event sampling and ecological momentary assessment data to sample perceptions about well-being at random intervals through a defined time period (e.g., sampling work and non-work satisfaction on several random days per month) and comparing sampled subjective well-being data to global perceptions of QOL.

In its social contract, the DoD describes a larger objective, as stated in the quadrennial defense review, as addressing "factors that influence the Military Services' continued readiness to fight and win the Nation's wars through recruiting, developing and retaining talented people." (Office of the Under Secretary of Defense for Personnel & Readiness, 2004, p. ii). If this is truly the case, outcome measures of interest should include personnel readiness, personal and professional development, and retention.

Few studies examine personnel readiness, primarily because no standard definition or model of readiness exists. Burnam et al. (1992) and Kerce (1995) both included outcome measures for personnel readiness but research to refine readiness measures, examine scale/index reliability and validity, and factors that affect readiness have not been conducted. McGonigle et al. (2005) propose a model of QOL program impact on military personnel and personnel readiness that could serve as a starting point for studies that identify factors that indicate personnel readiness (e.g., fitness, technical competence, organizational citizenship behavior, preparedness, commitment, and unit cohesion). Other personnel readiness factors could include non-work readiness factors such as family readiness and preparedness for deployment.

Currently, military studies of QOL, work life, organizational commitment, and job satisfaction examine retention intent. It is useful to identify factors that affect retention intent because theories of planned behavior (Ajzen, 1988; 1991) propose that attitudes, subjective norms, and perceived behavioral control affect intent, and intent is related to behavior. For example, a person's decision to leave military service is based on previously held attitudes about leaving, the norms associated with leaving, and the ability to voluntarily separate from military service. Learning about the perceptions of military personnel is useful in identifying and addressing factors that negatively affect retention so that changes can be made that affect the service member's decision to leave active duty.

In studies of retention intent and retention behavior, the validity of using self-report intent items to make conclusions about behavior has been called into question. Fitch and McCarty (1993), for example, found no significant relationship between employee's intent to quit and actual turnover at the group level. Szoc and Seboda (1984), however, examined the relationship between intent and actual retention behavior in the military and found that the strongest predictor of retention behavior is stated intent. Based on a meta-analysis of 34 studies that include both civilian and military populations, Steel and Ovalle (1984) report a correlation of 0.50 for the relationship between intention and turnover. They also report that population type (military versus civilian) was not a significant moderator variable for the relationship between intent and turnover. Modeling QOL to actual retention behavior would be a powerful way of demonstrating the actual effect of QOL on retention and cost models could be developed to quantify the cost/benefit trade-off of investing in service member QOL.

Studies of retention behavior should contain some mechanism for linking self-report data to personnel record data indicating actual retention behavior. Using personal identifiers such as social security numbers to study retention behavior rather than retention plans has not been conducted because of concerns regarding how identifiers would affect subjective ratings and data quality. Including identifiers on studies of sensitive behavior has been shown to influence self-report data (Olson, Stander, & Merrill, 2004), but studies of work life among Navy personnel comparing anonymous or identified surveys indicate no significant differences in response rates and data quality between identified and anonymous personnel surveys (Booth-Kewley, Edwards, & Rosenfeld, 1992; Olmsted, 2001).

There are limitations to many of these recommendations that need to be acknowledged. Military organizations exist for a nation's defense: their first priority is naturally carrying out national defense strategy. Balancing that perspective is the notion, with an all-volunteer force, that military organizations need to attract personnel to fill the jobs to carry out that strategy. Another limitation is that all of the military studies cited are conducted using cross-sectional samples of military personnel. While recurring cross-sectional surveys can aid in tracking attitudes of groups of people over time, it does not provide information as to how attitudes and perceptions change within people over time. Also, while there is a need to collect more information on the trait aspects and the state aspects of work life and non-work life, feedback from military survey respondents is that surveys are already too long. They also feel that they do not see the results of surveys put into action (Newell, Rosenfeld, Harris, & Hindelang, 2004). Fewer omnibus surveys and more surveys focused to samples, while more costly, may yield better quality data and lessen the risk of non-response bias. Finally, the most obvious limitation to these recommendations for those conducting military personnel research is the lack of funding. If we invest in learning more about the impact of QOL programs than about who uses programs, when, and how satisfied users are, we will discover (1) on a practical level whether programs are worth the investment and (2) how the lives of military personnel and their families are better as a result of using QOL programs.

With all of the QOL initiatives underway and research being conducted, a great deal of work remains in order to understand the effect of work life and non-work life on military personnel. World events, economic factors, social norms, and work/family balance is dynamic and ever-changing. As military leadership and QOL program managers work to improve the lives of military personnel and their families, the effectiveness of these programs in terms of their impact on people's lives needs to be continually evaluated. Investing in military personnel and their families is a cost-effective way of maintaining a ready military force, especially for militaries with an all-volunteer force that depends on the military's ability to be an employer of choice for people in a competitive work force.

The common, unifying theme of this chapter is that QOL matters. QOL matters in community-building, personnel readiness, retention plans, and spousal support of career decisions. Though QOL may be modeled and expressed in various ways, there is a statistically significant relationship between work factors, non-work factors, and

QOL. QOL represents the innately human element of military personnel. Soldiers, airmen, marines, and sailors are more than "human capital" or "personnel inventory"—they're people.

Notes

1. More information on social structure and exchange theory can be found in Cook & Whitmeyer (1992).
2. Two prevailing conceptualizations of QOL are global QOL and health-related QOL. The World Health Organization (1948) defined health-related QOL as "a state of complete physical, mental, and social well-being, and not merely the absence of disease or infirmity." Much of the focus in health-related QOL research centers on tracking public health or the effects of disease or the treatment of disease on an individual's health. While a discussion of health-related QOL has some bearing on a general discussion of QOL research, it is beyond the scope of this chapter. Hereafter, use of the term "QOL" refers to general QOL.
3. Top-down, bottom-up, and integrative models can also be studied in terms of the degree of independence between state and trait indicators. A segmentation model suggests that state and trait indicators are uncorrelated and have a direct effect on subjective well-being or QOL. Spillover and compensation models indicate an interrelationship between state and trait indicators.
4. This logic can apply to some programs such as the military housing program where military housing satisfies needs for shelter and residence. The logic fails when attempting to equate satisfaction with military childcare programs with needs for satisfying relationships with one's children.
5. Cluster evaluation is an approach commonly used by national grant foundations to "evaluate a program that is being administered at different [autonomous] program sites aimed at bringing about a common general change" (Sanders, 1997, p. 397). The end-users of a cluster evaluation are the local program managers as well as the corporate-level program managers, a common requirement for evaluating military QOL programs.

References

Ajzen, I. (1988). *Attitudes, Personality, and Behaviour.* Milton-Keynes, England: Open University Press.

Ajzen, I. (1991). The theory of planned behaviour. *Organizational Behavior and Human Developmental Processes, 50,* 179–211.

Alderks, C.E. (1998). *PERSTEMPO: Its Effects on Soldiers' Attitudes.* Army Research Institute for the Behavioral and Social Sciences, Alexandria, VA. ADA351766.

Andrews, F. M., & Withey, S. B. (1976). *Social indicators of well-being: America's perception of life quality.* New York: Plenum Press.

Baker F., & Intagliata, J. (1982). Quality of life in the evaluation of community support systems, *Evaluation and Program Planning, 5,* 69–79.

Beal, D. J., & Weiss, H. M. (2003). Methods of ecological momentary assessment in organizational behavior. *Organizational Research Methods, 6*(4), 440–464.

Bell, D. B., Schumm, W. R., & Martin, J. A. (2001, October). *How Family Separations Affect Spouse Support for a Military Career: A Preliminary View from the U.S. Army.* Paper presented at the Biennial International Convention of the Inter-University Seminar on Armed Forces and Society, Baltimore, MD.

Booth-Kewley, S., Edwards, J. E., & Rosenfeld, P. (1992). Impression management, social desirability, and computer administration of attitude questionnaires: Does the computer make a difference? *Journal of Applied Psychology, 77*(4), 562–566.

Booth-Kewley, S., & Thomas, M. (1993). *The Subjective Quality of Life of Navy Personnel* (TR-93-8). San Diego, CA: Navy Personnel Research and Development Center.

Bowen, G. L., Orthner, D. K., Martin, J. A., & Mancini, J. A. (2001). *Building Community Capacity: A Manual for U.S. Air Force Family Support Centers.* Chapel Hill, NC: A Better Image Printing.

Bowen, G. L., Martin, J. A., & Mancini, J. A. (1999). *Communities in Blue for the 21st Century.* Fairfax, VA: Caliber & Associates.

Bowen, G .L., Orthner, D., Martin, J. A., & Mancini, J. A. (2001). *Building Community Capacity: A Manual for U.S. Air Force Family Support Centers.* Chapel Hill, NC: A Better Image Printing.

Brenner, S. O., & Bartell, R. (1983). The psychological impact of unemployment: A structural analysis of cross-sectional data. *Journal of Occupational Psychology, 56,* 129–136.

Brief, A. P., Butcher, A. H., George, J. M., & Link, K. E. (1993). Integrating bottom-up and top-down theories of subjective well-being: The case of health. *Journal of Personality and Social Psychology, 64,* 646–653.

Bryant, F. B., & Marquez, J. T. (1986). Educational status and the structure of subjective well-being in men and women. *Social Psychology Quarterly, 49,* 142–153.

Buddin, R. (1998). *Building a Personnel Support Agenda: Goals, Analyses Framework, and Data Requirements* (MR-916-OSD). Santa Monica, CA: RAND Corporation.

Burnam, M. A., Meredith, L. S., Sherbourne, C. D., Valdez, R. B., & Vernez, G. (1992). *Army Families and Soldier Readiness* (R-3884-A). Santa Monica, CA: RAND.

Campbell, A., Converse, P. E., & Rodgers, W. L. (1976). *The Quality of American Life: Perceptions, Evaluations, and Satisfactions.* New York: Russell Sage Foundation.

Cantril, H. (1965). *The Pattern of Human Concerns.* New Brunswick, N. J.: Rutgers University Press.

Capon, J., Chernyshenko, O. S., & Stark, S. E. (2004). Applicability of civilian retention theory in the New Zealand military. *Proceedings of the International Military Testing Association,* Brussels, Belgium.

Cheng, S. T. (1988). Subjective quality of life in the planning and evaluation of programs. *Evaluation and Program Planning, 11,* 123–134.

Cohen, E. H. (2000). A facet theory approach to examining overall and life facet satisfaction relationships. *Social Indicators Research, 51*(2), 223–237.

Cook, K S., & Whitmeyer, J. M. (1992). Two approaches to social structure: Exchange theory and network analysis. *Annual Review of Sociology, 18,* 109–127.

Costa, P. T., & McCrae, R. R. (1984). Personality as a lifelong determinant of well-being. In C. Maletesta & C. Izard (Eds.), *Affective processes in adult development and aging* (pp. 141–156). Beverly Hills, CA: Sage.

Costa, P. T., McCrae, R. R., & Norris, A. H. (1981). Personal adjustment to aging: Longitudinal prediction from neuroticism and extraversion. *Journal of Gerontology, 36,* 78–85.

David, J. P., Green, P. J., Martin, R., & Suls, J. (1997). Differential roles of neuroticism, extraversion, and event desirability for mood in daily life: An integrative model of top-down and bottom-up influences. *Journal of Personality and Social Psychology, 73,* 149–159.

DeLongis, A., Folkman, S., & Lazarus, R. S. (1988). The impact of daily stress on health and mood: Psychological and social resources as mediators. *Journal of Personality and Social Psychology, 54,* 486–495.

Deputy Assistant Secretary of Defense, Office of the (Military Community & Family Policy). (2002). *A New Social Compact: A Reciprocal Partnership Between the Department of Defense, Service Members, and Families.* Washington, DC: Author.

Diener, E. (1984). Subjective well-being. *Psychological Bulletin, 95,* 542–575.

Diener, E., & Diener, C. (1995). The wealth of nations revisited: Income and quality of life. *Social Indicators Research, 36,* 275–286.

Diener, E., & Emmons, R. A. (1984). The independence of positive and negative affect. *Journal of Personality and Social Psychology, 47,* 1105–1117.

Diener, E., Emmons, R. A., Larsen, R. J., & Griffin, S. (1985). The Satisfaction With Life Scale. *Journal of Personality Assessment, 49*(1), 71–75.

Diener, E., & Larsen, R. J. (1984). Temporal stability and cross-situational consistency of affective, behavioral and cognitive responses. *Journal of Personality and Social Psychology, 47,* 871–883.

Diener, E., Lucas, R., & Oishi, S. (2002). Subjective well-being: The science of happiness and life satisfaction. In C. R. Snyder & S. J. Lopez (Eds.), *Handbook of Positive Psychology* (pp. 63–73). New York, NY: Oxford University Press.

Diener, E., Suh, E. M., Lucas, R. E., & Smith, H. L. (1999). Subjective well-being: Three decades of progress. *Psychological Bulletin, 125*(2), 276–302.

Directorate Quality of Life (2005, January 20) *What is Canadian Forces Quality of Life?* Retrieved January 20, 2005, from http://www.forces.gc.ca/hr/qol/Engraph/diagram2_e.asp

Ditton, T. B., Bolmarcich, J. J., Moore, T., Webb, J., & Quinlan, M. (2003). 2002 Quality of life in the U.S. Marine Corps Study. Dumfries, VA: Decision Engineering Associates.

Dobreva-Martinova, T., Villeneuve, M., Sharp, E., Otis, N., & Coulombe, D. (2004). Predicting turnover in the Canadian Forces using structural equation modeling. *Proceedings of the International Military Testing Association,* Brussels, Belgium.

Evans, D. R., & Cope, W. E. (1989). *Manual for the Quality of Life Questionnaire.* Canada: Multi-Health Systems, Inc.

Fiest, G. J., Bodner, J. F., Jacobs, J. F., Miles, M., & Tan, V. (1995). Integrating top-down and bottom-up structural models of subjective well-being: A longitudinal investigation. *Journal of Personality and Social Psychology, 64,* 442–452.

Fitch, T. A., & McCarty, E. A. (1993). *A Test of the Theory of Reasoned Action at the Group Level of Analysis.* Wright-Patterson AFB, OH: Air Force Institute of Technology.

Gade, P. A., Tiggle, R. B., & Schumm, W. R. (2003). The measurement and consequences of military organizational commitment in Soldiers and spouses. *Military Psychology, 15*(3), 191–207.

Gladis, M. M., Gosch, E. A., Dishuk, N. M., & Crits-Christoph, P. (1999). Quality of life: Expanding the scope of clinical significance. *Journal of Consulting and Clinical Psychology, 67*(3), 320–331.

Haring, M. J., Okun, M. A., & Stock, W. A. (1984). A quantitative synthesis of literature on work status and subjective well-being. *Journal of Vocational Behavior, 25,* 316–324.

Hart, P. M. (1999). Predicting employee life satisfaction: A coherent model of personality, work and nonwork experiences, and domain satisfactions. *Journal of Applied Psychology, 84*(4), 564–84.

Headey, B., Glowacki, T., Holmstron, E., & Wearing, A. J. (1985). Modeling change in perceived quality of life. *Social Indicators Research, 17*, 267–298.

Headey, B., & Wearing, A. J. (1989). Personality, life events, and subjective well-being: Toward a dynamic equilibrium model. *Journal of Personality and Social Psychology, 52*, 511–524.

Heady, B., & Wearing, A. J. (1991). Subjective well-being: A stocks and flows framework, In F. Stack, M. Argyle, & N. Schwarz (Eds.), *Subjective Well-Being: An Interdisciplinary Perspective* (pp. 49–73). Elmsford, NY: Pergamon Press.

Heller, D., Watson, D., & Ilies, R. (2004). The role of person versus situation in life satisfaction: A critical examination. *Psychological Bulletin, 130*(4), 574–600.

Hindelang, R. L., Schwerin, M. J., & Farmer, W. L. (2004). Quality of life (QOL) in the U.S. Marine Corps: The validation of a QOL model for predicting reenlistment intentions. *Military Psychology, 16*(2), 115–134.

Hotard, S. R., McFatter, R. M., McWhirter, R. M., & Stegall, M. E. (1989). Interactive effects of extraversion, neuroticism, and social relationships on subjective well-being. *Journal of Personality and Social Psychology, 57*, 321–331.

Kahneman, D. (1999). Objective happiness. In D. Kahneman, E. Diener, & N. Schwarz (Eds.), *Well-being: The Foundations of Hedonic Psychology* (pp. 3–25). New York: Russell Sage Foundation.

Kahneman, D., Diener, E., & Schwarz, N. (1999). *Well-Being: The Foundation of Hedonic Psychology.* New York: Russell Sage Foundation.

Katschnig, H. (1997). How useful is the concept of quality of life in psychiatry? In H. Katschnig, H. Freeman, & N. Sartorius (Eds.), *Quality of Life in Mental Disorders* (pp. 3–15). New York: Wiley.

Keane, J. M. (2001, January 5). *Well-being Strategic Plan.* Memorandum for distribution. Washington, DC: Department of the Army.

Keane, J. M. (2001, August 28). *Well-being Campaign Plan.* Memorandum for distribution. Washington, DC: Department of the Army.

Kelley, M. L., Schwerin, M. J., Farrar, K. L., & Lane, M. E. (2005a; in press). "A Participant Evaluation of the U.S. Navy New Parent Support Program." *Journal of Family Violence.*

Kelley, M. L., Schwerin, M. J., Farrar, K. L., & Lane, M. E. (2005b; in press). "An Evaluation of a Sexual Assault Prevention and Advocacy Program for U.S. Navy Personnel." *Military Medicine.*

Kerce, E. W. (1995). *Quality of life in the U.S. Marine Corps* (TR-95-4). San Diego, CA: Navy Personnel Research and Development Center.

Kerce, E. W. (1998). *Assessment of USMC Quality of Life (QoL) Program Contributions to Readiness, Performance, and Retention Volume 1: Design and Methodology* (TN-98-6) San Diego, CA: Navy Personnel Research and Development Center.

Kerce, E. W., Sheposh, J., & Knapp, S. (1999). *Assessment of USMC Quality of Life (QOL) Program contributions to Readiness, Performance, and Retention: Volume II, Pilot Test Results* (TN-99-5), San Diego, CA: Navy Personnel Research and Development Center.

Lance, C., Mallard, A. G., & Michalos, A. C. (1995). Tests of the causal direction of global-life facet satisfaction relationships. *Social Indicators Research, 34*, 69–92.

Lent, R. W. (2004). Toward a unifying theoretical and practical perspective on well-being and psychosocial adjustment. *Journal of Counseling Psychology, 51*(4), 482–509.

Lyubomirsky, S., & Lepper, H. S. (1999). A measure of subjective happiness: Preliminary reliability and construct validation. *Social Indicators Research, 46*, 137–155.

McGonigle, T. P., Caspar, W. J., Meiman, E. P., Cronin, C. B., Cronin, B. E., & Harris, R. R. (2005). The relationship between personnel support programs and readiness: A model to guide future research. *Military Psychology, 17*(1), 25–39.

Michalos, A. C. (1985). Multiple discrepancies theory (MDT). *Social Indicators Research, 16* (4), 347–413.

Michalos, A. C., & Zumbo, B. D. (1999). Public services and the quality of life. *Social Indicators Research, 48*, 125–156.

Naval Research Advisory Committee. (2001, March). *Quality of life: Renewing Commitment to Our People.* Naval Research Advisory Committee Report, Washington, DC: Office of the Assistant Secretary of the Navy (Research, Development, and Acquisition).

Netemeyer, R. G., Boles, J. S., & McMurrian, R. (1996). Development and validation of work–family and family–work conflict scales. *Journal of Applied Psychology, 81*, 400–410.

Newell, C. E., Rosenfeld, P., Harris, R. N., & Hindelang, R. L. (2004). Reasons for non-response in Navy surveys: A closer look. *Military Psychology, 16*(4), 265–276.

Office of the Under Secretary of Defense for Personnel & Readiness. (2004). *Report of the 1st Quadrennial Quality of Life Review.* Washington, DC: Author.

Okun, M. A., Olding, R. W., & Cohn, C. M. G. (1990). A meta-analysis of subjective well-being interventions among elders. *Psychological Bulletin, 108*, 257–266.

Olmsted, M. (2001, August). *2000 Navy-wide Personnel Survey: Testing the Navy's Quality of Work Life Survey on the Internet.* Paper presented at the American Psychological Association Convention, San Francisco, CA.

Olson, C. B., Stander, V. A., & Merrill, L. M. (2004). The influence of survey confidentiality and construct measurement in estimating rates of childhood victimization among Navy recruits. *Military Psychology, 16*(1), 53–69.

Peterson, D. L. (2001, July 18). *Air Force Personnel Overview.* Congressional testimony presentation to the Committee on Armed Services Subcommittee on Personnel. Washington, DC: United States Senate.

Rootman, I. (1996). Quality of life indicators and health: Current status and emerging concepts. *Social Indicators Research, 39*, 65–88.

Rosen, L. N., & Durand, D. B. (1995). The family factor and retention among married soldiers deployed in Operation Desert Storm. *Military Psychology, 7*(4), 221–234.

Ryan, R. M., & Deci, E. L. (2001). On happiness and human potentials: A review of research on hedonic and eudaimonic well-being. *Annual Review of Psychology, 52*, 141–166.

Ryff, C. D. (1989). Happiness is everything, or is it? Explorations on the meaning of psychological well-being. *Journal of Personality and Social Psychology, 57*(6), 1069–1081.

Ryff, C. D. (1995). Psychological well-being in adult life. *Current Directions in Psychological Science, 4*, 99–104.

Ryff, C. D., & Keyes, C. L. M. (1995). The structure of psychological well-being revisited. *Journal of Personality and Social Psychology, 69*(4), 719–727.

Ryff, C. D., & Singer, B. (1998). The contours of positive human health. *Psychological Inquiry, 9*, 1–28.

Ryff, C. D., & Singer, B. (2000). Interpersonal flourishing: A positive health agenda for the new millennium. *Personality and Social Psychology Review, 4*, 30–44.

Sanders, J. R. (1997). Cluster evaluation. In E. Chelimsky & W. R. Shadish (Eds.), *Evaluation for the 21st century: A handbook* (pp. 396–404). Thousand Oaks, CA: Sage.

Schumm, W. R., & Bell, D. B. (2000). Soldiers at risk for individual readiness or morale problems during a six-month peacekeeping deployment to the Sinai. *Psychological Reports, 87,* 623–633.

Schulz, W. (1995). Multiple-discrepancies theory versus resource theory. *Social Indicators Research, 34*(1), 153–169.

Schwerin, M. J., Michael, P. G., Glaser, D. N., & Farrar, K. N. (2002). A Cluster Evaluation of Navy Quality of Life Programs. *Evaluation and Program Planning, 25*(3), 303–312.

Segal, D. R., Rohall, D. E., Jones, J. C., & Manos, A. M. (1999). Meeting the missions of the 1990s with a downsized force: Human resource management lessons from the deployment of PATRIOT missile units to Korea. *Military Psychology, 11*(2), 149–167.

Sirgy, M. J., Cole, D., Kosenko, R., Meadow, H. L., Rahtz, D., Cicic, M., Jin, G. X., Yarsuvat, D., Blenkhorn, D. L., & Nagpal, N. (1995). A life satisfaction measure: Additional validational data for the congruity life satisfaction measure. *Social Indicators Research, 34,* 237–359.

Standing Committee on National Defence and Veterans Affairs. (1998, October). *Moving Forward: A Strategic Plan for Quality of Life Improvements in the Canadian Forces.* Ottawa, Ontario: Author.

Steel, R. P. & Ovalle, N. K. (1984). A review and meta-analysis of research on the relationship between behavioral intentions and employee turnover. *Journal of Applied Psychology, 69*(4), 673–686.

Sticha, P. J., Sadacca, R., DiFazio, A. S., Knerr, C. M., Hogan, P. F., & Diana, M. (1999). *Personnel Tempo: Definition, Measurement, and Effects on Retention, Readiness, and Quality of Life* (FR-WATSD-99-43). Alexandria, VA: Human Resources Research Organization.

Stone, A. A. (1987). Event content in a daily survey is differentially associated with concurrent mood. *Journal of Personality and Social Psychology, 52,* 56–58.

Szoc, R., & Seboda, B. L. (1984). *Follow-on Study of Family Factors Critical to the Retention of Naval Personnel.* Columbia, Maryland: Westinghouse Public Applied Systems.

Tellegen, A. (1982). Multidimensional Personality Questionnaire Manual. Minneapolis, University of Minnesota Press.

Tourangeau, R. (1984). Cognitive Sciences and Survey Methods. In T. Jabine, M. Straf, J. Tanur et al. (Eds.), *Cognitive Aspects of Survey Methodology: Building a Bridge Between Disciplines* (pp. 73–100). Washington, DC: National Academy Press.

U.S. Air Force Chief of Staff. (2002). *2002 Quality of Life Survey.* Randolph AFB, TX: Air Force Survey Branch, Air Force Personnel Center.

Vernez, G., & Zellman, G. (1987). *Families and Mission: A review of the Effects of Family Factors on Army Attrition, Retention, and Readiness* (N-2624-A). Santa Monica, CA: RAND.

Watson, D., Clark, L. A., & Tellegen, A. (1988). Development and validation of brief measures of positive and negative affect: The PANAS scales. *Journal of Personality and Social Psychology, 54,* 1063–1070.

Weingarten, H., & Bryant, F. B. (1987). Marital status and the meaning of subjective well-being: A structural analysis. *Journal of Marriage and the Family, 49,* 883–892.

White, M. A., Baker, H. G., & Wolosin, D. G. (1999). *Quality of life in the Marine Corps: A comparison between 1993 and 1998* (TR-99-1). San Diego, CA: Navy Personnel Research and Development Center.

Wiggins, J. S. (1973). Personality and prediction: Principles of personality assessment. Menlo Park, CA: Addison-Wesley.

Wilcove, G. L. (1994). *1994 Navy Quality of Life Survey* (TN-96-41). San Diego CA: Navy Personnel Research and Development Center.

Wilcove, G. L., & Schwerin, M. J. (2002). *1999 Navy Quality of Life Survey Results* (TN-02-03). Millington, TN: Navy Personnel Research, Studies, and Technology (PERS-1).

Wilcove, G., Schwerin, M., & Wolosin, D. (2003). An Exploratory Model of Quality of Life in the U.S. Navy. *Military Psychology, 15*(2),133–152.

Williams, K. J., & Alliger, G. M. (1994). Role stressors, mood spillover, and perceptions of work-family conflict in employed parents. *Academy of management Journal, 37*(4), 837–868.

Willis, G. B. (2004). *Cognitive Interviewing: A Tool for Improving Questionnaire Design.* Thousand Oaks, CA: Sage Publications.

Woefel, J. C., & Savell, J. M. (1978). *Marital and Job Satisfaction and Retention in the Army.* Army Research Institute for the Behavioral and Social Sciences, Alexandria, VA. ADA077974.

Wood, W., Rhodes, N., & Whelan, M. (1989). Sex differences in positive well-being: A consideration of emotional style and marital status. *Psychological Bulletin, 106*, 249–264.

World Health Organization. (1948). *Charter.* Geneva, Switzerland: Author.

Zika, S., & Chamberlain, K. (1987). Relation of hassles and personality to subjective well-being. *Journal of Personality and Social Psychology, 53*, 155–162.

CHAPTER 9

LIFE IN WARTIME: REAL-TIME NEWS, REAL-TIME CRITIQUE, FIGHTING IN THE NEW MEDIA ENVIRONMENT

Cori E. Dauber

Journalists, military personnel, and academics have focused for some time on the relationship between the military and the media. It is not hard to understand the intensity of the interest over the years, an interest that has produced an extensive literature. It has been understood for some time that public support is essential for a society to conduct war successfully—all the more so in a democracy.

That abstract understanding was brought home in a concrete way when the continued prosecution of the war in Vietnam ultimately became impossible. Because the role the press coverage played in the change of public opinion in that conflict remained controversial, in every subsequent conflict the precise limits on the way the press would be allowed to cover the battlefield were also a subject of controversy, and continued to mutate, as the press and the Pentagon engaged in a constant tug of war over exactly how much freedom of access the press would have.

The result was an enormous body of literature on the relationship between the military and the media, some of which was historical (Hammond, 1998; Landers, 2004; Seib, 1997) some normative (Sylvester & Huffman, 2004; Taylor, 1997; Thrall, 2000) and asking what the ideal structure of battlefield reporting should be. Nested within that literature was an additional, and large, body of social science work which tried to answer what role the press had played on attitude formation in previous conflicts—including that lingering question of whether or not the press really had lost Vietnam (Hallin, 1992).

All of that literature has, in a sense, been made obsolete by a perfect storm of technological development, Pentagon policy choice, business decisions, and the implications of the information revolution all coming together at the same place and time, which, first visible during Operation Enduring Freedom in Afghanistan, crested during Operation Iraqi Freedom. Understanding the way these developments came together, and the way the resulting media environment has impacted media coverage of the military is essential, because it likely defines the parameters of the way the public will learn about military operations—at least in embryonic form—for some time to come.

Reporting on War: The Case of Iraq

This chapter explores the impact of fighting in the radically new media environment on the American service member. As has been commented upon before, Operation Iraqi Freedom combined for the first time the embedding of hundreds of correspondents with American combat units, with brand new technologies making possible not just live, but real-time, coverage of the battlefield. Indeed, these technologies were so new that had the same embedding program been available for reporters in Afghanistan, they would not have been able to take advantage of them in the same way, and so new that up until military forces crossed into Iraq and reporters began efforts to broadcast, no one really knew if they would work. The most famous individual piece of equipment was without a doubt the "Bloommobile," made famous by the live reports of the late David Bloom on NBC and MSNBC. (Kusnetz, et al., 2003, pp. 19–23). It was all digital, often Internet-based, all satellite-dependent—and that meant that the 70 or 75 cases of equipment needed to get a television report on the air in Afghanistan required closer to *seven* in Iraq, a mere 18 months later (Wendland, 2000).

But for the American soldier or marine involved in the ground war, this was a less than revolutionary moment. Although many met, and created relationships with, members of the press corps (many of them positive), ground forces were neither watching—nor even particularly aware of—the coverage (Katovsky & Carlson, 2003).

From the perspective of those fighting the war, the revolutionary change came when the situation in Iraq (and, at around the same time, Afghanistan) became somewhat stable, not in the sense of pacified but as a mature theatre of operations. For the first time, thanks to satellite TV, and Internet hookups, soldiers, marines, and airmen (sailors on Navy ships had had this a while longer) could watch the broadcast coverage, access print coverage through online editions of newspapers and magazines and, in a variety of ways, provide commentary that would get back to the American public, also in real time. This mattered because while embedding created a revolutionary change on the coverage side, once troops reached Baghdad, the embedding program, at least as far as the national press corps was concerned, for all intents and purposes ended.

The reporters who had been embedded made it to Baghdad—and then went home. By the beginning of July 2003, from a high of roughly 700, the corps of embedded reporters in Iraq was down to 23 (Strupp, 2003). At that point they were replaced in Baghdad by reporters who had, almost without exception, the same characteristics as those who had been providing the coverage of military deployments that had created the demand for embedding from the military side in the first place: an

almost complete lack of awareness of military concerns, issues, sensibilities, and constraints. Some of the most important outlets in the country, including *The Washington Post*, *The New York Times*, and NBC, sent reporters with backgrounds in general
politics, business and financial, salacious crime, or even metro education beats.

The military retained the embedding program, and continued to try to get reporters to take those slots, very aggressively in fact, but for the most part the only journalists interested in doing so were those from local and regional outlets wanting to
report on a specific unit of interest to a local audience. This not only meant that after
the fall of Baghdad the Iraq conflict was being covered by reporters from national
outlets with less understanding of military issues, it also magnified the impact of having the bulk of the press corps centered in Baghdad and rarely leaving that city. Secretary of Defense Rumsfeld explained in an interview:

> We're open to embedding. There are probably a few embedded right now, but people are
> not embedded....And the reporters are, for the most part, in Baghdad, where they've got
> access to the facilities they want. So it's a—I've asked that same question you asked,
> Tony, and I've found that there are a few, but there—for the most part, the reporters
> aren't interested in embedding at the present time, it appears....I think what you find
> is people report what they see and that they think is newsworthy and that they think will
> get on the news. And if most of them are in Baghdad, they're going to report what's
> going on in Baghdad. Well, clearly, Baghdad is the most difficult place we've got. The sit-
> uation in the north is much better; the situation in the south is much better. And if
> you're going to have constant drum-beat with 24-hour news, it leaves an impression,
> not because there's a distortion, simply because it's an accurate representation of what
> those people happen to be seeing, that they happen to be seeing a relatively narrow slice
> of what's taking place in the country of Iraq.
>
> I was looking at some materials the other day where I suppose our forces, coalition
> forces, do something like 1,700 patrols a day, and of those, less than one-tenth of 1 per-
> cent end up with any conflict of any kind. That's a relatively small percentage. A
> very high percentage of those, however, occur in the Baghdad and the central regions.
> (Rumsfeld, 2003)

This focus on Baghdad would be the case until, of course, something big happened, at which point the national outlets sometimes wanted back in for a few days
—which just made it look to the public as if they were with the troops (as opposed
to in the hotels) far more than they actually were.

It was ironic, for example, that after the siege of Fallujah in April of 2004, an
offensive many observers believed was called off too soon precisely because of the
way it was being (unfairly) portrayed in the press (Peters, 2004) both at home and
abroad, one reporter wrote a piece arguing that the marines' performance had been
absolutely exemplary and above reproach. The problem, he argued, was the lack of
a strategy for getting that message out. He began his short article by writing, "When
Bravo Company of the First Battalion of the Fifth Marine Regiment led U.S. forces
into the heart of Fallujah in the predawn hours of April 6, I was the only journalist
present" (Kaplan, 2004). Yet it was during precisely that time frame that other
reporters, rather than re-embed, were drastically curtailing their reporting, so much

so that even their normal competitiveness was being set aside. In Fallujah the five U.S. television networks were pooling resources, with a Fox News cameraman and a CNN producer working with one or two others to produce footage, then making it available to all the networks. And a CNN official actually stated that this and other security measures meant that

> [w]e've sent out the smallest number of people possible when we feel we can and must send people out. But I think news consumers are being shortchanged to a degree, not just on television but in print, because journalists are not able to do their jobs effectively, and certainly the depth and breadth of reporting that you saw even a month ago was far more vast than what news consumers get today. (Jordan, 2004)

Of course, one could argue that it was progress for CNN to finally be admitting to its viewers that there were limitations on its reportage at the time, rather than after the fact, given that their vice president had waited until after the fall of Baghdad to admit that the network had routinely been suppressing stories for 12 years for fear they would anger the regime, and lose their status as the only Western news outlet with a permanent bureau there (Jordan, 2003).

The local and regional outlets were prepared to cover the war intensively from the beginning, and were given embed slots originally, along with the national ones. And it is these outlets that have continued to be interested in embedding for the same reason they were at the beginning—if they represent a community with military bases, then they see it as part of their mission to keep the community informed about those units when they deploy (Weber, 2003). Some of the finest coverage of the marines of the 1st Marine Division, home based in California, has without a doubt come from reporters from the *North County Times*. Their reporting has been so fine, in fact, and their reporters, often embedded, are so well-placed, that they have logged phone interviews on all three of the cable news networks, which would suggest that at critical moments, the cable outlets were caught without reporters in the key locations or with the key units. That proximity and familiarity has permitted not just higher quality reporting generally but also the avoidance of misleading mistakes:

> While the daily violence along Fallujah's northern border has become the norm for the Marines here, it apparently was news to a film crew from CNN. A crew from the 24-hour cable news network arrived a couple of days ago with apparently little in the way of context to prepare them for what they would see, according to military officials. On Monday, they were on the scene to film much of an intense firefight in which a Marine was killed and American tanks brought a mosque minaret tumbling down. And late Tuesday night, the crew captured the near-nightly visit from the Air Force AC-130 Spectre gunship as it blasted vehicles and buildings where suspected insurgents were hiding. Military officials Wednesday said the footage was played over and over during Tuesday's news reports in the states and was being billed as the much-ballyhooed "big offensive." It was no such thing.
>
> Nearly every night, with the exception of a few quiet nights in the last week, any combination of three gunships that work around Fallujah rock the dark city with thunderous blasts. But the fury of "Slayer," as the gunships are known by the grateful troops on the ground, was apparently too much for prime-time audiences and politicians when it

broadcast on international news—even though, in reality, it has made its presence known over Fallujah for weeks. Military officials on Wednesday said the TV footage caused such a stir on Tuesday that even some international leaders were making statements condemning the offensive that never was. (Mortenson, 2004)

What all of this has meant, is that without regular embedding, the coverage *after* the fall of Baghdad from the national outlets was of far lower quality than that during the combat phase.

Yet, never before had it been possible for the average service member to directly critique that coverage, and inject their critiques straight into the national conversation on a real-time basis. Now they could do so, both because they were consuming it in the same time frame as their friends and families back home, and because with email and the ease of maintaining their own Internet-based web pages, their commentary could reach a national, even global, audience in real time.

Framing the News

Explaining the importance of this move requires first backing up and exploring what the problems with the mainstream coverage were. It is a truism within the study of political communication that news events are not themselves self-evident, nor is the way those events should be covered by the media. Every day news outlets face choices when they confront a far larger variety of events around the world than their resources would permit them to cover. Assignment editors have to determine which of the events taking place, day by day, hour by hour, are *newsworthy*.

Once a reporter has been sent to cover a particular event, *how* that event should be covered is certainly by no means self-evident. The reporter is not, at least in the beginning, sent to cover a *story*. Rather, the reporter is sent to cover an *event*, something that has happened or is happening, and in doing so, the reporter confronts a near infinite list of information fragments (some of which will be so obviously unimportant that the reporter will almost unconsciously filter them out. "The Senator's tie was blue," is not a sentence one generally sees in news stories.) Other pieces of information may or may not be important.

The reporter needs some way to take all these items of information and package them so that they can be communicated to the audience in a way that is compelling and coherent—and that fits into the space allotted. The mechanism for doing so is a *narrative frame* (thus explaining why it's called a news story.) The narrative frame is essentially the story line, the overarching type of story, such as tragedy, or failure. It is not that the narrative frame is a subtle mechanism for trying to hide bias. Rather, there is literally no other way to tell a story: without the narrative frame the news report would simply be a jumble of facts, each one presented as if it were as important as the one before and the one after.

Once the reporter has chosen a narrative frame, all other choices cascade easily from that one (Jamieson & Waldman, 2003). Certainly it tells the reporter which items of information are important, and must go in the piece, and which are expendable or irrelevant, and can be left out. The importance of the narrative frame can be seen by taking the same event and looking at the way alternative frames radically alter the news story and therefore the event's very meaning. Consider, for example, a major front-page story in *The New York Times* prompted by the release of new information about air strikes during the war in Iraq (the event, or news hook).

The narrative frame chosen by the *Times* is quite clear: overzealous use of inadequate intelligence led to the deaths of innocent Iraqi civilians, at absolutely no gain for the military effort.

> The four case studies examined by the organization included the failed March 19, 2003, strike on Mr. Hussein and his sons at Dora Farms, which it said killed a civilian. According to Human Rights Watch, a failed April 5 strike that singled out General Majid in a residential area of Basra killed 17 civilians; a failed April 8 strike that was aimed at Mr. Hussein's half brother Watban Ibrahim Barzan in Baghdad killed 6 civilians; and the second raid on Mr. Hussein and one or both of his sons, on April 7 in the Mansur district of Baghdad, killed an estimated 18 civilians.

The reporters continued:

> General Moseley, the top Air Force commander during the war who is now the Air Force vice chief of staff, said in the interview last summer that commanders were required to obtain advance approval from Mr. Rumsfeld if any planned airstrike was likely to result in the deaths of 30 or more civilians. More than 50 such raids were proposed, and all were approved, General Moseley said.
>
> But raids considered time-sensitive, which included all of those on the high-value targets, were not subject to that constraint, according to current and former military officials. In part for that reason, the report by Human Rights Watch concluded, "attacks on leadership likely resulted in the largest number of civilian deaths from the air war." (Jehl & Schmitt, 2004, section 1, p. 1)

But the choice of that frame is not self-evident, best proven by showing that alternative frames are possible. For example, for more than ten years now, in every conflict the United States has fought, the use of airpower has gotten more and more precise, which has permitted it to be employed and deployed with greater lethality against who and what is targeted with less and less danger to civilians each time.

By the simple rhetorical move of not contextualizing these bombing campaigns historically, not mentioning how the campaign the *Times'* reporters are writing about compares to those before it, the *Times* chooses a narrative frame that makes the bombing appear almost criminal, rather than the historic achievement it actually is. By neglecting to mention such issues as what the alternatives to a bombing campaign might be, the issue is similarly decontextualized so that civilian casualties from a bombing campaign also cannot be compared to what casualties would have been under different scenarios.

Another possible frame would have been to focus on the fact that the strikes failed, in the sense that the leaders we attempted to kill with these attacks were still breathing at the end of the day. They did not fail in the sense that the bombs went where they were supposed to go—the failures were either of intelligence (the leaders were not where they were supposed to be) or they were somehow able to walk away. But, because these were not hardened military targets, the people near them were killed.

And that's only a second alternative frame. Jason Van Steenwyk, a "milblogger," or military service member who writes a daily web log, offered yet a third, when he wrote:

> In maneuver warfare theory, it is not necessary to kill the [high-value targets] HVTs in order to have the desired effect on the battlefield. It's nice, sure, but it's not necessary in order for the strikes to be successful. We target key individuals and headquarters facilities not so much to kill, but to disrupt the enemy's decision-making process. We go after them aggressively, we hit them hard, and we hit them again and again, and we don't let up, because we know that a headquarters staff which is constantly on the move is not nearly so effective at battle-tracking and making decisions as one left alone. We know that a commander who cannot use his satellite phone for fear of [being struck by a missile] cannot stay informed, cannot make sound decisions, and cannot inform his subordinate commanders of his decisions in a timely manner. We know that if we keep after the headquarters facilities, the nodes of communication, the commanders themselves, then intelligence reports are not processed, maps are not updated, knowledge is not disseminated. The units in the field are left blind and leaderless. They cannot mutually reinforce. They cannot inform one another of a threat to the flank or rear. They obviously cannot react to those threats.
>
> The effect on the battlefield is entire brigades and divisions bypassed—left out of the fight, because they cannot receive instructions to conduct counterattacks. The effect on the battlefield is entire formations destroyed piecemeal, because they cannot mutually reinforce, because they cannot react to events on the ground. Or if they are, they're reacting to yesterday's events while U.S. commanders are already executing tomorrow's.... The effect on the ground means a war shortened, victories attained by maneuver and not by attrition, and innumerable (though unquantifiable) lives saved.
>
> This is the moral and military calculus illuminating the decision to conduct raids on high-value targets. (van Steenwyk, 2004)

But just because multiple possible narratives can be imagined coming out of any given event does not mean that the possibility for more than one narrative is ever obvious —or even imaginable—in the construction of a given news story. News stories are, in fact, explicitly designed to suppress the fact that the narrative was a choice. At every step along the line the final product is the result of choices made by any variety of different people, beginning with the assignment editor and ending with the person responsible for final layout and page design (or, in broadcast, editing) but at every stage any evidence that human choices have shaped and developed the final product is ruthlessly suppressed. The news story is always produced in such a way as to create the impression that no human choices were relevant to the way the story came out at all. The news is "just there," it is "just reported" by journalists who do nothing more than write about, film, and tell the story of the—again, self-evident—facts. The news could not be reported unless people made choices, but the fact that people had to make choices (even if those choices are informed by defensible professional judgments) is eluded, in favor of a representation of the news as a far more simplistic process—reporter as human recording device, merely providing a window for the audience into what they would have seen and heard had they been there themselves.

Identical Choices Appear Self-evident

It's even easier to overlook the way human choices shape and form the news product because it is so rare for the major national outlets to report different stories, or to report the stories they cover in different ways. Some of this similarity is, as critics have noted, the overriding influence on even major national outlets of the choices made by *The New York Times* (Kohn, 2003). Some of the similarity is due to the influence of the wire services. (In a devastating critique on the behavior and practices of reporters from the mainstream outlets in Iraq, Noah Oppenheim, an executive producer from MSNBC sent to Baghdad to determine if the negative reporting from there was really appropriate, describes the news as "a jigsaw puzzle whose shape is dictated by an unholy deity, 'the wires'" (Oppenheim, 2003, p. 9).

The service *The Tyndall Report* demonstrates how rare it is for any of the three national nightly news broadcasts on the traditional broadcast networks to differ from the other two in decisions regarding the top three stories of the day (available at www.tyndallreport.com). They will, perhaps as much as once a week, differ in the order of the top three stories. But for them to not have the *same* top three stories is an event of some note.

The introduction of cable news networks did not much change things. Although CNN has changed its model over time, it was originally for the most part a "visual wire service," less used by subscribers for its news, in the sense of produced news pieces (stories), and more as a service providing access to live events. (That's part of why it has been forced to constantly try and play with its approach. A visual wire service is something in high demand in moments of breaking news—and in those moments its ratings would skyrocket—but not in particular demand when things settle back down again; Collins, 2004).

The second cable news network to enter the fray, MSNBC, was a joint corporate project of Microsoft and NBC. It was meant to position both companies to take advantage of the supposed coming synergy in communications technology, but it was also meant to put NBC into the cable news business at low cost. The same news piece could be produced for the same cost as always, but be used on three different networks, NBC, MSNBC, and the financial network, CNBC. But that meant that the story lines were those established by journalists, editors, and producers predominately from NBC (Collins, 2004).

The introduction of the most recent all-news network, Fox News, on the other hand, has made a real difference in the diversity of stories available to viewers. Critics more assume than argue that Fox "tilts" or "spins" to the right, giving its coverage such a conservative coloration that some have gone so far as to refer to it as "GOP TV" (Rich, 2004). Fox itself, of course, rigorously refuses to concede the point, consistently refusing to say more than that it provides a corrective to the "liberal bias" of other outlets (Auletta, 2003).

Whether one believes Fox or its critics, there is no question that of all the major national outlets it is Fox that regularly covers different stories than the other outlets, and covers the stories that it has in common with the other major outlets in substantively different ways. Fox has without a doubt engendered a response from representatives of the major outlets, media reviewers, and the media elite in general that frankly often borders on the near hysterical. This is nowhere as clear as in the response to their coverage of the war in Iraq.

An amazing amount of this criticism stemmed from Fox's decision to run an American flag graphic as part of its logo in the lower portion of the screen (Shaw, 2003). Such pieces are given particularly prominent play in the *Los Angeles Times*, whose editor published an op-ed on May 16, 2004, in which he wrote:

> All across America, there are offices that resemble newsrooms, and in those offices there are people who resemble journalists, but they are not engaged in journalism. What they do is not journalism because it does not regard the reader—or, in the case of broadcasting, the listener or the viewer—as a master to be served. In this realm of pseudo-journalism, the audience is regarded as something to be manipulated. And when the audience is mis-led, no one in the pseudo-newsroom ever offers a peep of protest. (Carroll, 2004)

He continued, "You may have guessed by now that I'm talking about Fox News" (Carroll, 2004). The piece was actually a close adaptation of comments made in a speech given at a university, and which had been given wide circulation around the Internet, so they were already well familiar to web loggers.

The paper's media critics followed suit, as for example in a piece published on April 11, 2003, arguing that "Fox slants like a drunk, who's guzzled a couple of six-packs. If only it did so honestly, calling itself the 'conservative alternative' or something like that, instead of pretending to be what it's not by having its anchors deliver these relentless on-screen mantras: 'We report, you decide' and 'real journalism, fair and balanced.' Fat chance" (Rosenberg, 2003).

Defining What's Newsworthy

That was during the combat phase. Once the combat phase was over, it was several months before it was well and truly clear what "phase" we were in. But by the end of the summer of 2003 it was clear that there was a massive reconstruction effort under-way—and that the mainstream media appeared uninterested in covering it. They were uninterested in covering anything other than "spot news," in other words, spe-cific events, which basically meant violence, for a long period only that against Amer-icans, rather than thematic news or in-depth analyses. They seemed uninterested in covering anything outside of Baghdad unless it was an event large enough to draw the entire Baghdad-based press corps to cover it (for example, the assassination of a moderate cleric in Najaf in August 2003; Associated Press, 2003; Behn, 2003; "Bomb explodes outside police headquarters," 2003; Walt & Cambanis, 2003).

This relative lack of focus on anything outside Baghdad was as much a function of practical necessity as anything else. With the end of the military movement to Bagh-dad, all that expensive equipment designed to permit reporters to broadcast on the move had been shipped back to the States, and broadcast journalists in particular were tied to the locations of their satellite uplink. Wherever it was—and inevitably it was on a rooftop in Baghdad—was where they needed to be to do their "live shots" for the morning news shows and for the evening newscasts, at a minimum. Cable outlet reporters had to be there more often. That meant they could only venture as far from their hotel as could be easily transited in time to hit their marks by 6:30 p.m. Eastern Standard Time—not leaving, of course, until their last live shot for the morning shows at roughly 8:30 a.m. Eastern (Pinkston, 2003).

Within a few months there were more and more voices suggesting that there was in fact no way for the American people to judge whether the reconstruction effort was going well or going badly, because nothing but bad news was getting through. This in turn led to a growing debate over the question of the *balance* in Iraq coverage. It was unusual among such debates in that it was not so much a debate over a liberal or conservative bias in the stories that were covered as much as a debate over the balance *between* the kinds of stories that were covered and those that were ignored altogether (Chrenkoff, 2004; Jarvis, 2004; Rosen, 2004; Simon, 2004).

The debate received enough attention that anchorman Dan Rather on CBS felt compelled to provide a weak attempt at contextualizing a particularly gloomy report on their nightly news show (since, for some reason, *bad* news that was not spot news was still getting covered.) On the Friday, September 19, 2003 broadcast he said, "A reminder that television sometimes has trouble with perspective, so you may want to note that in some areas of Iraq, things are peaceful" ("FNC and MSNBC Pick Up on Cyberalert Item," 2003). A few sentences, with no accompanying story and no visuals, before a single negative story, amidst a sea of negative stories, could hardly be considered sufficient contextualizing information. On September 23, 2003, *USA Today*, the nation's largest circulation newspaper carried an article with the headline, "War in Iraq is hell on headlines and perspective: Reporters contrast what they see with what viewers see" (Johnson, 2003, p. 10D).

Some of this soul searching may have been prompted by an opinion piece in the *Atlanta Journal Constitution* by Georgia's Democratic Congressman Jim Marshall. Marshall had just returned from a fact-finding trip to Iraq, and was not happy with the discrepancy between what he found and what he had been led to expect, given media reports. His words were harsh enough to get some attention:

> So it is worth doing only if we have a reasonable chance of success. And we do, but I'm afraid the news media are hurting our chances. They are dwelling upon the mistakes, the ambushes, the soldiers killed, the wounded…Fair enough. But it is not balancing this bad news with "the rest of the story," the progress made daily, the good news. The falsely bleak picture weakens our national resolve, discourages Iraqi cooperation and emboldens our enemy. (Marshall, 2003)

Representatives and defenders of the mainstream press quickly settled on two primary justifications for the choices being made. The first was that, essentially, good news did not count as news. This was pithily summed up in the slogan, "we don't report it when a plane lands safely." Complained network reporter turned media critic Bernard Goldberg:

They don't report when a plane doesn't crash. But you'd have to be a moron to not know that most banks in this country don't get robbed every day and most planes, thank God, don't crash. But the only way we could know what's going on in Iraq, the only way, is through the news media. So, I say the negative stories are absolutely legitimate. Continue giving us page-one negative stories. I want to see that. But also give us the rest of the story. Give us the positive things, because that's the only way we could know what's going on over there. (Goldberg, 2003)

Jeff Jacoby, columnist for the *Boston Globe*, also spoke directly to the way this mindset impacted public support for the Iraq mission. He wrote at length:

You read the paper or watch the nightly news, so of course you know about the bad things happening in Iraq. Last week a terrorist's bomb devastated a downtown street in Baquba, murdering 68 innocent Iraqis and wounding dozens more. Every day brings fresh kidnappings—some committed by Islamists bent on power, some by thugs interested only in ransom. Insurgent violence continues to flare, and by now more than 900 U.S. troops have lost their lives.

No wonder so many Americans think Iraq is a mess. And no wonder the latest polls show that nearly half of the public now believes the war in Iraq wasn't worth fighting.

The press tends to emphasize what's going wrong in Iraq because of an inbuilt bias for the negative—only the plane that crashes, not the 999 that land safely, make news. The result is that while the bad news in Iraq gets reported everywhere, the reports of good news you have to look for. (2004)

The mainstream press was not impressed with such complaints.

Bush's beef about news from Iraq is a variation on the famous complaint that the media never report about all the planes that land safely. And it's true: Many American soldiers have not been killed since the war officially ended. You rarely read stories about all the electricity that works, or the many Iraqis who aren't shouting anti-American slogans. For that matter, what about all the countries we haven't invaded and occupied in the past year? And what about the unreported fact that Saddam Hussein has been removed from power? Well, maybe that isn't actually unreported. But an unfilterish media would surely report it again and again in every story every day, in case people forgot. (Kinsley, 2003)

The problems with this logic are staggering. At first glance, of course, it makes some sense as a description for determining newsworthiness *in the United States*. But then, the United States is not an active combat zone, a country in the midst of a massive reconstruction after 30 plus years of dictatorship and neglect, a reconstruction effort that was being judged as worthwhile or not based on whether there is enough success to balance against the cost. When all that is reported is the cost in lives resulting from the violence, the impression the public is left with is massively skewed, both in terms of its ability to determine the mission's overall worth, and its ability to determine whether or not the majority of the Iraqi people support American efforts, since to a large extent the only Iraqis seen in the news for months on end were those engaged in violent acts, not those engaged in reconstruction efforts. This was a phenomenon made worse when journalists showed no interest in reporting repeated polling data, despite the fact that the conduct of polls should have been in and of itself news. As an example, when Gallup conducted a poll of citizens of Baghdad the *New York Times* did provide a stand-alone piece about the poll. And the piece mentioned one of the most important findings in that poll, that 67 percent of respondents believed their lives would be better in five years. But the finding that 62 percent believed that everything they were going through was worth it to get rid of Saddam and have a chance at freedom was ignored (Tyler, 2003). *USA Today* simply buried the story (which was a wire service pickup from AP on another topic entirely) simply stating, "A Gallup poll conducted in recent weeks…" giving the impression that polling in the country was in itself not something to take notice of ("Bomb Misses U.S. Patrol," 2003). In short, the standard for determining newsworthiness being applied is one appropriate for a stable, peaceful, developed country, not a devastated country recovering from 30 years of dictatorship.

Furthermore, that standard is not even one that is always used in the United States. There have been times, in fact, when planes landing safely have been extensively covered. For example, 15 months after a high-profile accident in Europe grounded the fleet, a British Airways Concorde, followed roughly an hour later by an Air France Concorde, landed (safely) with great fanfare at JFK Airport in New York, and received concomitant press attention (Associated Press, 2001; Baltierra, 2001; Hager, 2001). And after the attacks of September 11, 2001, the skies were closed to commercial air traffic, as it became apparent that multiple planes had been hijacked. The administration made the decision to keep American airspace closed for several days, until more was known about how the hijack teams had penetrated American security measures. When the airspace was reopened to commercial aviation, and planes began to land at various airports, almost every local media outlet covered the first landings at their local airports. In other words, it most certainly was a story that planes were landing safely (Alonso-Zaldivar & Malnic, 2001; Dyer, 2001; Paige, 2001; Schmeltzer & Worthington, 2001; Tamman & Carter, 2001; Zimmerman & Patel, 2001; for television coverage, see Claiborne, 2001; Gallagher, 2001; Pinkston, 2001).

The second argument made, although it was made less frequently and by fewer reporters, was that there was simply no good news to report, that in fact the impression given of Iraq as a scene of nothing but violence and chaos was quite accurate. This was generally coupled with a challenge to the critics, a charge that they found the bad news "not newsworthy," phrased most often as a question. "Is the bombing of the U.N. headquarters not newsworthy?" or "should the U.N. bombing be on page 23?" (Sesno & Kalb, 2003).

This argument, of course, was a straw man, since no one was questioning the fact that bad news was news worth covering. But it was a way of suggesting that those critiquing the balance were not *really* in favor of balanced news coverage, but actually wanted ideologically determined, biased coverage (just as Fox's slogan "fair and balanced" was supposed to mean "conservatively biased.") It was also a not so subtle way of reasserting the professional credentialing that was supposed to be required to make these decisions, another way of saying: Listen here. We're the news professionals, and we'll say what qualifies as good news judgment, not the amateurs (Sesno & Kalb, 2003).

The Impact of Media Decision Making on the Mission

None of this debate over the media agenda should be a peripheral question to the military. The way news stories are defined and framed directly impacts the military's ability to successfully complete the mission. This analysis begins with the argument laid out by Feaver and Gelpi (2004) that the conventional wisdom about the casualty shyness of the American public is a myth. As they articulate it, the public is not "casualty phobic" but rather is "defeat phobic." Based on an analysis of data (collected prior to September 11, 2001) they argue as follows:

> When it comes to opinion on the use of force, the public appears to break down into four distinct groups. On any given use of force, the president can probably count on roughly 30–35 percent of the public that are solid hawks, relatively indifferent to stakes, costs, or prospects of victory. The president can also expect a group of solid doves, ranging from 10 to maybe 30 percent of the public, who oppose the use of force regardless. The president must mobilize two other groups. One group is indeed casualty phobic, and its proportion may be as high as 20 percent, depending on the mission, its members support a hypothetical military mission until the question mentions hypothetical casualties or give zeros when asked how many casualties are acceptable. Hypothetical questions probably exaggerate the degree of public casualty phobia since they are imposed on the respondent without either the rally-'round-the-flag effect or the frame that these casualties are necessary for victory, which an effective president would set in the context of an actual mission; but the casualty-phobic group is nonetheless a concern for political leaders. The remaining 15–40 percent of the public is best thought of as defeat-phobic, people who support military missions provided that they are successful. These people supply the short-term "escalation dynamic" seen in many polls, where support can be found for reversing a temporary setback with an escalation that will seek victory.... This segment of the American public will not panic at the sight of body bags, but will turn on a mission that appears to have no prospect of meaningful victory. (Feaver and Gelpi, 2004, p. 186)

And, they note, of course, the sizes of the groups are likely to vary with the mission (p. 186).

If their argument is correct, then the question becomes, not what is necessary to achieve public support for a fast, conventional, warfighting mission, but instead, what are the conditions that have to be met for that support to sustain over the course of a long, potentially unconventional mission, possibly including a campaign against an insurgency or terrorist elements.

First, people have to believe that winning is possible. They simply need to believe that it is within our capabilities *to* win, that the mission is a feasible or viable one. Second, people have to believe that we are in fact winning. If they begin to perceive that we are losing, that we are throwing away our national treasure, that is the point at which public opinion will begin to turn. Third, people have to believe that individual deaths are purposeful, that they have meaning, that they *purchase* something.

If it begins to appear that day after day we are losing soldiers for no reason, even if the outcome of the overall mission is in doubt, support will turn.

But for any of those beliefs to sustain over time, for people to continue to believe that the mission can be won, is being won, and that individual deaths have had meaning, people have to be given information that would support those beliefs. Even if those beliefs are true on the ground, it doesn't matter, unless people are given that information.

Here the conventional wisdom about media and personal beliefs appears not to be true. It has generally been held that the mass media can function as "agenda setters," that is, they can determine what it is that people *think about* (Iyengar & Kinder, 1987) but cannot tell us *what to think about those topics*, cannot determine our attitudes and beliefs. However, those studies have looked at domestic policies, where people have a framework, a reference point, from their own lives. It is not clear at all that attitude formation would work the same way when the subject is war, where most people would not have a frame of reference.

A perfect example of the way coverage can influence perceptions about the way military operations are proceeding came during the first few days of the war with Iraq, comparing the tone of the news coverage against nightly spot polls. Despite network promises, the broadcast networks in fact returned to regular programming very quickly, settling for just extending their regular news shows slightly. But war coverage was available on the cable news outlets on an around the clock basis (and it is likely that the broadcast outlets bailing led to the stratospheric increases in cable news ratings during the war; Hartlaub, 2003). And the networks were providing somewhat more news than usual. It would have been difficult for people watching any television to avoid some war news, and anyone who wanted it had access to the cable nets.

Consider the presentation of the war's progress on the first Saturday, which was almost uniformly positive, in the sense that what was being conveyed was a sense of forward movement, success across the battlefield, unchecked progress. On CNN the first thing of substance said during the 3 p.m. hour (by Wolf Blitzer) was:

> Another tense night in Baghdad. Baghdad residents, some 5 million of them, experiencing today for the first time daytime bombing strikes, evening bombing strikes. The U.S. military, the U.S. Air Force clearly anxious to demonstrate they can fly and target positions in and around Baghdad, elsewhere in Iraq, in daytime as well as in nighttime. ("Baghdad waiting for next bombing wave," 2003)

During the same show, the first service member Christiane Amanpour interviewed was Marine Corporal Jeremy Archer, whose comment was that, "I expected a big war, I guess, but they're all giving up."

Amanpour then said, "Not all are giving up," and introduced the commander of one of the U.S. Marine units, Col. Thomas Waldhauser of the 15th Marine Expeditionary Unit, who tempered the Corporal's comments—barely.

He said, "They did resist. But once it appeared that they would deal with some overwhelming firepower, they have a tendency then to give up."

On MSNBC, NBC's embedded reporters were reporting similar observations. Chip Reid, traveling with the 1ˢᵗ Marine Division, reported:

> On another interesting note, so far in the military confrontations that they've had—there was really one major one in particular where they secured a very large oil plant to keep the Iraqi army from blowing it up, the Iraqi army has no interest in fighting. They were very heavily armed, they found out later. They found large caches of weapons in the mud huts and the underground forts, but none of them fought. All of them surrendered quite easily. ("Operation Iraqi Freedom," 2003)

ABC's Chris Bury began its 1 a.m. report with these words:

> Not even daylight has stopped the bombing. This morning, air raid sirens sounded again in Baghdad and overnight, another barrage struck government targets all around the Iraqi capitol. The ground invasion is now in its second full day. Allied forces say they have secured Iraq's major port and key oil fields in the south. American troops are moving towards Baghdad. The overriding aim of all this is to unravel Saddam Hussein's power base. A senior U.S. military official says, the bombing campaign has been, quote, "taking down elements of Iraqfs (sic) elite Republican Guard." And the commanders of an Iraqi army division surrendered to coalition forces near Basra. The division, about 8,000 soldiers, is said to have melted away. ("War with Iraq," 2003)

The next day, however, Sunday, March 23, there was negative news to report. There were casualties, and most dramatically, an Army maintenance unit, wandering disastrously off course and away from the rest of the enormous convoy it was supposed to be following, was ambushed. Suddenly Iraqi State TV and, more importantly, al Jazeera, were airing video of U.S. POWs (and other, more disturbing footage that U.S. outlets never showed more than a few seconds of: the bodies of other American soldiers from the same unit, apparently having been killed execution style).

And the media's mood turned.

These were not negative events amidst positive progress. They were "setbacks." And suddenly the tone of forward movement, invincibility, inevitability, turned instantly dark.

The very first sentence from Aaron Brown during CNN's 11 p.m. show was, "We're going to start this hour by touching again on the story of the American POWs" ("War in Iraq Under Way," 2003). After intense discussion of the POW story, Brown said, "the fighting in the area where young Joe Hudson was captured was extraordinarily intense." This led to a report from CNN's Alessio Vinci:

> Hours after the U.S. armored column came under attack in Nasiriyah, the body of one Marine was being wrapped in an American flag and carried to a waiting helicopter, which had just landed nearby. He was one of many marines to die in this intense battle to control an important supply route for U.S. forces trying to reach Baghdad to the north. The charred remains of one of the vehicles smoldering—a testimony to the ferocity of the fight as Iraqi forces used rocket propelled grenades to destroy the heavily armored personnel carrier, killing everyone on board . . . U.S. military commanders say helicopters and planes managed to destroy several Iraqi tanks, trucks and anti-aircraft batteries. But somehow, commanders say, they did not manage to prevent serious losses in the fiercest battle yet of the Iraqi conflict. ("War in Iraq Under Way," 2003)

That "yet" was a bit odd, since this was only the fourth day of the war. At any given point, there would always be one battle that was the fiercest "yet": the comment was a non sequitur. Michael Gordon, defense correspondent for the *New York Times*, told Brown that given the length of American supply lines, "they now have a fight in front of them and a fight behind them." Asked whether that risk was "inherent" in the plan, Gordon replied:

> Well, yes, I mean, I guess the question is whether it was a necessary risk. These are— there are not a lot of American troops in this fight, as I see it. I think this force is barely adequate for the task...And there are areas of Iraq which are a sanctuary. ("War in Iraq Under Way," 2003)

So the tone of the coverage between the two days took a sharp turn. The question is whether or not that change in tone in any way altered people's perceptions of the war. In fact, there is a way to determine that, since during that period major media outlets were sponsoring *spot polls*, polls put in the field overnight to measure responses to particular and limited events.

CBS News polling on the Saturday night, found 72 percent approval for George W. Bush's handling of the Iraq situation—but 75 percent approval when polling on the Sunday. On the other hand, in response to the question, will the war be successful, or long and costly, results from polling done between the 20th and 22nd found 62 percent believed successful, 32 percent believed long and costly. But polling done on the 23rd found only 53 percent believed successful, while 43 percent believed long and costly (CBS News Poll, 2003). This suggests that the coverage did change people's beliefs about how the war was going—something they could not determine on their own, but needed the media to tell them—but did not change, in the short term, their attitudes about whether the war itself was justified.

But if the link between reporting and polling results suggests coverage has the potential to alter attitudes about the war, while Feaver and Gelpi's work suggests the public needs to be convinced by what it is seeing in the media that very specific conditions are being met, then support will always crater in a long-term operation in the contemporary media environment. This has nothing to do with arguments about ideological bias. This is about ingrained biases on the part of the media over what can be defined as "newsworthy." All of the information that would serve to contextualize the casualties and therefore persuade people that those casualties are worthwhile, sustaining support, counts as *not newsworthy*. This is akin to the argument I made earlier about only reporting "planes landing safely" and spot news.

The imbalance resulting from their criteria was so evident that by the fall of 2003 it had even become a subject of conversation between journalists (internally, of course, and their soul searching never seemed to change their coverage patterns.)

> *USA Today* got hold of a memo from ABC News President David Westin that said the following—quote—"I've been troubled for some time about the reporting on the situation in Iraq. We often seem to be captive to the individual dramatic incident and subject to one that comes with great video." (Scarborough, 2003)

Simultaneously, for a variety of reasons, they just did not want to continue reporting an ongoing conflict at the same level of detail. After awhile there was a desire to move on to other stories and greener pastures. So the detail given in coverage of deaths during the march to Baghdad—details which amounted to a narrative frame, a frame which explained what those deaths purchased, and gave them meaning—eventually disappeared. At that point the narrative frame is gone and the deaths are presented in such a way that they by definition cannot be seen as having meaning because *no meaning is provided.*

On March 25, 2003, for example, Chip Reid noted as part of his report during the *NBC Nightly News with Tom Brokaw* that:

> This battalion [the 1st Marines, with whom Reid was embedded], working its way in the general direction of Baghdad, fighting all the way along as some small militia groups, or perhaps the forward unit of a larger unit were tormenting them all day and engaging in ambushes. There was one Navy corpsman who was killed and a marine badly injured, but there were 30 Iraqis killed and 40 taken prisoner. (NBC Nightly News, 2003a).

Yet by July 23rd of that year, Tom Brokaw, the primary anchor, was merely reading news headlines from Iraq (under the heading "Iraq Watch") rather than going to a reporter in Iraq for any real reporting, creating the illusion that NBC was covering Iraq without the need to devote any real time to the story. There is no time for anything more than the fact of American deaths to be presented. Note from the following excerpt that everything Brokaw says is compressed into almost the same number of words as what Reid had devoted to only the casualties in the earlier report:

> Other news on our Iraq Watch tonight, two more U.S. soldiers were killed today, one in an attack on a convoy near Mosul. Six were also wounded in that attack. A second soldier died in an attack 60 miles west of Baghdad in the so-called Sunni triangle. The U.S. captured another one of Iraq's most wanted today. He was a top man in Saddam's Republican Guard. He's number 11 on the list, the queen of hearts in that notorious deck of cards. (NBC Nightly News, 2003b)

The capture of a major figure in the former regime, which might be considered at least a minor victory, is barely even mentioned, let alone satisfactorily explained. Whether there is any link between that success and the deaths of any of the soldiers is certainly not explained.

The Role of the Internet

Every element of the way Iraq was covered after the fall of Baghdad, the context free news, the choices of what was and was not covered, worked to reduce support for the war. But what made this different was that the changed media environment also created the opportunity for far greater public reflexivity than ever before. Now there was not just the presence of a Fox News in the mix to ensure that the existence of good news stories was constantly being reinforced, and to constantly challenge the monopoly story lines of the mainstream networks. It was also the fact that this was the first Internet war. This was true in terms of the ways traditional media outlets offered information to their audiences. But it was also true in the sense that it was the first war where large numbers of deployed service members had regular access to *both* the media coverage of the war (through satellite television coverage—Armed Forces Television alone presenting programs from all the major networks—and the Internet, since essentially all print outlets now have web-based versions); they *also* had regular access to the Internet themselves—a mechanism that allowed them to comment on the media coverage to friends and family in a medium that permitted those comments to be spread far and wide.

An officer who deployed to Iraq with the 101st Airborne Division as a staff officer and spent eight months in Mosul wrote (in personal correspondence with the author):

> About a month after we arrived in Mosul, most units had a dayroom set up with TV's and satellite dishes with the AFN boxes. Many people (including me) pitched in with their tentmates and purchased a TV/Dish combo from the local economy (they became the hottest commodity on the street after Saddam skipped town)—total cost for a set was about $140 U.S. That's right—most of us had Satellite TV *in our tents*. Not many English-speaking channels, but CNNI was always on. Internet café's sprang up everywhere, and most people had Internet on their work computers. So, for the last eight months, media access was plentiful—I would imagine that is the case right now—it certainly is where I'm at in Kuwait right now. (2004)

The Internet made a difference because as troops saw the media coverage of Iraq, and found it to have little or no relationship to their experience of the situation on the ground, they were able to communicate a critique of the media's performance directly to the American people in several ways. First, of course, was through email to friends and family. (One email that circulated widely on the Internet, for example, came from an officer named Major Rydbom. Googling the name "Major Rydbom," produces more than two hundred results, including stories about his email in the traditional media, interviews with the major about his email, Internet sites devoted to debunking hoaxes confirming that his email is in fact genuine, as well as various sites linking to and reproducing the actual email itself.) Second was through their participation in media interviews in very small outlets. While the major national media might not want to know what Sgt. Jones thought about the way reconstruction was going—and certainly not what Sgt. Jones thought about the job they themselves were doing—every Sgt. Jones who went home, either at the end of a deployment or for a leave, was big news if he or she lived in a small town. And small town newspapers *did* care, quite a great deal, what Sgt. Jones thought, including what Sgt. Jones might think of the performance of the national outlets (Bolt, 2004; Hoffman, 2004; Kepple, 2004; Yates, 2004).

As recently as Desert Storm all those stories, in all those small circulation outlets, would have been collected on microfilm in regional libraries all over the country, and there would have been no way to pull them together to learn that there was a secondary narrative about how the war was going that was just as coherent as that told by the national media but that was competitive to it and exclusive of it—either one was right or the other was, but not both. At least, not until some academic got around to doing a study, a project that would have required travel to all those libraries all over the country, and therefore would have taken far too much time to ever constitute a part of any contemporaneous conversation. But now even weekly newspapers with a circulation of 5,000 have their own web pages.

The War Bloggers

All those emails, and all those newspaper stories, were out there. All that was necessary was for someone working the search engines to see that they *were* there, and then to pull them together. And in this war, those were there too, in the form of "bloggers," private citizens operating "web logs," or regularly updated web sites, with the entries appearing in reverse chronological order, and any items the blogger refers to hyperlinked or "linked," so that a reader could read them in their entirety, if he or she desired, with just one click. "War bloggers" were operating blogs devoted to support for the war on terror, many of which were started specifically to support the Iraq war and critique the media coverage of it, and the war bloggers were just itching to pull these items together into a coherent narrative (Reynolds, 2004). For example, one military blogger, using the pseudonym Greyhawk (2004), created a link to an article in order to illustrate that when there is good news to report, only the lone reporter from a unit's local paper bothers to show up to cover the event (Lynn, 2004).

But the other, final phenomenon that truly made this war unique was that Internet access was so readily available to so many service members that the "milblogger" was born—loosely, the blogger with a military record, but often one still on active duty. Many of these bloggers were literally blogging right from the combat zones.

Journalist and blogger Dan Gillmor has written:

> [The story of the new media technologies such as blogging] is also a story of a modern revolution, however, because modern technology has given us a communications toolkit that allows anyone to become a journalist at little cost and, in theory, with global reach. Nothing like this has ever been remotely possible before. . . . Big Media, in any event, treated the news as a lecture. We told you what the news was. You bought it, or you didn't. You might write us a letter, we might print it. (If we were television and you complained, we ignored you entirely unless the complaint arrived on a libel lawyer's letterhead.) Or you cancelled your subscription or stopped watching our shows. It was a world that bred complacency and arrogance on our part. Blogs and other modern media are feedback systems. They work in something close to real time . . . . Now, for the first time in history, the feedback system can be global, and nearly instantaneous. (Gillmor, 2004, p. 137)

The question could be asked of the bloggers, both the war bloggers as a group, and the smaller subsection who were actually milbloggers, whether the work they were doing to undermine the narrative of the dominant media would make any difference. After all, the mainstream media was considered "mainstream" for a reason. How many Americans were actually paying attention to bloggers—or for that matter, even knew what blogging was?

Even when the Democratic National Committee took the unprecedented step of credentialing bloggers as journalists for the 2004 Democratic National Convention the attention given to the phenomena by the traditional media outlets for the most part consisted of belittling it and those engaged in it. Much of the early coverage should be read primarily as a last ditch effort to stop the barbarians at the gate. *The New York Times* published a feature article essentially portraying bloggers as asocial losers in bathrobes with an addiction akin to alcoholism (Hafner, 2004).

When, in the late 1990s, software was developed that made it possible for anyone to blog with no knowledge of computer language whatsoever and it was made widely available for free, there was a massive explosion in the number of blogs, an explosion that has not stopped.

The most comprehensive research done to date suggests that millions of blogs have been created and anticipated that by the end of 2004 there would be 10 million on the major hosting services. An enormous number of blogs, millions in fact, are really no more than personal diaries posted on the web—and many of those are kept by teenage girls ("Most Blogs Never Seen," 2003).

But the number of blogs in their totality, particularly the personal diaries, does not constitute the blogosphere as it matters to political discourse or as it matters to media critiques. The personal diaries constitute an entirely insular world, relevant only to those who are writing the posts and their friends and family, while the political, media, and military blogs can receive tens of thousands of hits or more a day. Some of the more popular ones have larger audiences than many newspapers, in fact. It is those blogs, the ones that link to news items and to one another, in an interactive web of material, that are a growing force with an increasing role to play in the way people understand the media (or rather, "Big Media," or "Old Media," or even, "Legacy Media," the blogosphere's preferred terms for the more traditional means of informing an audience about the news; Kiely, 2003).

With the most influential of those sites getting tens of thousands of hits a day, perhaps hundreds of thousands if there has been a breaking news story of particular interest, it's still easy to wonder how important this nascent "thing," the blogosphere, might be, whether blogs are a form of journalism, of "citizen's media" as some have claimed, an addendum to journalism, a way for audiences to critique journalism. After all, a few thousand people in the grand scheme of things is still not all that many people.

At least not until those numbers are put into perspective. Bloggers had a field day with a Pew study that found that "only" between two and seven percent of Internet users in the United States kept blogs. Consider what Edward Driscoll Jr. (2004) was able to do with that figure:

> This is the sort of cynical, "glass half empty/glass half full" story that bloggers love to parse, and many Weblogs had a field day with it. Scott Ott,…put things into sharp perspective. In one of his typical *satiric news articles*, he wrote that if only about two percent of Internet users actually write Weblogs, it means that there are more bloggers *writing*, than people reading *USA Today* (whose circulation is 2.6 million), *The New York Times* (1.6 million) or *The New York Daily News* (805,000).

Ott doesn't mention CNN, but since the article most prominently appeared on CNN's Website, it's probably worth noting that in the United States, CNN's typically daily viewership is only about 450,000 viewers. (The Fox News Channel, the cable news ratings leader, gets an average of 799,000 viewers during their broadcasting day.) (Driscoll, 2004)

The Impact of Blogging on the Media

Political and media bloggers in several specific cases had an observable impact on Big Media's behavior, forcing them to cover stories they were clearly not otherwise going to cover or forcing them to cover stories in ways they would not otherwise have chosen. It is generally recognized that the first time this happened was the media storm over racially charged comments made by Senator Trent Lott at the 100th birthday party of Senator Strom Thurmond, comments that eventually led to his downfall from the position of Senate Majority Leader. In fact, those comments initially made barely a ripple. It was only after several days of key political blogs (particularly blogs from the right) complaining about the fact that the Senator was paying no price for the comments—and, separately, complaining about the fact that Big Media did not seem to care at all—that major media outlets were roused to give the story any attention at all. Once they began to cover it, of course, the trajectory of the story was all but inevitable (Scott, 2004).

But of course the case that really put the bloggers and the blogging phenomenon on the map was that of the forged documents used by CBS regarding President Bush's National Guard service. When CBS put the documents on their web site, it took less then 24 hours before bloggers, working with their readers, were able to demonstrate that the documents were a forgery, drawing on experts in typography, Air Force formatting requirements of the 1970s, and computer software and desktop publishing. Within days the mainstream media had picked up the story, adding more information based on interviews with the experts CBS itself had used, and CBS's case rapidly collapsed, until it was finally forced to apologize and begin an internal investigation. But the work of the bloggers had been so central that many mainstream outlets were citing blogs in their pieces, and bloggers were interviewed on the air: heady stuff indeed for asocial losers in bathrobes (Boyd, 2004; Humphries, 2004; Levin, 2004).

Blog Readers

Still, it remains difficult to know how many Americans are regularly reading blogs, or how heavily they are relying on them for news or judgments about the news. But it is possible to know something, based on recent survey data, about those who *are* reading blogs.

61 percent of blog readers responding to the survey are over 30, and 75 percent make more than $45,000 a year.

Moreover, blog readers are more cyber-active than I'd hoped: 54 percent of their news consumption is online. 21 percent are themselves bloggers and 46 percent describe themselves as opinion makers. And, in the last six months:

50 percent have spent more than $50 online on books.

47 percent have spent more than $500 online for plane tickets.

50 percent have contributed more than $50 to a cause or candidate, and 5 percent have contributed more than $1000.

(This survey shows that blog readers are older and more affluent than most optimistic guestimates. Only 25 percent of NYTimes.com readers have contributed anything online in the last year.)

Blog readers are media-mavens: 21 percent subscribe to the *New Yorker* magazine, 15 percent to the *Economist*, 15 percent to *Newsweek* and 14 percent to the *Atlantic Monthly*. (Copeland, 2004)

What is particularly important about this group, however, is their attitude toward "Big Media."

Likewise, blog readers are united in their apathy about traditional news sources: 82 percent of blog readers say that television is worthless or only somewhat useful as a source of news and opinion. 55 percent say the same about print newspapers. 54 percent say the same about print magazines.

Meanwhile, 86 percent say that blogs are either useful or extremely useful as sources of news or opinion. 80 percent say they read blogs for news they can't find elsewhere. 78 percent read because the perspective is better. 66 percent value the faster news. 61 percent say that blogs are more honest. Divided on so much else, blog readers appear united in their dissatisfaction with conventional media and their rabid love of blogs. (Copeland, 2004)

Although this survey incorporates international blog readers, domestic polls have for some time shown increasing dissatisfaction with the mainstream media, increasing perceptions that it is unprofessional, agenda driven, biased, and generally failing in its mission to inform the American people. The CBS implosion only magnified those attitudes (Gillespie, 2004). What these survey results would seem to indicate is that those who are *most* dissatisfied are beginning to find an alternative.

It's possible that this could explain why my arguments about reactions to casualties are correct, yet support for the war continued to decrease. That is, the public, left to its own devices, would have continued to support the war despite casualties, but the way those casualties were presented by the media eroded support. The blogosphere, in other words, is simply too new a medium, just finding its collective voice, and was not able to counteract relentlessly negative media coverage of the war over a period of months. It has the power, then, to force Big Media's hand at specific moments, on specific individual events (like the Trent Lott story, or the CBS documents), but not to alter in a major way the coverage of an ongoing story. It has a committed and devoted following, and millions have become aware of it as they themselves have experimented with some form of Internet commentary (and through the CBS story), but it is not yet able to sway overall public opinion on a major ongoing story. Yet, that is.

Or, alternatively, I am correct, and Big Media was driving support for the Iraq war down, but it was the blogosphere that was keeping that support from cratering further and faster. Because the overall number of devoted blog adherents may be small, but their self-description as "opinion leaders" (the kind of people who once would have been described in the literature on mass communication effects as "gatekeepers") is correct.

This is complicated by the fact that simply determining the relationship between media coverage and public opinion is notoriously difficult, all the more so for an event that has lasted as long as the Iraq war. Just some of the difficulties would include controlling for the major shifts in the way the media has covered the story over time, the fact that it is almost impossible now to measure the opinion of audience members who have not been exposed to multiple forms of media, yet different media have covered the story differently during the same period (print versus broadcast versus cable), not to mention the not insignificant question of trying to segregate the impact of the administration's message—say, after a major presidential address—from the media's coverage of it, even if we're only talking about which sound bite they chose to pull from a speech versus which one the White House might have wanted them to pull. And all of that is before one even looks at such traditional and non-media specific issues as the impact of slightly altering polling questions, the effect of the presidential campaign, or the effect of failed expectations. The challenges are daunting.

But in truth, at the end of the day it may not be necessary to produce hard quantitative data that the existence of the blogosphere altered public opinion about the war to prove that it mattered. The difficulties in proving the relationship between public opinion and media have been there since mass media have been there. If it can be proved that more and more people are turning to the blogosphere for commentary on the news (or for their news) then its importance is clear. This is a completely new way for people to receive news from war zones. We may need to think through completely new ways to study its impact.

Milbloggers

There have as yet been virtually no scientific surveys or opinion polling done of military personnel serving in the post-September 11th era that have been made available in the open literature. One was a poll primarily for purposes of determining service members' electoral preferences and attitudes toward the mission in Iraq (although only insofar as that data contributed to predicting electoral behavior) ("Service Men and Women Upbeat," 2004). Another was a sociologist's survey of attitudes pertinent directly to morale, but the researcher did not include questions regarding the way press bias or the perception of press bias might impact troop morale (Blackfive, 2004). Nevertheless, there is no shortage of anecdotal evidence for the claim that serving military personnel, including those who deployed to Afghanistan and Iraq found the press coverage of events in Afghanistan and, most especially, Iraq, to be often distorted, sometimes just out and out wrong, and very often biased.

There is substantial anecdotal evidence that, whether or not it was the primary motivation in their decision to begin blogging, the milbloggers in particular find the press coverage biased. One blogger, in an interview with an online journal, was explicit about not only the type of bias but the reason:

> As far as the media goes they miss many aspects of the real war and focus on their political agenda. The thought that the media is unbiased is ridiculous. The slant found in reporting is usually negative toward whatever action the U.S. undertakes. Many stories of humanitarian aid are going unnoticed along with stories from around the country. (Haibi, 2004)

Wrote another:

> I believed the press was ideologically biased. I do not discuss politics with my troops all that much, but there was a strong sense among many soldiers that the press is reflexively liberal and could not be trusted. There was also a good deal of frustration that the press covered only bad news, ignored rebuilding projects, and focused on trivial happenings in and around the Baghdad Green Zone when the real action was out in Ramadi. (Personal communication from anonymous milblogger, 2004)

A third concurred, making an important distinction regarding the coverage:

> I feel as though press coverage of the military has been fairly supportive, it's the coverage of the conflict in general that is biased. The media would have you believe that the Four Horsemen along with the Angel of Death have orchestrated some sort of blood orgy here. As far as the wages of war go, this one is a pittance. But soldiers only hear of this sentiment second-hand in emails from friends and family. (Personal communication from anonymous milblogger, 2004)

Wrote another:

> Most reporters for the major television networks are camped out in Baghdad and only report on the attacks in and around that area. We've had a number of print journalists "embedded" in our units during certain operations and in several cases the interviews they conducted with soldiers were taken very much out of context. Most articles I have seen talk about the difficulties and problems we're having in certain areas and neglect the successes we're seeing in other areas. I understand the need to report on the "newsworthy" attacks but I feel that the American public doesn't get the entire picture from the articles and reports in the American media. (Personal communication from anonymous milblogger, 2004)

Thus, many are motivated to use their blogs as platforms for critiques of the media coverage. Even when they are not *explicitly* responding to specific media pieces or themes (or "memes" as they are called in the blogosphere) the milbloggers often represent their postings, using the opportunity provided by this new and as yet undefined medium of blogs, to describe for people not in the military what life in the combat zone (or perhaps just life in the military) is "really like," as itself a form of media critique. One milblogger who writes anonymously, (as many do), commented in private correspondence with the author:

> I decided that we were losing the information battle. I concluded that soldiers (like me) need to get better at getting the word out. In my estimate, this is an unheralded, but *very*

necessary, adjustment that we need to make in this new information age. For decades, our profession has promoted the "quiet professional." We go out there, do great things, let our wives and mothers hang up our medals, and go on with our lives. Any talk of "I did this" and "I did that" was shunned. The only ones who were fit to speak of their accomplishments were the ones who were no longer able to speak. This worked well when the public received their information from DOD-manufactured newsreels that played in movie theaters. But today…we can no longer afford to be quiet. I'm not willing to stand idly by while the brave and noble sacrifices of some of my best friends are desecrated by the likes of…[Michael] Moore and Dan Rather…I really do believe that… the mass media is vulnerable to their influence.

We need to figure out how to make our voices heard without coming across as the glory-seekers…that we so bitterly despise. We need to write more letters to newspapers. We need to call radio shows when we get home. We need to blog. I like blogging, because I can discuss all these great things that I did without anyone knowing who I am. People can react to it, ask questions—it's interactive. And I'm completely anonymous. There's no real credibility issues (sic)—nobody has questioned my credibility yet. I correctly anticipated that the content of my writing would leave no room for doubt. Blogging is the best medium I've found so far to counter the news-for-profit machine that so capably deprives the American people of the "complete" picture that they all want and deserve. (2004)

The argument is that in providing a more realistic view of what the military does and what military people are like, they are providing a necessary corrective to the flawed view provided by the media. Thus it is perceptions of press bias that seems to be at least part of the motivation for blogging. In response to written questions, one milblogger wrote:

Did you believe press coverage of the military was biased? Did the rest of your unit?

Yes we felt a lot of the news coverage on certain TV news was biased, mainly CNN.

Did your impression of press bias in coverage of the military have anything to do with your decision to begin a blog?

Yes, I decided to start a blog before I left to keep my family and friends in the know as to what we were seeing and thinking here, so they didn't just get the press's view. (Personal communication from anonymous milblogger, 2004)

Future Directions

This is the first war fought in this new media environment, but it certainly will not be the last. Indeed, the time gap between an event and the reporting of an event has now compressed in many cases to virtually zero; the compression between the reporting of a controversial event and the commentary on the reporting from those who were eyewitnesses and participants is now decreasing at a mind-boggling rate (Missick, 2004). Indeed, it is decreasing almost as rapidly as the number of milbloggers—and the size of their audiences—is increasing.

Thus, the anecdotal evidence that American service members deployed to the combat zones after September 11th (and even those who did not so deploy) believed that the press coverage of their activities was, if not out-and-out biased, so incomplete as to be misleading, is overwhelming. Would quantitative research support that finding? Did the perception about press coverage, if it holds up empirically, in any way impact troop morale? As the ease of Internet access (and milblogging as an option) spreads, how many service members will avail themselves of the opportunity in the months and years to come?

The questions that remain to be answered, therefore, are unlikely to be answered without specifically targeted polling. Since most public polls in the United States do not identify respondents' military status as a matter of course (and since most public polling companies do not specifically go out of their way to target that population demographic in the general population, and would need to make special arrangements to reach deployed personnel) only proprietary polls would be able to provide quantitative data for any of the questions raised by this chapter.

While, as this study has indicated, there have been some preliminary public polls done of the way Americans have used blogs as a supplement to their media use, there are no polls I am aware of that look specifically to their use of milblogs, or at whether they are particularly skeptical of news regarding military issues. Since, unlike other bloggers, the milbloggers are not only providing perspective coming from authentic experience but are now sometimes competing with war correspondents in giving eyewitness accounts, determining whether audiences exposed to their writings respond differently to the mainstream media than those who have not been so exposed would be of great use.

Changes in Pentagon policies (embedding), and in business models, (the birth of the 24-hour news cycle), came together with the information revolution to change the media environment in which American wars will be fought forever. This chapter lays the groundwork for understanding the implications of those changes, which is all that can be done until the dust has settled a bit more. But the age when a few dominant media voices could present a singular, unchallenged narrative, and presume that their story line would not only be accepted but inevitably appear as nothing more than an objective recounting of the facts on the ground is long gone. The mere multiplication of voices is in itself a form of media critique, because in and of itself it makes clear that the mainstream media's chosen narratives are indeed the product of particular *choices*, not the unavoidable Truth. Indeed, merely changing the frame can radically change which facts matter, and which don't, until different versions of the story are barely recognizable as the same event. As rapidly as the media environment has changed for the personnel on the ground, so by definition does the range of media options available to the general public, and potentially the versions of any given narrative. The research is only just beginning.

References

Alonso-Zaldivar, R. and Malnic, E. (2001, September 14). A return to the skies; limited air travel resumes, amid stringent security, most airports reopen. *Los Angeles Times*, p. A–1. From Lexis-Nexis news service.

Associated Press. (2001, November 7). Concorde flights resume. Retrieved October 5, 2005, from http://www.cbsnews.com/stories/2001/11/07/world/main317223.shtml

Associated Press. (2003, September 2). Mourners demand vengeance for cleric's death. *The Guardian*. Retrieved October 5, 2005, from http://www.guardian.co.uk/Iraq/Story/0,2763,1034138,00.html?=rss

Auletta, K. (2003, May 26). Vox Fox: how Roger Ailes and Fox News are changing cable news. *The New Yorker*, 58–73.

Baghdad waiting for next bombing wave; coalition forces move to capital. (2003, March 22, 15:00). *CNN Live Event* [Television broadcast]. CNN. [Transcript]. Available from Lexis-Nexis news service.

Baltierra, M. (2001, November 7). *World News Now* [Television broadcast]. ABC. [Transcript]. Available from Lexis-Nexis news service.

Behn, S. (2003, August 29). Ba'athists, Shi'ites, both eyed in al-Hakim's death. *Washington Times*. Available from http://www.washingtontimes.com

Blackfive. (2004, April 26). Operation Iraqi Freedom: Troop morale survey. Post to blog, *Blackfive…reminiscent of Ghenghis Khan*. Retrieved October 5, 2005, from http://www.blackfive.net/main/2004/04/operation_iraqi.html

Bolt, G. (2004, September 25), Soldier says Iraq is turning around. *Eugene, Oregon Register-Guard*. Available from http://www.registerguard.com

Bomb explodes outside Baghdad police headquarters. (2003, September 2). *International Herald Tribune*. Available from http://www.iht.com/articles/108526.html

Bomb misses U.S. patrol, kills Iraqi. (2003, September 24). *USA Today*. Retrieved October 5, 2005, from http://www.usatoday.com/news/world/iraq/2003-09-24-iraq-roadside-attack_x.htm

Boyd, R. (2004, September 13). How four blogs dealt a blow to CBS's credibility: Bush show in doubt. *New York Sun*, p. 1.

Caroll, J. (2004, May 16). Psuedo-Journalists betray the public trust. *Los Angeles Times*. Retrieved October 5, 2005, from http://www.latimes.com/news/opinion/commentary/la-op-carroll16may16,1,3379470.story

CBS News Poll. (2003, March 26–27). Retrieved October 6, 2005, from http://www.pollingreport.com/iraq8.htm

Chrenkoff, A. (2004, August 30). Good news from Iraq. Post on blog, *Winds of Change*. Retrieved October 5, 2005, from http://windsofchange.net/archives/005438.php

Claiborne, R. (2001, September 15). *World News Tonight Saturday* [Television broadcast]. ABC. [Transcript]. Available from Lexis-Nexis news service.

Collins, S. (2004). Crazy like a fox: The inside story of how Fox News beat CNN. *New York: Portfolio*, 54–55.

Copeland, H. (2004, May 19–21). Blogads: Blog reader survey. Retrieved October 5, 2005, from http://www.blogads.com/survey/blog_reader_survey.html

Driscoll, E. B. (2004, March 15). Is the blogosphere half-empty, or half-full? Tech Central Station. Retrieved October 5, 2005, from http://www.techcentralstation.com/031504B.html

Dyer, S. (2001, September 14). Sole woman first passenger to fly out of Akron, Ohio area airport. *Akron Beacon Journal*. Available from Lexis-Nexis news service.

Feaver, P., & Gelpi, C. (2004). *Choosing your battles: American civil-military relations and the use of force*. Princeton: Princeton University Press.

FNC and MSNBC pick up on Cyberalert item on Dan Rather's caveat. (2003, September 29, Vol. 8, No. 179). Retrieved October 5, 2005, from http://www.mrc.org/cyberalerts/2003/cyb20030929.asp

Gallagher, T. (2001, September 13). *Special Report with Brit Hume* [Television broadcast]. Fox News Channel. [Transcript]. Available from Lexis-Nexis news service.

Gillespie, M. (2004). Media credibility reaches lowest point in three decades. *The Gallup Organization*. Available from http://www.gallup.com

Gillmor, D. (2004, July). *We the media: Grassroots journalism by the people, for the people*. Sebastopol, CA: O'Reilly Media, Inc.

Goldberg, G. (2003, October 17). *Scarborough Country* [Television broadcast]. MSNBC. Available from Lexis-Nexis news service.

Greyhawk. (2004, August 8). Home. Post to blog, *Mudvillegazette*. Retrieved October 5, 2005, from http://www.mudvillegazette.com/archives/001140.html

Hafner, K. (2004, May 27). For some, the blogging never stops. *The New York Times*, p. G-1.

Hager, R. (2001, November 7). *The Today Show* [Television broadcast]. NBC. Available from Lexis-Nexis news service.

Haibi, E. (2004). (Army medic stationed in Mosul with the Stryker Brigade, writer of the blog, *A Candle in the Dark*). Quoted in Glaser, M. (2004, September 24). U.S. "Milibloggers (sic), Iraqi bloggers discuss war-time experiences. *USC Annenberg Online Journalism Review*. Retrieved October 5, 2005, from http://ojr.org/ojr/glaser/1096404261.php

Hallin, Daniel, C. (1992). *The "uncensored war": The media and Vietnam*. (2nd ed.) Berkeley: University of California Press.

Hammond, William. (1998). *Reporting Vietnam: Media and military at war*. Lawrence: University of Kansas Press.

Hartlaub, P. (2003, April 11). War no boon for major networks. Cable news prospering, but ratings for NBC, CBS and ABC decline. *San Francisco Chronicle*. Available from Lexis-Nexis news service.

Hasso, F. S. (2003, April, 17). Who covered the war best? Try al-Jazeera. *Newsday*. Republished by Common Dreams. Retrieved October 5, 2005, from http://www.commondreams.org/views03/0417-01.htm

Hoffman, L. (2004, June 29), Efforts to rebuild made progress in many areas. Available from http://tennessean.com

Humphries, S. (2004, September 22). Blogs look burly after kicking sand on CBS. *Christian Science Monitor*. Available from Lexis-Nexis news service.

Iyengar, S. and Kinder, D. R. (1987). News that matters: Television and American opinion. University of Chicago Press.

Jacoby, J. (2004, August 1). The news in Iraq isn't all bad. *The Boston Globe*. Retrieved October 5, 2005, from http://www.boston.com/news/globe/editorial_opinion/oped/articles/2004/08/01/the_news_in_iraq_isnt_all_bad/

Jamieson, K. H., & Waldman, P. (2003). *The press effect: Politicians, journalists, and the stories that shape the political world*. United Kingdom: Oxford University Press.

Jarvis, J. (2004, May 15). Iraq assignment desk: The rebuilding beat, post to the blog, *Buzz machine*. Retrieved October 5, 2005, from http://www.buzzmachine.com/archives/2004_05_15.html#007058

Jehl, D. and Schmitt, E. (2004, June 13). The struggle for Iraq: Intelligence: Errors are seen in early attacks on Iraqi leaders. *The New York Times*, Section 1, p. 1.

Johnson, P. (2003, September 23). War in Iraq is hell on headlines and perspective. *USA Today*, p. 10D.

Jordan, E. (2003, April 11). The news we kept to ourselves. *The New York Times*, p. A-25.

Jordan, E. (2004, April 22). [Interview]. *PBS Newshour* [Television broadcast]. PBS Television. [Transcript]. Retrieved October 5, 2005, from http://www.pbs.org/newshour/bb/media/jan-june04/media_04-22.html

Kaplan, R. (2004, May 31), The real story of Fallujah: Why isn't the administration getting it out? *OpinionJournal.com*. Retrieved October 5, 2005, from http://www.opinion journal.com/editorial/feature.html?id=110005147

Katovsky, B., & Carlson, T. (2003) *Embedded: The media at war in Iraq, an oral history*. Guilford, Connecticut: Lyons Press.

Kepple, B. (2004, November 10), City soldier sees Afghan army growing stronger. *Manchester Union-Leader*. Retrieved October 5, 2005, from http://www.newhampshire.com/articles/showularticle.cfm?id=46874

Kiely, C. (2003, December 30). Freewheeling "bloggers" are rewriting rules of journalism. *USA Today*. Retrieved October 5, 2005, from http://www.usatoday.com/news/politicselections/nation/2003-12-30-blogging-usat_x.htm

Kinsley, M. (2003, October 16). Filter tips. *Slate*. Retrieved October 5, 2005, from http://slate.msn.com/id/2089915/

Kohn, B. (2003). *Journalistic fraud: How the New York Times distorts the news and why it can no longer be trusted*. Nashville, Tennessee: WND Books.

Kusnetz, M., Arkin, W. M., Meigs, M., & Shapiro, N. (2003). *Operation Iraqi Freedom: NBC News*. Kansas City, KS: Andrews McMeel Publishing.

Landers, James. (2004). *The weekly war: Newsmagazines and Vietnam*. Columbia: University of Missouri Press.

Levin, J. (2004, September 10). Rather suspicious: Searching for answers in the Killian memo controversy. *Slate*. Retrieved October 5, 2005, from http://slate.msn.com/id/2106553/

Lynn, A. (2004, August 3). GIs throw a wild party for Iraqi kids. *Tacoma News Tribune*. Retrieved October 5, 2005, from http://www.knoxstudio.com/shns/story.cfm?pk=IRAQ-KIDS-08-06-04&cat=II

Marshall, J. (2003, September 22). Media's dark cloud a danger: Falsely bleak reports reduce our chances of success in Iraq. *Atlanta Journal Constitution*. Available from http://nl.newsbank.com

Missick. (2004, December 9). Rumsfeld grilled by soldiers? Post to the blog, *Sgt. Missick, A Line in the Sand: A View of Operation Iraqi Freedom through the Eyes of an Iraqi Soldier*. Available from http://www.missick.com/warblog.htm

Mortenson, D. (2004, April 28), Politics rears head in Fallujah, *North County Times: The Californian*. Retrieved October 5, 2005, from http://www.nctimes.com/articles/2004/04/29//military/iraq/22_27_484_28_04.txt

Most blogs are never seen and never updated. (2003, October 31). *The Write News*. Retrieved October 4, 2005, from http://www.writenews.com/2003/103103_abandoned_blogs.htm

NBC Nightly News with Tom Brokaw. (2003a, March 25). [Television broadcast]. Available from Lexis-Nexis news service.

NBC Nightly News with Tom Brokaw. (2003b, July 23). [Television broadcast]. Available from Lexis-Nexis news service.

Operation Iraqi Freedom. (2003, March 22, 14:00). *Countdown: Iraq* [Television broadcast]. MSNBC. [Transcript]. Available from Lexis-Nexis news service.

Oppenheim, N. D. (2003, December 15). Flacks and hacks in Baghdad: What it's like to report from Baghdad, *The Weekly Standard*, 9.

Paige, W. (2001, September 14). Flight lifts heavy hearts back to skies. *Denver Post*, p. A-03. Available from Lexis-Nexis news service.

Peters, R. (2004, May 20). Kill Faster! *New York Post*. Retrieved October 5, 2005, from http://www.defenddemocracy.org/research_topics/research_topics_show.htm?doc_id=226344&attrib_id=7511

Pinkston, R. (2001, September 15). *CBS Evening News* [Television broadcast]. ABC. [Transcript]. Available from Lexis-Nexis news service.

Pinkston, R. (2003, September 13). *Finding facts in a war zone*. Talk presented at the Public Seminar on The New Age of War Reporting at the University of North Carolina at Chapel Hill School of Journalism and Mass Communication, NC.

Reynolds, G. H. (2004). The blogs of war. *The National Interest, 75*(1), 59–64.

Rich, F. (2004, September 19). This time Bill O'Reilly got it just right. *The New York Times*, Section 2, p. 1.

Rosen, J. (2004, May 26). The reporting from Iraq is not too negative. But it is too narrow. Post to blog, *Press Think*. Retrieved October 5, 2005, from http://journalism.nyu.edu/pubzone/weblogs/pressthink/2004/05/26/iraq_story.html

Rosenberg, H. (2003, April 11). Objectivity is lost to Fox News' barbs. *Los Angeles Times*. Available from http://www.latimes.com

Rumsfeld, D. (2003, October 10). Interview with Tony Snow, *Weekend Live with Tony Snow* [Television broadcast]. Retrieved October 5, 2005, from http://www.defenselink.mil/transcripts/2003/tr20031010-secdef0753.html

Scarborough, J. (2003, October 17). *Scarborough Country* [Television broadcast]. MSNBC. [Transcript]. From Lexis-Nexis news service.

Schmeltzer, J., & Worthington, R. (2001, September 14). Flights trickle out of reopened airports. *Chicago Tribune*. Retrieved October 5, 2005, from http://www.chicagotribune.com/business/columnists/jimkirk/chi-0109140353sep14,0,4862370.story?coll=chi-business-hed

Scott, E. (2004). "Big Media" meets the "bloggers": coverage of Trent Lott's remarks at Strom Thurmond's birthday party. *Kennedy School of Government Case Program* (C14-04-1731.0).

Seib, Philip. (1997). *Headline diplomacy: How news coverage affects foreign policy*. Westport, CT: Praeger.

Service men and women upbeat on Bush, war in Iraq, Annenberg data show. (2004, October 15). Press release for *National Annenberg Election Survey (NAES'04)*. Retrieved October 5, 2005, from http://www.annenbergpublicpolicycenter.org/naes/2004_03_military-data_10-15_report.pdf

Sesno, F. and Kalb, M. (2003, November 18). *Comments*. Conference on the Military and the Media, National Defense University, Ft. McNair, Washington, DC.

Shaw, D. (2003, April, 20). A skeptical journalist isn't an unpatriotic one. *Los Angeles Times*. Available from http://www.latimes.com

Simon, R. (2004, May 21). The new reactionaries. Post to the blog, *Roger L. Simon*. Retrieved October 5, 2005, from http://rogerlsimon.com/archives/00000976.htm

Strupp, J. (2003, July 9). Only 23 embedded reporters left in Iraq, *Editor and Publisher*. Available from http://www.editorandpublisher.com

Sylvester, J. L., & Huffman, S. (2004). *Reporting from the front: The media and the military.* Boulder, CO: Rowman and Littlefield.

Tamman, M., & Carter, R. (2001, September 14). Travelers endure some glitches at Hartsfeld. *The Atlanta Journal Constitution.* Available from Lexis-Nexis news service.

Taylor, Philip. (1997). *Global communications, international affairs, and the media since 1945.* New York: Routledge.

Thrall, A. (2000). *War in the media age.* Cresskill, NJ: Hampton Press.

Tyler, P. (2003, September 24). The struggle for Iraq: The Iraqis; in a poll, Baghdad, residents call freedom worth the price. *The New York Times,* p. A-16.

Van Steenwyk, J. (2004, June 12), The New York Times blows it again. Big time. Post to Web log, *Iraqnow.* Retrieved October 5, 2005 from http://iraqnow.blogspot.com/2004/06/new-york-times-blows-it-again-big-time.html

Walt, V., & Cambanis, T. (2003, August 31). U.S., Iraqis hold 19 men in bombing. *Boston Globe.* Retrieved October 5, 2005 from http://www.boston.com/news/world/articles/2003/08/31/us_iraqis_hold_19_men_in_bombing/

War in Iraq under way. (2003, March 23, 23:00). *CNN Live Event* [Television broadcast]. CNN. [Transcript]. Available from Lexis-Nexis news service.

War with Iraq: Continuing coverage. (2003, March 23, 1:00 a.m.). *Special Report* [Television broadcast]. ABC. [Transcript]. Available from Lexis-Nexis news service.

Weber, C. (2003, April 16). Regional papers court military readers. *The Washington Post.* Retrieved October 5, 2005, from http://www.washingtonpost.com/wp-dyn/articles/A38187-2003Apr16.html

Wendland, M. (2003, March 6). From ENG to SNG: TV Technology for Covering the Conflict with Iraq. Retrieved October 5, 2005, from http://www.poynter.org/content/content_view.asp?id=23585

Yates, P. (2004, September 18). Amarillo reservist gains perspective from tour in Iraq, *The Amarillo Globe-News.* Retrieved October 5, 2005, from http://www.amarillo.com/stories/091804/new_amareserv.shtml

Zimmerman, S., & Patel, J. (2001, September 16). Planes trickle through. *Chicago Sun Times.* Available from Lexis-Nexis news service.

CHAPTER 10

POULTRY AND PATRIOTISM: ATTITUDES TOWARD THE U.S. MILITARY

Janice H. Laurence

Can you eat chicken in the military? This question was actually posed by a teenager who was taking part in a recruiting study. The inquiry may be absurd but it conveys the lack of knowledge about the U.S. military. This is but one of the misperceptions of the military held by our nation's youth. Others are less benign. Some youth believe that once you join, you have to stay for life. Others cite battle death rates at 20 percent or higher (Wilcox, 2001).

Perceptions and misperceptions of the military are more than interesting anecdotes or social curiosities. Despite the size, might, and worldwide deployment of U.S. forces, many U.S. citizens don't truly know the military—at least not "up close and personal." The ensuing analysis and discussion are based only on U.S. studies but are intended for many audiences including the U.S. military recruiting and personnel managers and our international counterparts who wish to benchmark or learn from U.S. experiences.

To fill its ranks with volunteers, the U.S. military recruiting community seeks to create awareness of and interest in the military. Perceptions—awareness—knowledge; these are the building blocks of attitudes. Attitudes are a complex system of perceptions, beliefs, feelings, and action tendencies. According to Allport (as cited in Ajzen & Fishbein, 1980, p. 17): "An attitude is a mental and neural state of readiness, organized through experience, exerting a directive or dynamic influence upon the individual response to all objects and situations with which it is related."

Given their role as mediators of behavior (Wilson, Lindsey, & Schooler, 2000), attitudes toward the military are important to understand and influence. However, understanding general attitudes toward the military is not sufficient. According to the theory of reasoned action, it is more specific behavioral intentions that are predictive of behavior. Behavioral intentions, in turn, have both an attitudinal component as well as a social or normative component. Thus, if the goal is to predict and/or influence military enlistment and retention behaviors, it is necessary to gauge salient specific attitudes and influencers.

For over 30 years, the United States has garnered its troops without conscription. Volunteer recruitment has been challenging, especially in meeting the demands for enlisted personnel who outnumber officers almost six to one. Although economists have played a significant role in enlistment policy and practice, psychologists and other social scientists also have much to contribute. In addition to assessing job demands and applicant qualifications, contributions of military psychology include measuring attitudes, interests, and motivation for military and other careers (Laurence, 2003).

The Military's Challenge

Each year, the military services enlist approximately 200,000 new recruits for the active duty forces. These so-called accessions round out the enlisted force strength of approximately 1.2 million members. In addition, there are over 200,000 active duty officers with some 18,000 officers commissioned annually. Still others are needed to fill the billets of the Reserve Forces that comprise over 736,000 enlisted members and almost 200,000 officers. To meet its substantial workforce demands, the services recruit from the nation's youth. Approximately 9 percent of the population comprises the prime military manpower pool of 18–24 year olds (DoD, 2002). On the surface, there appears to be ample manpower for both the military and civilian workforce. Of course, these figures have yet to exclude those not in the labor force, those who do not meet military qualifications, and those with no taste at all for the armed forces.

Without a draft to press people into service, U.S. Department of Defense market researchers continue to probe into the attitudes, values, and perceptions of the prime recruitment pool (Sackett & Mavor, 2003). In addition, it is important to gain the perspective of those who influence youth—parents, friends, educators, and the like. Further, society in general imparts indirect or subtle effects on youth. With fewer veterans in our midst, there are fewer exemplars to stimulate awareness of the profession of arms. The media also send varying messages with regard to military life. And of course, deployments and war have profound effects. These issues and factors among the recruitment pool will be addressed along with relevant views and opinions of those who have made the decision to enlist.

Not only is the military trying to recruit ample numbers of youth, they are also looking for quality. In selecting its members, the military screens on the basis of aptitude, physical fitness, health, and moral character in addition to age and citizenship. Thus, it is important to influence those who qualify for the military and not just take in those predisposed to serve. Further, representation of population subgroups is also important. Ideally, the benefits and burdens of service should be shared equally. Representation by race/ethnicity is particularly salient. The military has oftentimes been referred to as an "employer of last resort." This epithet has been levied in response to the overrepresentation of the underprivileged, especially blacks, in uniform.

Although gender is not an explicit screen,[1] women are not as actively recruited as men. Representation levels and roles for women in the military continue to be debated. Table 10.1 presents representation levels among incoming recruits (i.e., accessions) for women by race/ethnicity for selected years.

Even positive social trends can have negative effects on military enlistment. For example, among the "disturbing" trends with unsettling military manpower implications is increasing college attendance rates. More members of the prime recruitment pool (18–24 year olds) are attending college—a career path that has been at odds with enlisting in the military. College enrollment rates are above 60 percent for 17–21 year old high school graduates (DMR, 2001). Link to this the fact that unemployment rates are inversely related to educational attainment and the news is even more challenging from a recruiting perspective. For example, Bureau of Labor Force statistics reveal that 16 through 24 year olds with less than a high school diploma have unemployment rates that range from 6 to 8 percent. The rates for high school graduates, those with some college, and college graduates are 4, 3, and 2 percent, respectively. Thus, with more college-bound youth with relatively good employment prospects, the military struggles to compete for recruits. However, there is some "good" news. And again, the news may be good from the standpoint of military recruiting but not in terms of human capital. The news is that not all of those who enroll in college complete college. In fact, for those who go to two-year colleges, at least one-third drop out (DMR, 2002).

The changing workforce—in terms of educational aspirations, complexion, and attitudes—will affect military recruiting. The military must work hard to "flip" the qualified subset of the 85 percent of those with a negative propensity toward a

Table 10.1
Percentage of Non-Prior-Service Accessions Who Are Female and of Various Racial/Ethnic Categories for Selected Fiscal Years (Percentages for the 18–24 year old civilian population in parenthesis)

FY	Female	White	Black	Hispanic	Other
1973	5.0	76.7	17.1	5.4	.8
1975	8.9	75.0	17.9	5.3	1.8
1980	13.5	70.3	22.1	4.7	2.9
	(50.9)	(78.2)	(12.6)	(6.7)	(2.5)
1985	12.7	74.3	18.6	3.7	3.4
1990	13.2	69.3	20.7	7.0	3.1
	(51.1)	(71.9)	(13.9)	(10.8)	(3.4)
1995	17.6	68.3	18.4	9.0	4.3
2000	18.8	62.5	20.0	11.2	6.3
	(50.2)	(65.6)	(14.3)	(15.0)	(5.1)

military career. The burgeoning ethnic, racial, and gender diversity will have accompanying prospects and problems. Representation trends for women and minorities, such as those shown above in Table 10.1, are likely to be affected.

Indeed, the military will have to depend more heavily on women and minorities. Hispanics will soon become the dominant minority group, surpassing blacks who tend to join and stay in the military at rates well above their population proportions. This is significant in light of the relatively high drop out rates and relatively low representation of Hispanics in the military to date. And these are national demographic trends. Demographics may be more traditional in the Midwest and Northeast as compared to the relative military recruiting strongholds of the South and West.

The above mentioned population trends and projections are important to consider. However, these military manpower issues have been addressed primarily from an economic perspective, with pay, benefits, and bonuses pitched as likely solutions. Models of recruiting and retention behavior are deficient without considering psychological factors such as family tradition, social networks, unit cohesion, patriotism, and civic consciousness. Indeed, attitudinal variables, such as perceived importance of the role of the military, acceptance of service rules and regulations, and satisfaction with opportunities for promotion have been identified as significant correlates (Faris, 1984). However, these variables are seen as limiting economic factors; they have not been studied or manipulated in their own right. Psychological variables—attitudes in particular—are relevant and can be modified through such means as socialization. Military personnel planners ought to concern themselves with attitude formation, change, and strength. Attitudes are formed or modified through cognitive, affective, or behavioral means (Chaiken, Wood, & Eagly, 1996).

Enlistment Intentions

So who is ready, willing, and able to join and make a career of the profession of arms? Despite the numerous benefits and opportunities to be derived from military service, given that military personnel are trained to actively engage in or support a dangerous enterprise and must sacrifice their personal freedom and a stable home life, this is not an overly popular career calling. The public sector, in general, is less attractive to youth as a work setting; and the military is at the bottom of the heap. About three quarters of high school seniors rated the private sector as desirable or acceptable whereas only one quarter of them so rated the military. Other government employment and public service had middle of the road rating (DMR, 2001).

Approximately 15 percent of youth ages 16 – 21 express some interest in joining the military (Boehmer, Zucker, Ebarvia, Seghers, Snyder, Marsh, et al., 2003; Warner, Simon, & Payne, 2001) in some capacity. As shown in Figure 10.1, for young men and women, the latest reported level of interest is 23 and 10 percent, respectively. Propensity to serve in the Active Duty forces is reported to be a bit higher than propensity to join the Selected Reserve (see Figure 10.2). The gender gap remains but is narrower for Reserve propensity. Gender tensions (e.g., recurring instances of harassment and marginal status) as well as remaining career pattern

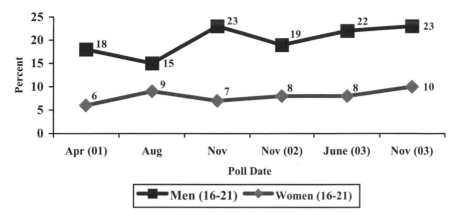

Figure 10.1
Military Propensity Trends

Source: Boehmer, Zucker, Ebarvia, Seghers, Snyder, Marsh et al., 2003, December. Department of Defense (2003), Briefing: *Youth Poll 6.* (JAMRS). Washington, DC: Defense Human Resources Activity.

differences by gender no doubt contribute to the substantially lower propensity levels among women relative to men.

Unfortunately, the perception of the military as an employer of last resort is not without at least a kernel of truth. Propensity is higher among minorities, high school dropouts, lower academic achievers and those from lower socio-economic strata. Propensity is lower among women and high-aptitude youth, with better-educated parents, and who are planning to go to college. Interestingly, Hispanic youth express the highest levels of positive propensity but their representation rates do not reach their population proportions. This disparity may be influenced by their educational and citizenship status. Over half (55 percent) of foreign born Hispanics ages 25 and older are not high school graduates. A summary of propensity by race/ethnicity is provided in Figure 10.3 below. That is, Hispanics have lower high school graduation rates than other racial/ethnic groups. Also, they may shy away from federal service to avoid highlighting their own or their relatives' immigration status.

Data on high school seniors over the years 1984 to 1991 (with follow-ups one or two years after graduation) have revealed that correlations between propensity and actual enlistment are high among women ($\eta = 0.38$) and very high among men ($\eta = 0.57$) (Bachman, Segal, Freedman-Doan, & O'Malley, 2000). Enlistment rates are lower among those with college-educated parents, high grades, and college plans. Rates are higher among men, blacks, Hispanics, and those who view military work roles as attractive. Family factors in addition to demographics also are related to enlistment. Although behavioral theories, and the theory of reasoned action in particular, have been shown to be predictive of enlistment and retention, the requisite

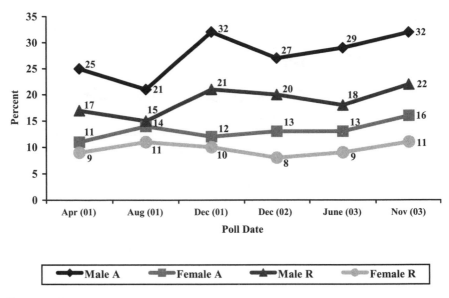

Figure 10.2
Military Propensity Trends (Active & Reserves)

Source: Boehmer et al., 2003, December.

data are not collected systematically (Sackett & Mavor, 2003). Little attention has been devoted to discovering the relationship between the routinely collected demographic characteristics and attitudes, values, and behaviors, which in turn influence propensity and result in enlistment behavior. For example, understanding the family values and obstacles to educational outcomes among Hispanics could well elucidate the relatively high propensity but low enlistment rates among this group. Such study would be in keeping with the tenants of the theory of reasoned action, which considers normative influences and expectations about success in the *attitude–behavior* link.

Attitudes have been shown to be a significant predictor of propensity ($r = 0.45$) (DoD, 2003). Overall, youth have a positive view of the military, rating it about 8 out of 10 in terms of "favorableness." Certainly, research shows that the more promilitary one's attitudes, the higher are propensity and enlistment. But again, it is not enough to elicit agreement that the military does a good job or that there should be an increase in military spending. In addition to attitudes toward the military roles and mission and in general, attitudes toward working in the military are important. Youth who see the military as an acceptable workplace and who see opportunities and fair treatment in that environment are more likely to enlist. In contrast, youth who want to put down roots and who dislike supervision may find the military distasteful (Bachman et al, 2000).

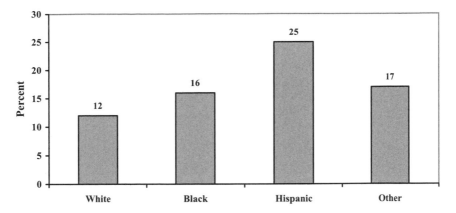

Figure 10.3
Probably or Definitely Serve in the Military in the Next Few Years (June 2003)

Source: Boehmer et al., 2003, December.

In particular, it is not just attitudes toward the military in general but attitudes toward skill development, patriotism, risk tolerance, and quality of life t hat predict enlistment behavior. That is, attitudes are formed and/or strengthened on the basis of assessing such factors as job security, pay, personal freedom, travel, pride in country, proximity to family and friends, and physical fitness. Job characteristics are extremely or very important. Youth want to enjoy their work. Further, they seek job security, good income, personal freedom, adequate retirement benefits, promotion opportunities, an opportunity to learn a valuable trade, and equal pay and opportunity for all racial/ethnic groups (Bartling & Eisenman, 1992). Civilian jobs tend to be rated as more enjoyable than the military given that the latter is less likely to be perceived as providing for such important characteristics as personal freedom, geographic stability, good income, enjoyable work, and identification with coworkers.

Although enlistment plans bear a substantial relationship to actual enlistment this connection must be expanded to better account for actual enlistment behavior (Bachman, 1983). A person could have attitudes and norms aligned with the military but fail to meet entry standards. Certainly, in addition to interest, it is important to consider eligibility for military service. Approximately 58 percent of youth would not meet physical/medical, moral character, or dependent[2] screens. Asthma, diabetes, medication for attention deficit and other disorders, and obesity take their toll. Drug or alcohol use and arrest records are additional enlistment roadblocks (DMR, 2001). Indeed, the path from attitudes to behavior is not simple. Such complexity should not lead to abandoning the path but to a deeper hunt for relevant attitudes and reasoned action on the part of youth while accounting for other key factors.

In addition to attitudes about the military, one must consider attitudes about job opportunities and fair treatment, factors that are correlated with plans and preferences for enlistment. Civilian employment opportunities influence enlistment rates. In times of severe unemployment enlistment rates rise. Although the military is rated positively in terms of educational opportunities and chances to assume responsibility, youth have negative perceptions regarding "followership" and fair treatment. Youth react negatively to the military's perceived autocratic supervisory style (Bachman, 1983).

Along with attitudes themselves, norms have a smaller but significant correlation (DoD, 2003) with enlistment intentions and subsequent behavior. Youth also consider whether normative group members (e.g., parents, teachers, counselors) would be supportive if they joined.

Recall from the above-mentioned application of the theory of reasoned action that military enlistment behavior is influenced by attitudes and subjective norms. Attitudes are a function of beliefs that a behavior will lead to certain outcomes in conjunction with the importance of those outcomes. Norms are derived from significant influencers and the motivation to comply with referent others. Engaging in the actual behavior of interest—enlistment—is also influenced by self- and institutional assessments of skills and abilities. Figure 10.4 provides a schematic of this enlistment decision model.

The above model further postulates that beliefs and outcomes about the military influence attitudes. And herein lies one of the problems for enlistment intentions. When asked to rate their knowledge of the military, youth did not feel they were very knowledgeable. The mean score was 5.6 on a 10-point scale (1 = not at all knowledgeable to 10 = extremely knowledgeable). Information may be disseminated

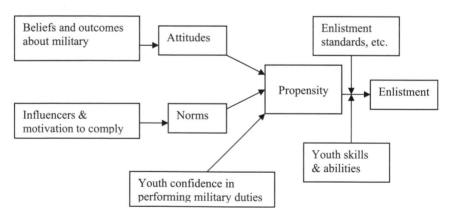

Figure 10.4
Theory of Reasoned Action Applied to the Military Enlistment Decision

Source: Boehmer, Zucker, Ebarvia, Seghers, Snyder, Marsh et al., 2004. *August 2003 influencer poll 1.* Arlington, VA: Joint Advertising, Market Research and Studies.

through advertising but influencers represent important filters that contribute to the normative component of the *reasoned action*. The knowledge gap is evident also within the military recruiting community. Despite persistent efforts to gauge propensity or enlistment intentions, the military knows relatively little about attitudes, values, and beliefs held by youth and influencers. The information below goes beyond demographics and general propensity. However, it provides only a foundation for the required knowledge base regarding values, attitudes, and perceptions of youth and those who offer them career advice.

Understanding the New Generation

Generation gaps are nothing new—from *traditionalists* (born 1900–1945) through *baby boomers* (born 1946–1964) and *generation Xers* (born 1965–1980) to today's *millennials* or *net generation* (born 1981–1999), the generations are different, having been shaped by their unique constellation of factors and experiences (Lancaster & Stillman, 2002). The military, to a great extent, is "stuck" in the traditionalist mode. It is hierarchical and paternalistic with long career pipelines and lock step paths. For the most part, this tact worked for boomers but comes up short with Xers and millennials, especially in light of eroding or eroded benefits. Generation X workers want to amass marketable skills rather than time with a single employer; they are building their resumes rather than job tenure. Recent generations tend to value status, workplace flexibility, technology, continuous learning opportunities, and quality of life. They want a more casual and carefree workplace with less hierarchy.

Top reasons to join the military are money for education, job training, patriotism, and pay. The top disincentives are military lifestyle, other career interests, threat to life, and long commitment. For women, family obligations also rank high on the list. Millennials want meaningful work and want to participate in the decision making process. The notion of a boss is not commonplace. Further, the overwhelming majority of them (88 percent) believe that people should be free to look, dress, and live the way they want (Yankelovich, 2001). Hence, for the generation of and approaching enlistment age, not only is military service not a popular career option but relatively few would recommend it as a post-high school option.

Actually, many of the job characteristics sought by today's youth are not new revelations (Sackett & Mavor, 2003). It may behoove the military to adjust to the new generation and market accordingly—as much as possible. In response to the millennials, An "Army of One" replaced "Be All That You Can Be" as the marketing theme for the Army. But it will take more than a new slogan to attract and keep today's youth. How much of a make-over can the military take? Can the military afford to beef up its benefits? Civilian companies and organizations are supporting continued education, which could undercut the military's recruiting strategy. The private sector has other perks too—flexible benefits in cash and kind.

Worlds Apart?

Does youth's at best modest interest in joining the military, not to mention lack of knowledge and perceptions that counter this career path, signal a big chasm between military members and civilians? Thus, are only a relative "in synch" few destined to be attracted to the profession of arms?

Some might suggest that there is indeed a stubborn gap between the military and civilian society with the former more conservative than the latter (Wiegand, & Paletz, 2001). Indeed, according to Franke (2001) military officers tend to be more conservative than those in civilian leadership positions—and the gap is widening. Many might conclude that there is little hope for compatibility between the military and civilian sectors. Generation X tends to be materialistic and individualistic; independent and self-sufficient. The values of today's youth seem to be at odds with teamwork, community, civic virtue, citizenship, and national identity. Their attitudes, values, and motives are inconsistent with public service including the military. They eschew wars on foreign soil. Yet, research on attitude change suggests that knowledge and socialization offer hope of narrowing the divide. This heartening prediction comes from a comparison of 1995/1996 survey responses from students at the United States Military Academy (a.k.a., West Point) and Syracuse University (Franke, 2001).

Cadets became more conservative in their attitudes the longer they were at West Point. They became less self-oriented, more patriotic, and military/warrior views loomed. Syracuse students, on the other hand, became more liberal. Within both groups, over time there were fewer middle-of-the-road views. Another, earlier study of attitude change in college points to the influence of college major. It is notable that the typical major is in the social sciences at Syracuse whereas engineering is the norm at West Point.

Evidence regarding the importance of information and hence major for attitude formation was provided in a longitudinal study at a Canadian military college (Guimond, 1999). It is commonly accepted that changes in sociopolitical attitudes are most likely to occur in the young adult years. Further, going to college during these impressionable years induces such change. Attitudes change and crystallize during this time. In addition to the role of social influence, information or cognitive processes are also keys to attitude formation or development. That is, liberal attitudes have been thought to take hold if one embraces the college community as a positive reference group. Conservative, or no change, in attitudes is posited if family and friends outside of college are the positive reference group.

Going beyond the normative influences, attitude change as a function of the academic program (engineering versus social science/humanities) was investigated. Overall, among these military students, change in a conservative direction was observed from the first to the third year. But, different patterns of attitude change were found depending upon major. Humanities/social science majors became somewhat more liberal or stayed the same whereas engineering students became much more conservative in their attitudes. Regardless of major, military ethos scale scores rose for those who identified highly with their peers. In short, cohesive groups exert more influence than noncohesive groups and military identification has a social basis whereas sociopolitical views had an informational basis (Guimond, 1999).

Narrowing the seeming polarization between civilian and military attitudes may not be insurmountable. Just as society is changing, so too is the military, albeit at a slower pace. Over the decades, the military has included more minorities, women, and married members. Such increasing diversity should affect attitudes.

Women are a particularly notable group with regard to military attitudes. Controlling for economics, education, political affiliation, knowledge of current events, and so forth, women have been found to be more liberal and less supportive of military action (Bendyna, Finucane, Kirby, O'Donnell, & Wilcox, 1996). Survey data have shown that women are less likely to favor the use of force, more pessimistic about war's outcomes and effects, and more reluctant to accept casualties. Within the military, there is somewhat of a clash between men and women. This clash is likely influenced by the typically traditional values and conservative attitudes of military men and the nontraditional values and more liberal attitudes of military women (Laurence, 2004).

In a comparison of students from military academies, Reserve Officers Training Corps (ROTC), and a civilian university, military students held the most traditional authoritarian beliefs and gender role attitudes (Kurpius, & Lucart, 2000). According to the authors, authoritarianism is related to militarism, conservatism, nationalism, and religiosity. It is also related to dogmatism, tough-mindeness, and conventionalism. Given the military's increasing reliance on women, it is important to understand their attitudes. Further, increasing gender diversity requires that the attitudes of *incumbents* be managed as well. Indeed there is evidence, and promise, that information can be instrumental in developing and strengthening attitudes. Given the motivation to comply with influencers, it would seem that educating referent groups would be a smart move in influencing attitudes.

Influencing Attitudes and Action

Even the popular press is supportive of the military, with few negative depictions (Wiegand, & Paletz, 2001) in *The New York Times, The Washington Post, The Washington Times*, and military papers such as *The Army Times*. People may have lost trust in the federal government but not in the military. Although officers believe that the media is too interested in scandals and negative stories, actual stories suggest that leaders are dedicated to the mission and address problems honorably. If anything the military media (e.g., *The Army Times*) paint the military as more conservative than does the civilian media and thus widen the gap with civilian society.

Attitudes and hence behavior are influenced by modeling and promoted or constrained by social norms. Thus, veterans are powerful influencers of attitudes and actual enlistment behavior (Warner, Simon, & Payne, 2001). Propensity is higher among youth whose parents served in the military (Faris, 1984). Unfortunately there are fewer veterans to inspire youth (DMR, 2001).[3] For example, in 1990 over 40 percent of fathers of 18 year olds were veterans. In 1998, that figure was down to 26 percent; and by 2005, it is expected to be down to 16 percent. Parents, regardless of military experience, express favorable attitudes toward the military but this does not necessarily mean that they favor enlistment for their own children. Youth and adults have positive perceptions of the military and the troops but this does not mean they are likely to join or suggest this career path. The military is not likely to be recommended to youth as a post-high school option (Yankelovich, 2002). Attending college, getting a job, or attending a trade school were more likely to be the options recommended by adults. Whereas 54 percent recommended going to college and 27 percent recommended full-time employment, only 22 percent of adults recommended military service. Men were more likely than women to recommend the military to youth (28 versus 18 percent). But saying that you would recommend the military is not the same as actually giving advice. Less than a third of American adults offered such advice to youth in 2002 (Yankelovich, 2002).

Older generations are more likely to recommend the military than are baby boomers or so-called echo boomers or generation Xers. Men are more likely to recommend the military than women. But, by and large, those who influence today's youth are not advocates of military service. Such adults might not talk someone out of joining the military but they do not advocate enlistment.

A survey of adults, ages 22 to 85, who directly influenced youth indicates that they have favorable opinions of the military but they are not likely to recommend joining (Boehmer, Zucker, Ebarvia, Seghers, Snyder, Marsh, et al., 2004). This is especially true in the case of parents' recommendations for their own children. On a 10-point scale, about 30 percent of influencers gave the military the top rating in terms of favorableness; with 69 percent of the ratings between 8 to 10 and 84 percent of the ratings between 7 and 10. The Air Force was rated highest, and the Army and National Guard were tied for least favorable. The Navy came in second. When these adults were asked about options they might suggest to youth after high school, the top choice was college (90 percent), next was a job (20 percent), and the military came in third (12 percent). Subjective norms moderate the effect of attitudes for influencers as well. Influencers' social networks tend not to be supportive of military enlistment (Boehmer et al., 2004). Further, important career outcomes such as staying near friends and family, safe environment, personal freedom, and a good paying job that makes one happy are perceived to be less likely in the military.

In contrast to Vietnam-era lows, confidence in and support for the military has been on the upswing in recent years. General positive attitudes have intensified following the September 11th attacks (Paul, 2002). Confidence in the military had not rebounded to pre-Vietnam highs but confidence is high relative to other government institutions such as Congress. Public opinion poll results show that the majority of Americans (over 60 percent) have quite a lot or a great deal of confidence in the military and about 70 percent think it is important to be number one in the world militarily. Stronger confidence is found among men, Republicans, older and less educated Americans, and people from the South and Western regions. About 9 in 10 backed the response in Afghanistan. Continued confidence in the military may depend on results.

Although they express positive attitudes toward the military (though not about enlistment), like youth themselves adult influencers lack knowledge about this institution. On a 10-point scale the mean knowledge rating was 6.3 and only 31 percent of adult influencers rated their knowledge at 8 or higher (Boehmer et al., 2004).

The joint value of influencers and knowledge was demonstrated in analyses of data from the Army Communications Objectives Measurement System (ACOMS), which linked parents and children respondents. Youth perceptions of parental attitudes predicted enlistment propensity; however youth perceptions of parents' attitudes and actual parental attitudes did not necessarily coincide (Legree, Gade, Martni, Fischl, Wilson, Nieva, et al., 2000). Misperceptions of parental attitudes may reflect either a failure to communicate or inaccurate interpretations of parents' messages. Also, parents' attitudes have an independent effect. A structural equation model of the enlistment decision provides evidence that a prospective recruit gains awareness of the military through advertising and through key influencers. This awareness results in beliefs about the military and then the recruit evaluates his or her need for the product. Beliefs and evaluations influence attitudes and intentions toward enlistment. Thus parents act as key influencers by converting youth propensity into enlistment behavior.

The importance of influencers was highlighted in interviews with 17–25 year old men awaiting reception into the military in the Delayed Entry Program (DEP). Their intentions to enlist were attributed to influencers with favorable military attitudes. Also events such as air shows, parades, and other military events were regarded as inspirational, as was participation in the high school Junior Reserve Officers Training Corps (JROTC) program (Achatz, & Ruiz, 2001). These men who signed enlistment contracts emphasized the military's tangible rewards. Their comments suggested that the Marine Corps is attractive to those interested in law enforcement or those who wish a physical challenge. The Air Force appeals to those interested in aviation.

As in the first Gulf War, few casualties have been realized in connection with the fighting in Afghanistan. However, mounting and unanticipated casualties in the current Iraq War are influencing perceptions and attitudes toward the war and the military (Pundum, 2003). Periodic polls of some 1,000 Americans, ages 18 and older, indicate that the war in Iraq is taking its toll on military attitudes. Support for sending troops to Iraq has been reported to be as high as 77 percent with 69 percent saying that the United States was justified. Despite such abstract support, only around 30 percent said they were more likely to recommend enlisting because of Iraq, whereas 46 percent said they were less likely. Parents (especially mothers) are reported to be even less likely to recommend enlistment than nonparent influencers. Early in the war (April 2003) approximately 40 percent of these respondents said that they were less likely to recommend joining the military because of these events. By May of 2004, the corresponding figure was 54 percent. Women are less likely to recommend the military than are men and the impact of the war in Iraq has been more negative for them. The Abu Ghraib prison scandal also soured enlistment recommendations, again especially among women (JAMRS, 2004).

Maintaining Positive Attitudes

Generating positive attitudes toward the military and enlistment in youth and parents is a good marketing strategy. But, another wise investment is maintaining and strengthening positive attitudes in those already serving. New generations will be difficult to retain as well as to recruit. Once they become "all they can be" they will leave, especially if their enlistment motives were not particularly strong (Lee & Tremble, 2004). They don't want to pay dues or to patiently wait to pass through the predetermined career pipelines. With the end of the draft, the military ultimately adjusted its recruiting strategy but it has yet to crack the retention code. Further, while tangible benefits have been targeted there has been but scant attention paid to the intangibles so as to enhance job satisfaction. Economists have ruled and tried to solve all with money but ignored other forms of compensation. Competitive employers must satisfy financial needs, personal needs, provide for the future, and provide a sense of mission or contribute to societal value.

With regard to retention, psychological factors such as cohesion, commitment, morale, esprit de corps, and a sense of purpose are important but often overlooked. Economic factors alone will not solve the recruiting and retention issues. In fact, non-economic factors (pride in service) are more significant than economic factors (satisfaction with pay and benefits) in predicting retention among junior enlisted personnel (Lee & Tremble, 2004; Moore, 2002). The military fails to sustain the motivations of many of its personnel; hence retention is a recurring concern. Re-enlistment is more heavily influenced by intrinsic rewards such as leadership, interest, relationships with comrades, and meaningfulness of service (Faris, 1984).

In addition to enlistment propensity, understanding commitment propensity is important for enhancing retention. There is evidence that job attitudes at entry affect satisfaction and retention. More specifically, personal characteristics are associated with initial job attitudes and these influence subsequent attitudes and behaviors. A stronger desire for an organizational career and more familiarity with the organizations core values leads to lower turnover. Less effort is required to socialize such individuals (Lee, Ashford, Walsh, & Mowday, 1992). But such research on continuance and attitude strength while in service is the exception rather than the norm.

Tangentially relevant are attitude surveys with mid-level officers (O-3 and O-4) attending command and staff colleges that have revealed a preference for traditional over nontraditional missions (Avant & Lebovic, 2000). Prior to September 11, 2001, and the waging of a war on terror, officers ordered missions in terms of appropriateness as follows: (1) general war, (2) regional war, (3) counterinsurgency, (4) anti-terrorism, (5) humanitarian assistance, (6) sanctions enforcement, (7) peace enforcement, (8) peacekeeping, and (9) drug interdiction. Military leaders indicate that although they prefer old missions, they support old and new alike. Further, they are attentive to civilian cues and consensus, though they see little of the latter. Attending to satisfaction—among officers and enlisted members—not only with missions but with aspects of service life that are identified as crucial to retention is in order.

Since the end of the Cold War, U.S. forces have been sent not only to Iraq and Afghanistan but also to Panama, Kuwait, Somalia, Haiti, Rwanda, Bosnia, Kosovo, Macedonia, Libya, Liberia, and Guantánamo Bay. U.S. forces maintain a routine presence in the Sinai, Korea, Saudi Arabia, and Europe. They have also participated in hurricane, flooding, and wildfire disaster relief and counterdrug efforts. Surprisingly, deployment in connection with long hostile duty has been shown to result in higher reenlistment. However, similar back-to-back deployments have reduced reenlistment (Reed & Segal, 2000). For example, in 1995, soldiers from the 10th Mountain Division (Light) at Ft. Drum, NY, reported peacekeeping to be boring. Further, although most accept peacekeeping, as deployments increase, they are less likely to support using the military for outside humanitarian relief. Indeed there is a negative impact of multiple deployments on morale (attitudes) and reenlistment (behavior).

Future Directions

Today's youth believe that it is important to make a contribution to society and participation in community service projects has risen over the past two decades. However, such civic calling has not resulted in easy times for military recruitment and retention. Trends in enlistment propensity along with economic conditions and societal attitudes toward the military are useful but deficient gauges for understanding and influencing enlistment behavior. Demographic and economic trends are informative. And, enlistment intentions are predictive of actual enlistment, though less so for women and minorities. With declining propensity, recruiting budgets and economic incentives can be (and have been) fortified. But among the shortcomings of this approach is a lack of understanding of the considerations that underlie behavioral intentions and ensuring actions. Attention to psychological factors would enhance recruiting and retention.

The theory of reasoned action posits that values, past behavior, personality, media habits, and so forth are moderated by attitudes and subjective norms in influencing behavior. It is important to understand attitudes—the positive or negative evaluation of sought-after and achievable outcomes for various demographic groups. It is also important to gain knowledge of the basis for and motivation to comply with internalized norms that influence whether or not one engages in the behavior.

Some research has been conducted to ascertain *what* underlies and *who* contributes to beliefs and attitudes toward serving in the military. In large part, attitudes toward benefits alone have been assessed with less emphasis on the perceived burdens of service life. In addition to obtaining reactions to pay, bonuses, and educational benefits, it is wise to gauge reaction to the nomadic lifestyle, family separation, treatment of subgroups, and potential for injury or death. And though types of influencers have been identified (e.g., parents, teachers, and guidance counselors), scant attention has been devoted to understanding their specific attitudes toward the military. The military, youth, and credible influencers must exchange pertinent knowledge and stimulate awareness and evaluation of job characteristics and other dimensions deemed critical to career and life course.

Understanding attitude formation, strength, and change with regard to salient aspects of military service offers promise of better serving military recruitment and youth career goals. Indeed salient information and assessment of such information is invaluable for attitude formation and the potential for attitudes to predict behavior. As a start, here's one tidbit of knowledge: You can eat chicken in the military.

Notes

1. Gender is used as an explicit screen for some military occupational specialties. In the Army, women are not assigned to jobs that have a high probability of direct combat. Women are also precluded from serving aboard submarines in the Navy and are excluded from Special Forces in all services.
2. Dependent screens refer to regulations barring single parents with custody of their children from enlisting in the military. Alternative custodial arrangements must be made prior to enlisting.
3. The term "veteran" is used for any former service member regardless of combat experience. The influence of recent combat veterans, including reservists, has not yet been studied.

References

Achatz, M., & Ruiz, M. (2001). *Attitudes on enlistment: Interviews with new recruits.* Arlington, VA: Defense Manpower Data Center.

Ajzen, I., & Fishbein, M. (1980). *Understanding attitudes and predicting social behavior.* Englewood Cliffs, NJ: Prentice-Hall.

Avant, D. & Lebovic, J. (2000). U.S. military attitudes toward post-cold war missions. *Armed Forces and Society, 27*(1), 37–56.

Bachman, J. G. (1983). American high school seniors view the military: 1976–1982. *Armed Forces and Society, 10*(1), 86–104.

Bachman, J. G., Segal, D. R., Freedman-Doan, P. & O'Malley, P. M. (2000). Who chooses military service? Correlates of propensity and enlistment in the U.S. Armed Services. *Military Psychology, 12*(1), 1–30.

Bartling, C. A., & Eisenman, R. (1992). Attitudes of American youth concerning military and civilian jobs. *Adolescence, 27*(106), 407–412.

Bendyna, M. E., Finucane, T., Kirby, L., O'Donnell, J. P., & Wilcox. C. (1996). Gender differences in public attitudes toward the Gulf War: A test of competing hypotheses. *The Social Science Journal, 33*(1), 1–22.

Boehmer, M., Zucker, A., Ebarvia, B., Seghers., R., Snyder, D., Marsh, S. M., Fors, J., Bader, P., & Strackbein, B. (2004, March). *August 2003 influencer poll 1.* Arlington, VA: Joint Advertising, Market Research and Studies.

Boehmer, M., Zucker, A., Ebarvia, B, Seghers., R., Snyder, D., Marsh, S. M., Fors, J., Radocchia, J. A., & Strackbein, B. (2003, December). *June 2003 youth poll 5.* Arlington, VA: Joint Advertising, Market Research and Studies.

Chaiken, S., Wood, W. L., & Eagly, A. H., (1996). Principles of persuasion. In E. T. Higgins & A. W. Kruglanski (Eds.), *Social psychology: Handbook of basic principles* (pp. 702–742). New York: Guilford Press.

Defense Market Research (DMR) Executive Notes. (2002, January 16). *The "dropout market" among students at 2-year colleges.* Retrieved December 11, 2002, from www.dmren.org/ DMREN/execute/secure/documents/view/en_dropout_market_2_year.html

Defense Market Research (DMR) Executive Notes. (2001, March 16). *Future plans of high schoolers.* Retrieved December 11, 2002, from www.dmren.org/DMREN/execute/secure/ documents/view/en_future_plans_high_schoolers.html

Department of Defense (DoD; 2003, November). *Fall 2003, Youth Poll 6.* Defense Human Resources Activity. Briefing.

Department of Defense (DoD; 2002). *Population representation in the military services: Fiscal year 2001.* Washington, DC: Office of the Assistant Secretary of Defense (Force Management Policy).

Faris, J. H. (1984). Economic and noneconomic factors of personnel recruitment and retention in the AVF. *Armed Forces and Society, 10,* (2), 251–275.

Franke, V. C. (2001). Generation X and the military: A comparison of attitudes and values between West Point cadets and college students. *Journal of Political and Military Sociology, 29*(Summer), 92–119.

Guimond, S. (1999). Attitude change during college: Normative or informational social influence? *Social Psychology of Education 2,* 237–261.

Joint Advertising, Market Research and Studies Program (JAMRS; 2004, May). *Impact of Abu Gharib on Likelihood to Recommend. DHRA Briefing.*

Kurpius, S. E. R., & Lucart, A. L. (2000). Military and civilian undergraduates: Attitudes toward women, masculinity, and authoritarianism.*Sex Roles,* 43(3/4), 255–265.

Lancaster, L. C., & Stillman, D. (2002). *When generations collide.* New York: Harper Business.

Laurence, J. H. (2004, February). *Women in the military: Mutual contributions.* Invited lecture presented to the United States Military Academy, Department of Behavioral Science and Leadership. West Point, NY.

Laurence, J. H. (2003). Test consumers: Testing and military careers. In J. Wall, & G. Walz (Eds.), *Measure up: The ultimate resource on assessment and testing issues for educators* (pp. 313–321). Greensboro, NC: ERIC/CASS.

Lee, J. K., & Tremble, T. R. (2004). An event history analysis of first-term soldier attrition. *Poster presented at the 19th annual conference of the Society for Industrial and Organizational Psychology.* Chicago, IL.

Lee, T. W., Ashford, S. J., Walsh, J. P., & Mowday, R. T. (1992). Commitment propensity, organizational commitment, and voluntary turnover: A longitudinal study of organizational entry processes. *Journal of Management, 18*(1), 15–32.

Legree, P. J., Gade, P. A., Martin, D. E., Fischl, M. A., Wilson, M. J., Nieva, V. F., McCloy, R., & Laurence, J. H. (2000). *Military Psychology, 12*(1), 31–49.

Moore, B. L. (2002). The propensity of junior enlisted personnel to remain in today's military. *Armed Forces & Society, 28*(2), 257–278.

Paul, P. (2002, February). Attitudes toward the military. *American Demographics, 24*(2), 22–23. Retrieved December 11, 2002, from www.demographics.com

Purdum, T. S. (2003, March 27). Delicate calculus of casualties and public opinion. *New York Times*, Late Edition-Final, Section B, p. 1, col. 3. Retrieved March 27, 2003, from www.nytimes.com

Reed, B. J. & Segal, D. R. (2000). The impact of multiple deployments on soldiers' peace-keeping attitudes, morale, and retention. *Armed Forces and Society, 27*(1), 57–78.

Sackett, P., & Mavor, A. (Eds.) (2003). *Attitudes, aptitudes, and aspirations of American youth: Implications for military recruitment.* Washington, DC: The National Academies Press.

Warner, J. T., Simon, C. J., & Payne, D. M. (2001, April). *Enlistment supply in the 1990's: A study of the Navy College Fund and other enlistment incentive programs* (DMDC Report No. 2000-015). Arlington, VA: Defense Manpower Data Center.

Wiegand, K. F., & Paletz, D. L. (2001). The elite media and the military-civilian culture gap. *Armed Forces & Society, 27*(2), 183–204.

Wilcox, A. G. (2001). *Recruiting the next generation: A study of attitudes, values, and beliefs.* Unpublished master's thesis, Naval Postgraduate School, Monterey, CA.

Wilson, T. D., Lindsey, S., & Schooler, T. Y. (2000). A model of dual attitudes. *Psychological Review, 107*(1), 101–126.

Yankelovich Monitor (2002, December). *Impressions of the military* (September 2002 Omni-Plus Results). Norwalk, CT: Yankelovich, Inc.

Yankelovich Monitor (2001, February). *An overview of America's generations.* Norwalk, CT: Yankelovich, Inc.

PART V

FUTURE DIRECTIONS

CHAPTER 11

MILITARY CULTURE: COMMON THEMES AND FUTURE DIRECTIONS

Thomas W. Britt, Amy B. Adler, and Carl Andrew Castro

Guy Siebold begins this volume by describing the culture of the military from the perspective of a junior enlisted service member caught up in the politics and social pressures of the military during wartime and as a psychologist tasked with studying the values that characterize military culture. As he tells his personal story, Siebold weaves in the perspective those 30 years of analyzing the U.S. military has brought him. After years of witnessing U.S. military culture first hand, Siebold hypothesizes that the U.S. military seeks not only to be great, but also good. Siebold notes that civilians assume they can trust and be protected by a service member in uniform, and that most service members care about living up to such values as honesty, respect, and helpfulness. Thus, when service members violate these standards, whether through abuse of prisoners, cheating scandals, or assault, such incidents are upsetting because both the public and other service members operate under the assumption that service members hold high moral and ethical standards.

The importance of values in the socialization of service members is highlighted in the chapter by Grojean and Thomas, who discuss the complex path through which abstract values influence the performance and decision making of military personnel. Castro then goes on to discuss the importance of the specific value of courage among military personnel, emphasizing that service members need to be courageous not only physically, but morally as well.

Although much of the research by Grojean, Thomas, and Castro focuses on values from the U.S. military, Soetters, Popenete, and Page describe the existence of a *supra-national* military value system that appears to transcend national borders. However, these authors also note that the values emphasized by the armed services within a particular nation may differ in important ways, and that these differences have the potential to contribute to conflict during military operations. Understanding the similarities and differences in the value systems of military personnel from different nations will be critical given the multinational composition of most modern military operations.

Siebold's first-person account emphasizes the importance of such values as fairness and competence occurring in the context of small work groups. The chapters in this volume dealing with group diversity emphasize the importance of values such as fairness when dealing with the variety of individuals willing to make the ultimate sacrifice in the defense of their country. Wisher and Freeman emphasize the importance of addressing the unique issues service members in the reserves and National Guard face in preparing for deployment, and provide suggestions for training these individuals so they are fully-functioning members of deployed forces. Pierce provides an historical overview of the incorporation of women into the military, and discusses the workplace issues facing women, including the effects of bias on promotion, the presence of sexual harassment, and the health impact of deployment. Finally, Herek and Belkin address the controversial issue of homosexuals serving in the military. These authors make a strong case for not considering sexual orientation when determining who should serve in the armed services, and discuss the successful inclusion of homosexual personnel in militaries from other nations.

At various points in his first-person account, Siebold emphasizes that service members trust their leaders will take care of them, and count on leaders to sustain the organization and make decisions that reflect caring and consideration. Schwerin discusses the important issue of understanding quality of life provided to service members and their families, and illustrates the immense resources that are spent to improve quality of life. He notes the need for research to determine the effectiveness of particular programs in raising the quality of life among military personnel and their families.

Siebold also observes that one of the major changes in military culture in the 21st century has been the heightened coverage of military issues by the media and on the Internet, and that in many cases these outlets focus more on the problems being encountered than on positive developments. In her unique chapter on media coverage of the military, Dauber concurs and provides an analysis of traditional media coverage and how the process of such coverage is being transformed and even short-circuited by military bloggers, those who post stories on the Internet directly without going through standard news outlets. This exciting development gives new meaning to the phrase "frontline news coverage" and is influencing the way the media packages military stories. Also relevant to a discussion of how the military is portrayed to the general public is Laurence's chapter on recruitment in the military. Laurence discusses how potential military recruits often have misperceptions regarding the true behaviors and values that are expected of service members, and how these misperceptions can affect the decision making of potential recruits.

Each of these chapters provides a provocative view of how the culture of the military is formed, developed, and challenged by larger social changes. Whether by conceptualizing the specific values that define military culture, by identifying the issues that the military and groups of individuals face in their potentially tough transition into military culture, or by examining how the military is viewed from both inside and outside the armed forces, these chapters create a framework for viewing the multidimensional structure of military culture. This framework leads to the recognition of five core principles that can guide the understanding of military culture.

Core Principles for Military Culture

1. Military organizations demand service members possess particular values. There is a military culture that transcends national boundaries, as well as differences between militaries from different nations.

2. Military values influence the actions and behaviors of service members, as well as how service members from different nations interact with each other. Values influence the development of identity as a service member, which then influences military performance. Value differences between nations can lead to inadvertent conflict during multinational operations when the behavioral consequences of the values clash.

3. The more a subgroup within the military deviates from the current military culture, the greater the necessity for formal policy and training strategies to ensure successful integration and cohesion. As service members fully incorporate military values (e.g. respect for others, the golden rule) into their identity, the integration of subgroups committed to the goals of the military will be facilitated.

4. An effective military organization assumes responsibility for supporting the health and well-being of service members and their families. This responsibility spans both work and non-work factors that influence service member quality of life.

5. The ultimate success of the military is a function of how the military is perceived by society. Attitudes toward the military are influenced by how the message of the military is communicated through the media and advertising.

Future Directions

Several historical shifts signal the need for renewed focus on traditional concerns. The increased use of military reservists calls for a thorough understanding of the impact of activation on the psychology of serving in the reserves, on the stressors that civilian communities encounter, and on methods to facilitate the reintegration of reservists into their home and civilian work lives. The need to smooth the way for reservists is paramount for ensuring that the military can sustain itself during heightened periods of operations tempo. How reservists and other military personnel are treated will set the stage for generations for the development of potential recruits' attitudes toward the military.

Other historical shifts point to the need to assess systematically the impact of new media outlets on public opinion and perception of the military. Exactly how effective is embedded reporting in communicating the military perspective? How can this communication be sustained during long engagements or periods of garrison-based activity? What impact does blogging and access to the Internet have on morale, family support, and ultimately, performance? Comprehensively researching these topics in the field may be daunting but at the very least a basic assessment of the impact of email and Internet on family relationships, public opinion, and accurate reporting needs to be conducted.

Throughout the development of military psychology, from a field primarily mired in selection to one that now includes a broad array of inter-disciplinary topics, the need to predict performance and health has been paramount. A critical task now facing military psychologists in the new millennium is how to incorporate the role of positive psychology. Positive psychology is ideally suited to address how individuals and groups adapt to challenges, how they succeed in meeting these challenges, and how interventions can be created to build on the strengths of individuals, groups, and organizations. By integrating the tenets of positive psychology, the content, structure, and development of military values can be more effectively examined.

The scientific study of military culture can be addressed by many different disciplines, including political science, sociology, psychology, communication, and anthropology. While psychological research on military culture has been relatively scant, recent research has highlighted the importance of values for individuals coming to identify with the role of service member and understanding times when military personnel from different nations have conflicts on multinational operations. Future research should examine how the endorsement of particular values predicts performance in operational settings, and whether instruction on military values is effective in preventing lapses in ethical judgment.

Ultimately, the military requires a value-driven service member. A value-driven service member is guided by a value system that facilitates adaptive decision making and action, and that allows the service member to make tough choices when values are in conflict. The value-driven service member will be effective not only in operational settings (e.g., combat), but also when interacting with service members from diverse groups and the larger civilian society. A military organization with value-driven members will create and sustain a culture that can serve as a model for the rest of society and that can live up to the reputation that Siebold encountered in a bus station as a young recruit so many years ago.

INDEX

About the Contributors

AMY B. ADLER is a research psychologist with the U.S. Army Medical Research Unit–Europe, Walter Reed Army Institute of Research (WRAIR), in Heidelberg, Germany. She is science coordinator at the unit, has deployed in support of peace-keeping operations, and is interested in deployment-related stress and early interventions. She and Thomas Britt edited a book published by Praeger Press in 2003, *The Psychology of the Peacekeeper: Lessons from the Field.*

AARON BELKIN is associate professor of political science and director of the Center for the Study of Sexual Minorities in the Military at the University of California Santa Barbara. His research interests include civil–military relations, strategic bombing, the causes of war, and sexuality and the armed forces. In his latest book (SUNY Press, 2005) he asks whether strategies that domestically vulnerable leaders pursue to minimize the risk of a coup may in some cases increase the risk of war.

THOMAS W. BRITT is an associate professor in the Department of Psychology at Clemson University. He was a uniformed research psychologist in the U.S. Army from 1994 to 1999 and deployed in support of peacekeeping, humanitarian, and contingency operations. His research interests include the search for factors that enhance resiliency and morale among soldiers serving on different types of military operations. Together with Amy Adler, he edited the book, *The Psychology of the Peacekeeper: Lessons from the Field* (Praeger Press, 2003).

CARL ANDREW CASTRO is a lieutenant colonel and research psychologist in the U.S. Army. He is chief of the Department of Military Psychiatry at the WRAIR. He has served tours of duty in Bosnia, Kosovo, and Iraq. His research interests include understanding the impact of deployments on the health and well-being of soldiers and families and how values improve individual performance.

CORI E. DAUBER is associate professor of communication studies at the University of North Carolina at Chapel Hill, and is a research fellow at the Triangle Institute for Security Studies. Her research focuses on the way the media covers war and the military, and weaknesses in the press coverage of the global war on terror. Her work has appeared in a variety of academic journals, including *Security Studies, Armed Forces and Society,* and *Rhetoric and Public Affairs,* and she authors and maintains the web site critiquing press coverage of the military, www.rantingprofs.com.

MICHAEL W. FREEMAN is a senior research scientist with Old Dominion University Research Foundation and deputy director of the Advanced Distributed Learning Initiative, Office of the Secretary of Defense, U.S. Department of Defense. A former career Army officer, he has over 25 years experience in military training and distributed learning, including service as a consultant to the Army Science Board on training issues. His research interests include the integration of online courseware, games, and collaborative environments to enable distributed learning.

MICHAEL W. GROJEAN is an industrial/organizational psychologist and director of the Aston Centre for Leadership Excellence, Aston Business School, Aston University in the United Kingdom. He served a total of 23 years active duty, as both a noncommissioned officer and a combat arms officer, deploying in numerous peacekeeping and combat operations, and he retired from the Army as a major. His research interests span leadership, leader development, organizational citizenship, personality, and values.

GREGORY M. HEREK, a professor of psychology at the University of California at Davis, has published more than 80 empirical, theoretical, and policy papers on sexual orientation, HIV/AIDS, prejudice, and related topics. He testified at congressional hearings on military personnel policy in 1993, and he has submitted expert declarations and assisted with amicus briefs for numerous court cases related to sexual orientation and the military. With Jared Jobe and Ralph Carney, he edited *Out In Force: Sexual Orientation and the Military* (University of Chicago Press, 1996). A fellow of the American Psychological Association and the American Psychological Society, he received the 1996 APA Award for Distinguished Contributions to Psychology in the Public Interest.

JANICE H. LAURENCE is the director of research and analysis within the U.S. Office of the Under Secretary of Defense (Personnel & Readiness). She also teaches and advises company officers within the Naval Postgraduate School's Leadership Education and Development Program at the U.S. Naval Academy. Trained as an industrial/organizational psychologist, Dr. Laurence has 25 years of experience conducting and managing policy studies and applied research and analysis related to workforce and human capital analyses, particularly in the military setting. She is the editor of *Military Psychology*, the official journal of the Society for Military Psychology, a division of the American Psychological Association.

JOSEPH T. PAGE JR. works for BAE Systems Information Technology where he serves as a network communications manager for the U.S. Department of Defense in Germany. He served as a U.S. Army officer from 1968–1991 and had assignments in Korea, Vietnam, Italy, Germany, and throughout the United States in both command and staff positions. His research interests focus primarily on cultural differences among career military personnel and the importance of cultural awareness and training in support of global military operations.

PENNY F. PIERCE is an associate professor in the School of Nursing and faculty associate at the Institute for Social Research at the University of Michigan in Ann Arbor. She has been in the Air Force Reserve since 1973 and has held the position of squadron commander in two aeromedical evacuation units. Her research has focused on military women's health and postdeployment well-being and retention following wartime service.

CRISTINA-RODICA POPONETE is a Ph.D. candidate in sociology at Tilburg University, the Netherlands, and a junior lecturer in organizational theory. She is a civilian sociologist at the Romanian Air Force Academy. Her research interest includes the search for enhancing cultural interoperability in multinational operations.

MICHAEL J. SCHWERIN is a survey methodologist in the survey research division at RTI International. Dr. Schwerin served as an active duty research psychologist for the U.S. Navy and now serves in the Navy Reserves. He has led a number of quality of life research projects for Navy Personnel Research, Studies, & Technology. His research interests include examining the relationship between quality of life and military outcomes (e.g., readiness and retention), survey research methods, and identifying (and correcting) sources of cognitive error in self-report measures.

GUY L. SIEBOLD is a research psychologist in the Force Stabilization Research Unit, U.S. Army Research Institute for the Behavioral & Social Sciences, with three decades of experience conducting psychological and sociological research on military issues. His publications focus on training, unit dynamics, and personnel matters with special emphasis on training as a military advantage, language training, cohesion, motivation, leadership, and morale. Dr. Siebold completed four years in the Air Force, including a tour in Vietnam. He holds both a law degree and a doctoral degree in social psychology.

JOSEPH L. SOETERS is a professor of social sciences and organization studies at the Royal Netherlands Military Academy and Tilburg University. From 1999 to 2003 he acted as Dean of Studies at the Academy. He has also published over 150 articles, book chapters, and edited books. His main focus of interest is international military co-operation. In addition he works on diversity management, the impact of civil–military co-operation (CIMIC) activities in areas of deployment, the background of civil wars and terrorism, terror management theory, management perspectives on the set-up of deployments overseas, and issues related to developmental co-operation.

JEFFREY L. THOMAS is a U.S. Army major and research psychologist assigned to the WRAIR. He has conducted psychological research for the U.S. Army in deployed, training, and garrison military environments. His research interests span occupational health psychology, clinical intervention, and industrial and organizational disciplines in support of soldiers, leaders, and military units.

ROBERT A. WISHER is a senior research psychologist and director of the Advanced Distributed Learning Initiative, Office of the Secretary of Defense, U.S. Department of Defense. He worked within the defense laboratories for 20 years, conducting field research on manpower, personnel, and training issues. His research interests center around the use of technology for military training, education, and performance support.